Politics in the New South

SUNY series in African American Studies

John R. Howard/Robert C. Smith, editors

Politics in the New South

Representation of African Americans
in Southern State Legislatures

Edited by

Charles E. Menifield and Stephen D. Shaffer

STATE UNIVERSITY OF NEW YORK PRESS

Published by
State University of New York Press, Albany

© 2005 State University of New York

For information, address State University of New York Press,
194 Washington Avenue, Suite 305, Albany, NY 12210-2384

Production by Michael Haggett
Marketing by Anne M. Valentine

Library of Congress Cataloging-in-Publication Data

Politics in the new South: representation of African Americans in southern state
legislatures / Charles E. Menifield and Stephen D. Shaffer, editors.
    p. cm — (SUNY series in African American studies)
    Includes bibliographical references and index.
    ISBN 0-7914-6531-4 (alk. paper)—ISBN 0-7914-6532-2 (pbk.: alk. paper)
    1. Representative government and representation—Southern States. 2. African
American legislators—Southern States. 3. Legislative bodies—Southern States.
4. State government—Southern States. 5. African Americans—Southern States—
Politics and government. 6. Southern States—Politics and government—1951–7.
7. Southern States—Race relations—Political aspects. I. Menifield, Charles.
II. Shaffer, Stephen Daryl, 1953– III. Series.

JK2488.P65 2005
328.75'092'396073—dc22   2004062577

10 9 8 7 6 5 4 3 2 1

Contents

Tables   vii

Preface   xi

Acknowledgments   xiii

Chapter 1   An Introduction to Southern Legislative Coalitions   1
            Stephen D. Shaffer, Charles E. Menifield,
            Peter W. Wielhouwer and Keesha M. Middlemass

Chapter 2   African Americans in the Arkansas General
            Assembly: 1972–1999   17
            Janine A. Parry and William Miller

Chapter 3   African Americans in the Contemporary Florida
            Legislature   43
            Steven Tauber

Chapter 4   Black Representation in Georgia   73
            Peter W. Wielhouwer and Keesha M. Middlemass

Chapter 5   Representation of African Americans in the Contemporary
            Mississippi Legislature   107
            Stephen D. Shaffer and Charles E. Menifield

Chapter 6   Cohesiveness and Diversity among Black Members
            of the Texas State Legislature   131
            Michelle G. Briscoe

Chapter 7 An Overview of African American Representation
in Other Southern States   157
Charles E. Menifield, Stephen D. Shaffer and
Brandi J. Brassell

Chapter 8 Politics in the New South: Looking Ahead   179
Charles E. Menifield, Stephen D. Shaffer and
Barbara A. Patrick

References   201
About the Contributors   217
Index   221

Tables

2.1	African American Legislators in the Arkansas House of Representatives	20
2.2	African American Legislators in the Arkansas Senate	21
2.3	African American Committee Chairs in the Arkansas House of Representatives	22
2.4	African American Committee Chairs in the Arkansas Senate	23
2.5	Education Issues in the Arkansas General Assembly	26
2.6	Crime, Health, and Abortion Issues in the Arkansas General Assembly	29
2.7	Race/Ethnicity Issues in the Arkansas General Assembly	31
2.8	Economic Development Issues in the Arkansas General Assembly	33
2.9	Government Reform Issues in the Arkansas General Assembly	35
3.1	African American Legislators in the Florida House of Representatives	47
3.2	African American Legislators in the Florida Senate	48
3.3	African American Committee Chairs in the Florida House of Representatives	57
3.4	African American Committee Chairs in the Florida Senate	58
3.5	Political Incorporation Index for African Americans in the Florida Legislature	60
3.6	Roll Call Votes in the Florida Legislature on Abortion	62
3.7	Roll Call Votes in the Florida Legislature on Crime Issues	64

3.8 Roll Call Votes in the Florida Legislature on Tax Issues 65
3.9 Roll Call Votes in the Florida Legislature on Education Issues 67
3.10 Roll Call Votes in the Florida Legislature on
Government Reform Issues 68
3.11 Roll Call Votes in the Florida Legislature on Race Issues 69
3.12 Roll Call Votes in the Florida Legislature on Health and
Welfare Issues 71

4.1 African American Lawmakers in the Georgia House of
Representatives, 1979–2000 81
4.2 African American Lawmakers in the Georgia Senate,
1979–2000 82
4.3 African American Committee Chairs in the Georgia
House of Representatives, 1979–2000 83
4.4 African American Committee Chairs in the Georgia
Senate, 1979–2000 84
4.5 Roll Call Votes in the Georgia General Assembly on
Elections and Government Reform Bills 87
4.6 Roll Call Votes in the Georgia General Assembly
on Education Bills 89
4.7 Roll Call Votes in the Georgia General Assembly on
Health Care and Health Insurance Bills 90
4.8 Roll Call Votes in the Georgia General Assembly on
Social Welfare Bills 92
4.9 Roll Call Votes in the Georgia General Assembly on
Race-Related Bills 95
4.10 Roll Call Votes in the Georgia General Assembly on
Crime and Gun Control Bills 97
4.11 Roll Call Votes in the Georgia General Assembly on
Economic Development and Tax Bills 99
4.12 Georgia Legislative Black Caucus Priority Roll Call
Votes, by Topic, 1992–1999 103
4.13 Georgia Legislative Black Caucus Priority Roll Call
Votes, by Year, 1992–1999 104

5.1 African American Legislators in the Mississippi House
of Representatives 109
5.2 African American Legislators in the Mississippi Senate 110
5.3 African American Committee Chairs in the Mississippi
House of Representatives 112

5.4 African American Committee Chairs in the Mississippi
Senate 113
5.5 Roll Call Votes in the Mississippi State Legislature on
Education Issues 117
5.6 Abortion Issues in the Mississippi State Legislature 119
5.7 Crime Issues in the Mississippi State Legislature 121
5.8 Race Related Issues in the Mississippi State Legislature 122
5.9 Economic Development and Government Reform
Issues in the Mississippi State Legislature 124

6.1 African American Legislators in the Texas House of
Representatives 135
6.2 African American Legislators in the Texas Senate 136
6.3 African American House Members, Districts and Black
Populations of Districts 136
6.4 African American Committee Chairs in the Texas House
of Representatives 140
6.5 African American Committee Chairs in the Texas Senate 140
6.6 Texas Legislative Black Caucus Recorded Vote Outcomes,
1997 142
6.7 Texas Legislative Black Caucus Condensed Recorded
Vote Outcomes 142
6.8 Roll Call Votes in the Texas State Legislature on
Education Issues 145
6.9 Roll Call Votes in the Texas State Legislature on Crime
and Criminal Justice Issues 147
6.10 Roll Call Votes in the Texas State Legislature on Health
and Family Issues 148
6.11 Roll Call Votes in the Texas State Legislature on
Race Relevant Issues 150
6.12 Roll Call Votes in the Texas State Legislature on
Government Regulation and Economic Development
Issues 151

7.1 African Americans in the Alabama State Legislature 158
7.2 Black Committee Chairs and Vice Chairs in the Alabama
Legislature, 2000 159
7.3 African Americans in the Louisiana State Legislature 162
7.4 Black Committee Chairs and Vice Chairs in the Louisiana
Legislature, 2000 163

7.5   African Americans in the North Carolina General
         Assembly   165
7.6   Black Committee Chairs and Vice Chairs in the North
         Carolina General Assembly, 2000   167
7.7   African Americans in the South Carolina General
         Assembly   169
7.8   Black Committee Chairs and Vice Chairs in the South
         Carolina General Assembly, 2000   170
7.9   African Americans in the Tennessee General Assembly   171
7.10   Black Committee Chairs and Vice Chairs in the
         Tennessee General Assembly, 2000   173
7.11   African Americans in the Virginia General Assembly   174
7.12   Black Committee Chairs and Vice Chairs in the Virginia
         General Assembly, 2000   175
7.13   Representation of Black Legislators in the Modern South   176
7.14   Representation of Black Legislators in the Modern South
         in Committee Chairmanships, 2000   177

8.1   Representation of Black Legislators in the Modern South   181
8.2   Representation of Black Legislators in the Modern South
         in Committee Chairmanships   183
8.3   Correlates of Black Caucus Victory on Legislation   186
8.4   Coalition Formation in State Legislatures in the Modern
         South   189

Preface

Following the passage of the Voting Rights Act of 1965, there was a considerable increase in the number of African Americans registering and voting in the Southern states. This increase led to a record number of African Americans and other racial minorities in state assemblies and local governments. The purpose of this research is to ascertain whether or not this increase in descriptive representation has led to substantive legislative changes in the Southern states in the last two decades of the twentieth century.

Each chapter will address several questions: Has the number of African Americans increased over time? Are African Americans homogenous with regard to their voting behavior? Have African Americans successfully formed coalitions with other Democrats or Republicans in order to secure the passage of legislation? What has been the influence of the African American vote on different types of legislation? Are African Americans securing leadership positions in state legislatures?

Using roll-call data on key votes from several legislative sessions in Arkansas, Florida, Georgia, Mississippi, and Texas, we answer these and many other questions.

Acknowledgments

First and foremost, we would like to thank each of the contributors to this volume, along with our graduate (Barbara A. Patrick and Brandi J. Brassell) and undergraduate research assistants (April Higgins). We are also indebted to staff, faculty, and department heads at Mississippi State University and the University of Memphis who provided us with the infrastructure and support (mentally and physically) that we needed to complete this project. Further, we appreciate the assistance from the staff in the School of Urban Affairs and Public Policy at the University of Memphis and the College of Arts and Sciences at Mississippi State University.

We would also like to thank the editors at the State University of New York Press for their support and encouragement. Acquisitions Editor Michael. A. Rinella provided valuable suggestions on an earlier draft of the manuscript that resulted in the final draft being a more comprehensive study. Copy Editor Michele Lansing made numerous changes to the manuscript that improved its readability and led us to provide additional helpful information to readers. Senior Production Editor Michael Haggett was very supportive and understanding of the challenges that we faced in working with a team of scholars from across the nation, as we revised the book into its final form.

Lastly, we acknowledge the exceptional contribution that the *Journal of Black Studies* has made to the study of African American politics, and that the *Clarion-Ledger* has made to the study of Mississippi politics, contributions that we have liberally drawn upon and recognized throughout this book.

Chapter 1

An Introduction to Southern Legislative Coalitions

Stephen D. Shaffer, Charles E. Menifield,
Peter W. Wielhouwer, and Keesha M. Middlemass

The South remains the most culturally distinct and fascinating region in the United States, prompting even today the convening of a biennial Symposium on Southern Politics at the Citadel. A region whose secession from the nation over 100 years ago prompted the bloodiest conflict in American history continues to dominate the political landscape. Referred to as *The Vital South* (Black and Black 1992) in one contemporary presidential election study, the current Republican president and all three of the last Democratic presidents have hailed from Dixie. The South also plays a pivotal role in the United States Congress, as it was not until the Republicans were able to gain a majority of congressional seats from Dixie in the 1994 elections that their party achieved control of both congressional chambers for the first time in forty years.

Racial conflict has characterized much of the South's history, and even today modern-day lynchings, jail hangings, church burnings, segregated college fraternities and sororities, and underfunded black colleges in Dixie prompt national concern. V. O. Key (1949), in *Southern Politics in State and Nation*, demonstrated how white citizens employed their one-party Democratic monopoly to maintain white supremacy by disfranchising African Americans through numerous voting devices. Even as late as the 1960s and 1970s, white legislators in states such as Mississippi employed multi-member districts to dilute the black vote in state legislative districts, and gerrymandered congressional districts to ensure white majorities in each district (Parker 1990; Davidson and Grofman 1994). As white Southerners began to realize the futility of continued resistance to integration, and during the stagflation of the 1970s became more concerned over economic issues that united the races, biracial electoral coalitions within Southern

1

Democratic parties emerged and usually fended off challenges from the increasingly strong Republican Party (Lamis 1990). By the turn of the century, however, "white flight" among conservatives to the Republican Party yielded a Southern landscape where a very competitive, two-party system had finally been established (Lamis 1999).

Southern state legislatures are fascinating institutions to study, since they serve as the nexus for these intriguing forces of an empowered African American populace, a rising Republican Party, and a transformed white Democratic faction. After decades of struggle by African American civil rights leaders and federal initiatives such as the 1965 Voting Rights Act, a sizable group of African American Democrats was finally being elected to Southern state legislatures in the closing decades of the twentieth century. As African Americans gained greater influence over Southern Democratic parties, state Republican parties benefited by conversions of white conservatives and "Dixiecrats" to their ranks. Republican electoral gains that had emerged in presidential elections as early as 1964 finally reached down to the state legislative level, and by the turn of the century, the Grand Old Party (GOP) held control of one or both legislative chambers in six of the eleven states of the old Confederacy (Shaffer, Pierce, and Kohnke 2000). With Southern legislatures polarized between liberal African American Democrats and the "lily-white" Republicans, the diminishing ranks of the white Democrats likely play a pivotal role in state policy making.

Our book examines the nature of legislative coalitions during the last two decades of the twentieth century in Arkansas, Florida, Georgia, Mississippi, and Texas and the implications of those coalitions for the representation of African American interests. Hanna Pitkin (1967), in *The Concept of Representation*, provides a conceptual analysis of legislative representation that proposes several ways of envisioning representation: formalistic, descriptive representation, symbolic, acting for the represented, and virtual representation.

DEFINING REPRESENTATION

The "descriptive representation" school of thought argues that the composition of a legislature must accurately reflect the demographic characteristics of the community it purports to be representative of (Pitkin 1967). This approach to representation is not related at all to the actions or behavior of the representatives, "[r]ather, it depends on the representative's characteristics, on what he *is* or is *like*, on being something rather than doing something. The representative does not act for others; he 'stands for' them, by virtue of a correspondence or connection between them, a resemblance or reflection" (Pitkin 1967, p. 61). Pitkin finally concludes that descriptive representation is merely one dimension of the overall concept of representation, but is limited because it allows for little-to-no creativity, initiative, or individuality on the part of the elected official; he or she may simply present the opinions of the constituents. In the end, Pitkin concludes that descriptive representation is insufficient for guaranteeing that the representative will act in the substantive interests of the constituency, or of the nation as a whole.

For groups in American society who have historically been excluded from formal political institutions, however, there is a perception that a critical first step in obtaining substantive representation may be obtaining descriptive (or even symbolic) representation. For example, in arguing for election reform, Lani Guinier (1993) maintained that people with common interests should have the maximum opportunity to elect representatives of their group to office. One result of that would be the election of representatives with physical characteristics of those groups, and this would increase the likelihood that the group's interests would also be substantively represented in the legislature. This would be because "those who are group members are more likely to represent similar interests. Group members also may share common cultural styles or operating assumptions. [Therefore], group members are more likely to be perceived by their constituents as representing them . . . the presence of racial group members symbolizes inclusion of a previously excluded group" (Guinier 1993, p. 1618).

Many African American political leaders have adopted the descriptive form of representation, urging the drawing of majority-minority districts to maximize the number of African American lawmakers, arguing that black lawmakers can best act for their African American constituents. Mansbridge (1999) strongly expounds the value of descriptive representation, particularly when "communication is impaired, often by distrust" between the elected officials and their constituents (p. 652). She points out that history often shows that a person who has experienced the legacy of a group of oppressed people can as an elected or appointed official appreciate and understand their experiences. One who does not have that legacy may not be able to fully comprehend the group's experiences and win its trust, a situation that creates distrust, a lack of communication by the citizens to their elected official, and a failure to represent the group's interests.

Mansbridge (1999) also contends that descriptive representation creates a social meaning for the ability to rule. Historically, minority groups have not been able to promote minority interests because they lacked positions of power to do so. However, the ability to elect someone who exhibits demographic characteristics similar to one's own provides symbolic rewards for minority citizens.

This is especially the case when placed into the context of past overt and institutionalized racism and discrimination, which legitimizes the need for descriptive representation. Mansbridge basically argues that history has a reinforcing quality when it comes to politics. Voters want to see someone in office who looks like them (Menifield 2001). Black voters tend to support black candidates, Hispanic voters tend to support Hispanic candidates, and women voters sometimes prefer women candidates. While critics of descriptive representation (such as Swain 1993) point out that white Congress members may provide as much substantive representation of minority constituents as do black representatives, this does not eliminate the fact that minority groups in general feel a kinship to those who exhibit similar demographic characteristics.

Nonetheless, some scholars find that descriptive representation does not necessarily lead to substantive representation. Swain (1993), for example, found that the creation of majority-minority districts hurt minority interests, as more conservative white Republicans were elected from "bleached" districts and as moderate white Democrat incumbents were displaced (see also Grofman 1997; Bullock 1995a; Hill 1995). Moreover, Lublin (1997) argued that majority-minority districts had a negative impact on substantive representation of African Americans, as the aggregate responsiveness of the House of Representatives decreased with the addition of more majority-minority districts. The conclusion that one could draw is that the victory of groups promoting the creation of majority-minority districts is a Pyrrhic one, as the subsequent cost of that victory was the loss by the Democratic Party of control of the U.S. House after the 1994 elections.

Other critics of the descriptive form of representation point out that demographic characteristics are typically only modestly correlated with political attitudes, and that a political body that is representative of a population in important demographic respects may be very unrepresentative in terms of political attitudes (Kirkpatrick 1975; Swain 1993; Endersby and Menifield 2000).

Concerns about descriptive and substantive representation often present themselves in urban politics. For example, research based on the theory of political incorporation suggests that city councils are important vehicles for increasing minority representation and power in urban political institutions (for example, see Browning et al. 1997). Alternatively, Clarence Stone (1989) has argued a theory of regime politics, in which the predominantly white business community in Atlanta created alliances with black elected officials—especially the mayor's office—in order to develop a degree of influence over city policy. In a symbiotic relationship, holders of elected offices worked with the business interests (and their economic strength) across racial lines in order to accomplish collectively beneficial ends. In this case, descriptive representation alone misrepresents the complicated process of making and managing coalitions to make and implement public policy in cities.

Can descriptive and substantive representation be achieved simultaneously? Davidson and Grofman (1994) argue that they can, citing evidence from an analysis of racially diverse political bodies. When a racially defined group of people is excluded from political institutions, the members remain second-class citizens, but when they are involved in the process and included in the institutions, members become more trusting in the system, producing a crystallization of their substantive interests (Davidson and Grofman 1994, p. 16). There is also an inherent value in having members of a minority group descriptively represented, as they are able to raise issues about topics that majority representatives may be reluctant to consider (Swain 1993).

In our book, we examine a descriptive form of representation with respect to institutional power sharing by examining the extent to which African American lawmakers occupy the chairmanships of legislative committees. We also examine the representation of African American interests from the perspective of lawmakers "acting for" the represented, which we call "substantive representation," through an analysis of key roll-call votes on the central policy debates that have shaped the quality of life for African Americans in the Southern states.

CONGRESSIONAL STUDIES OF REPRESENTATION

Considerable research has focused on representation in the U.S. Congress, so we shall single out only a few studies that are suggestive of what we may find in Southern state legislatures. As early as the 1963–1964 congressional session, Joe Feagin (1972) found that on five civil rights bills, Southern white Democrats were moving toward the national trend of moderation. Moderate white Democrats were especially prevalent in areas where white residents were less fearful of black residents, such as in heavily white districts, in prosperous urban areas, and in areas having a higher-status African American population.

Mary Alice Nye and Charles Bullock (1992) extended the study of Southern voting on federal civil rights issues from 1963 through 1982. They found that even Congress members from the Deep South (more rural, lower-income states, also having the highest concentrations of African Americans, which are Alabama, Mississippi, Louisiana, Georgia, and South Carolina) began to moderate during the 1970s, and that regionwide a district's racial composition was no longer related to the Congress members' votes. District urbanism continued to predict greater support for civil rights, with an increasing number of Republican congressmen voting in a more conservative direction.

Kenneth Wink and Allison Hayes (2001) examined the most recent 1991–1998 period when a sizable number of African American Democrats and white Republicans were representing Dixie and expanded the focus to a diverse range of issues by employing Americans for Democratic Action (ADA) pressure group ratings of Congress members. They found that white Democrats from the South were essentially moderate in ideology, while African American Democrats were liberal. The standard deviation of ADA scores from states where racial redistricting had occurred to maximize the election of African Americans to Congress was higher than in other states, as greater numbers of liberal black Democrats and conservative white Republicans were elected at the expense of moderate white Democrats. They concluded that the well-meaning effort to carve out as many black majority congressional districts as possible made centrist coalition-building efforts less likely to occur.

An excellent book-length treatment of African Americans in the modern U.S. House of Representatives is Carol Swain's (1993) *Black Faces, Black Interests: The Representation of African Americans in Congress*, which thoroughly examines both descriptive and substantive representation. Swain found that by 1992 African American Congress members were "well represented in all committees, and high seniority had led to five chairmanships" (p. 40), and concluded that they were "assimilating, just as other ethnic representatives have" (p. 44) ... and "increasingly becoming more like white liberal Democrats" (p. 44). Focusing on four roll-call indicators of black interests that measure liberal social welfare and civil rights issues, she found that white Democrats were more supportive of black interests than were Republicans, and that white Southern Democrats were nearly as supportive as Northern Democrats. In two case studies of white Democrats representing Southern districts that were 40% black, Swain found that these white Southerners performed a delicate tightrope act, balancing the interests of liberal black constituents and white conservatives, and concluded that they did a "credible job of representing blacks" (p. 168).

Swain (1993) also examined two case studies of a vanished species—white Democrats representing majority black constituencies—and found that both had used their seniority to promote African American interests in their districts and nationally. Recognizing the value of descriptive representation where majority black districts are represented by African American Congress members, Swain nevertheless rejects the notion that only black elected officials can represent such districts, pointing out that "many white members of Congress perform as well or better on the indicators used in this book than some black representatives"

(p. 211) and urging African Americans to "make alliances with like-minded representatives from other races and ethnic backgrounds" (p. 225).

Kenneth Whitby's (1997) *The Color of Representation: Congressional Behavior and Black Interests* thoroughly examines substantive representation in the U.S. House of Representatives from 1957 through 1992 by studying roll-call voting of all Congress members on important civil rights measures and on issues included in the Leadership Conference on Civil Rights scale. After a series of sophisticated multiple regression analyses, including members' race, party, region, and district characteristics, Whitby demonstrates how members fall into five groups that range from African American Democrats, who are most liberal, to Republicans (from the South and non-South), who are most conservative, with white Southern Democrats in the middle ideologically (white Northern Democrats are on the left, but not as liberal as black Democrats). Whitby's informative temporal analysis illustrates how, over time, "Southern Democrats are voting less conservatively and more like their party colleagues from the non-South" (p. 35). Despite these "liberalizing" trends in white support for civil rights, Whitby concludes that on racial issues Congress usually makes only "minor to moderate modifications in existing civil rights laws" (p. 137). He also points out that race still matters, even in substantive public policy terms, since more black congressmen can result in "more effective anti-discrimination policies in the areas of education, employment, and housing" (p. 139), or "higher increases in minimum wages and unemployment compensation to help alleviate some of the economic hardships that fall disproportionately on blacks and other minorities" (p. 139).

Robert Singh's (1998) *The Congressional Black Caucus: Racial Politics in the U.S. Congress* also examines descriptive and substantive representation, though from a more restricted focus on the Black Caucus as an institution. Singh points out that while most committees by 1995 had at least one black member, only 20% had ranking committee members who were black (likely committee chairs if the Democrats had kept control of Congress), a level of descriptive representation that is nevertheless comparable to the Black Caucus's strength in the entire House Democratic Caucus (19%). Menifield and Jones (2001) found that African Americans were able to maintain their presence on these and other committees (as ranking minority leaders) up until the end of the century, despite serving under a predominantly Republican-controlled Congress.

Relying on seven well established roll-call scales to measure substantive representation since 1980, Singh (1998) found that Black Caucus members were ideologically cohesive, being liberal, pro-labor union, high on Democratic Party unity, and low in support for Republican presidents. The thirty-seven white

Democrats who were "Associate Members" of the Congressional Black Caucus were nearly as liberal as caucus members, differing from members primarily by representing white majority districts. Indeed, roughly half of white Democratic Congress members enjoyed liberal ADA scores of 75% or more. Singh concludes that while the Caucus's role in policy making "has been limited, incremental, and defensive" (pp. 210–11), its "presence and activism has proven valuable" (p. 210) in articulating and defending African Americans' interests in the federal system.

Menifield and Jones (2001) also conducted a similar study and found that African American Congress members (the Congressional Black Caucus) were the most liberal group in Congress. Using ADA ratings for 1984, 1989, 1994, and 1999, they found that African Americans were rated as the most liberal group of Congress members on social, economic, and foreign policy issues when compared to Democrats, Republicans, women, and Hispanics. In fact, they were, at minimum, 10% more liberal than any other group. In addition, they also found the group to be the most cohesive when voting on these three types of legislation. Vote cohesion consistently remained in the 90% range, with the lowest scores found on foreign policy legislation. "By voting as a bloc on legislation suggests a lot of agreement within the Caucus" (p. 28). Further, as the group has increased in size, its ability to affect legislation and form coalitions has increased significantly.

STATE LEGISLATIVE REPRESENTATION STUDIES

Research into state legislative representation has been more limited, partly because of the absence of computerized or published roll-call data at the state level, unlike the sophisticated congressional roll-call data sources that exist. In "Revisiting the State of U.S. State Legislative Research" for *Legislative Studies Quarterly*, Gary Moncrief, Joel A. Thompson, and William Cassie (1996) conclude, that "While there has been research on the consequences of women in state legislatures, similar research on the effect of African American or Hispanic legislators has been lacking" (p. 310). They attribute this paucity of studies to the fewer numbers of minorities serving in the legislatures but point out that this situation is changing, particularly in the South.

Early legislative studies reflected the difficulties of studying representation in the face of very limited numbers of minority representatives. In a case study of the California legislature, Robert Harris (1970) interviewed all six African American lawmakers and found that half believed that their white colleagues treated them unequally. Others believed that their race entered more indirectly into their daily work, or criticized the legislature for being an overly conservative institution. Perry (1976) found similar results in his study of African Americans serving in the Missouri legislature in the period 1969–1970. He asserted that the thirteen African American legislators found it difficult to assimilate into the legislature. Despite continued improvements in increasing the number of African Americans over time, they were unable to obtain positions of power and influence. Further, they were unable to organize and subsequently form strategies that would allow them to form a voting bloc or to form coalitions with other Democrats. In both scenarios, they would have been more successful in passing their legislation.

In a case study of the 1976–1977 Mississippi state house of representatives, Charles Bullock and Susan MacManus (1981) were unable to find a simple linear relationship between white lawmakers' votes on redistributive social welfare issues and the black population size of their districts. More revealing, despite the small numbers of lawmakers, while whites were evenly split on these twenty-eight roll-call issues, the four African Americans favored these redistributive issues 94% of the time.

The federal Voting Rights Act of 1965 greatly increased the numbers of African Americans in state legislatures, particularly in the South. Charles Bullock (1992) found a strong relationship between the black population size in a district and the election of African American lawmakers, with black candidates most likely to be elected in districts that had over a 60% black population. Bernard Grofman and Lisa Handley (1991) came to a similar conclusion, pointing out that Southern districts over 65% black elected African American legislators almost 90% of the time. They found the greatest increase in African American representation in states covered by the Section 5 pre-clearance provision of the Voting Rights Act, and in states shifting from multi-member to single-member districts. One state that nevertheless rebuffed this regional trend even into the 1980s was Mississippi, where Grofman and Handley found only 15% of majority black senate districts electing African Americans. In addition, a study of eleven states, which included four Southern states, suggested that even as late as 1988, African American women faced special hurdles in getting elected to state legislatures. Electorally disadvantaged by their gender as well as their race and therefore held to higher standards than other candidates, black women lawmakers were more likely than white lawmakers or black men to hold graduate degrees and a high-prestige occupation (Moncrief, Thompson, and Schuhmann 1991).

Studies of the increased numbers of African Americans were at first confined to only two or three Southern states and did not ascertain the policy preferences of black lawmakers. Robert Harmel, Keith Hamm, and Robert Thompson (1983) examined African American vote cohesion and interrace agreement in the lower chambers of the Texas, South Carolina, and Louisiana legislatures in the 1977 session and found vote cohesion higher among African Americans than among white lawmakers. Finding greater interracial agreement in Texas metropolitan areas and in more racially tolerant Southern Louisiana parishes (counties), their study suggests the importance of examining interstate differences in the concept of state political culture. Addressing the descriptive representation question of leadership positions and seniority in the 1977 Texas house and 1977–1978 South Carolina house sessions, Hamm, Harmel, and Thompson (1983) found that white and black legislators with seniority or who held such leadership positions as committee chairs or party leaders were more active in introducing bills or amendments and were more successful in seeing them enacted into law than were legislators lacking seniority or leadership roles. Indeed, a lawmaker's seniority and institutional positions were more important than his or her race or party membership, leading the authors to conclude that African American lawmakers would become more successful in the legislative process as they became "more fully integrated" (p. 186) over time.

Case studies in individual states were begun to examine the enactment of specific types of policies that were of interest to African Americans. Examining the Alabama, Georgia, and Louisiana state senates in 1980, Mary Herring (1990) found that the percentage of registered voters in a district that was black positively affected white and black lawmakers' votes on wealth redistribution, civil rights and liberties, and overt racial issues. However, this relationship decreased after controlling for a legislator's race, particularly in Alabama. In short, black lawmakers were most responsive to black interests, and states varied in their political cultures, with Alabama being particularly slow in accommodating black political empowerment.

Cheryl Miller (1990) examined the success of the Black Caucus's agenda in the 1987 North Carolina legislature and concluded that success was enhanced by both situational factors and political skills. Situational variables were caucus cohesion, size, members' seniority and, given their importance in reporting out legislation, committee chairmanships. Miller argues that a key political skill is the ability of black lawmakers to form coalitions with their white colleagues, an increasingly common phenomenon as the rising numbers of GOP lawmakers encourage Democratic Party leaders to turn to their African American colleagues for support. Using legislation from the 1997–1998 session in North Carolina and Maryland, King-Meadows and Schaller (2001) found that African Americans were the most cohesive groups in the states and that they used strategies to secure legislation beneficial to their African American constituents. They argued, "Whether motivated by race or necessity, caucus cohesion affects not only outcomes, but the coalition building *process*. Cohesiveness facilitates the effective and strategic allocation of resources dedicated toward building biracial coalitions" (p. 182).

A national study of the quality of black legislative life in the early 1990s, published in two journals, examines the extent of descriptive representation in the committee system, among other issues. Black lawmakers were more likely than white lawmakers to report experiencing discrimination in the legislative system and to complain that their committee chairmanships did not include the most powerful committees, such as the taxing and spending committees (Button and Hedge 1996). African American lawmakers who were more senior or who represented more affluent districts were more likely to chair committees than their colleagues, and black committee chairs were less common in the five Deep South states than in the rest of the nation (Hedge, Button, and Spear 1996).

Turning briefly to substantive representation, Button and Hedge's (1996) study touched on self-reported ideology and found that white Democrats were essentially moderate, while black Democrats were to the left of center and Republicans to the right of center. These group differences suggest that African Americans pursuing their legislative agenda through coalition building would have more success by joining with white members of their own party than by crossing party lines. Edith Barrett (1995), in a 1992 mail survey of black women state legislators across the nation (and a geographically matched sample of white residents and black men), found that black and women lawmakers were more liberal than white legislators and men on a women's issue dimension, a minority issues factor, and on the issue of jobs. When asked to list their three greatest concerns, black women appeared to be the most distinctive of the four race-gender groups, expressing the greatest concern of any group over the issues of education, health care, jobs, and economic development. As in Herring (1990), the racial composition of a district loses its significance as a predictor of support for progressive issues when the race of the legislator is included in the analysis, since African Americans tend to represent majority black districts and tend to hold liberal views on minority and women's issues.

The *Journal of Black Studies* released a special issue in the summer of 2000 devoted to examining African American politics at the state level. The journal contained seven articles that examined Virginia (Clemons and Jones 2000), Mississippi (Orey 2000), North Carolina (Sullivan 2000), Georgia (Holmes 2000), South Carolina (Legette 2000), Tennessee (Wright 2000), and Missouri (Menifield 2000). Although mostly descriptive in nature, these articles also elucidate the rate of elections of African Americans, committee chairmanships, and the formation of state-level black caucuses. However, most important is the discussion of the role of the caucus in the passage of legislation. Using roll-call data from the 1987–1988 legislative session, each chapter assessed the voting behavior of caucus members relative to other members of the legislature, with special attention paid to legislation proposed by African American legislators. Generally speaking, the authors collectively noted that African American legislators served as the primary mouthpiece for African American citizens in their respective states and were the most likely to pursue legislation that would have direct benefits to African Americans.

Further, they noted that these caucuses were very cohesive and much more likely to pass their legislation when they had a large number of caucus members or members in influential positions. However, overall, African American legislators were not as successful as white legislators in passing legislation. Orey (2000) points out in his study of Mississippi that "There exists anecdotal evidence where progressive White legislators and Black legislators coalesced to produce progressive legislation. However, these cases appear to be marginal with respect to bills introduced by Black legislators" (p. 811). Menifield (2000) found that although the black state delegation had penetrated the power hierarchy in the Missouri general assembly, institutional power had not translated into substantive legislation beneficial to the state's black community.

A few books have examined descriptive or substantive representation concerns involving African American state legislators. One of the earliest was Hanes Walton's (1985) *Invisible Politics: Black Political Behavior*, which is a wide-ranging analysis of African American socialization, attitudes, voting behavior, and representation in political institutions. In a chapter on black legislative behavior that also examines black power from local aldermanic positions to the U.S. Congress, Walton relies primarily on dissertations to briefly examine black state lawmakers in Georgia and in three non-Southern states in 1969, 1971, or 1972. He finds that black elected officials were generally assigned to minor or moderately important committees rather than to the most important committees, and that chairmanships followed the same pattern. Walton also concludes that black lawmakers primarily sponsored "people-oriented legislation" (p. 216) such as health, education, welfare, consumer protection, and crime but had limited success in enacting their bills into law. Holmes (2000) found similar patterns in his longitudinal study of the Georgia assembly from 1970 to 1988. This lack of committee assignments was further exacerbated by the poor relations and cooperation among the caucus members. The Black Caucus enjoyed more success in later years by backing winning gubernatorial candidates and then pressuring them to deliver on their campaign promises. Holmes concluded that "coalition building efforts are essential to gain passage of legislation and fund programs beneficial to Georgia's more than 1.5 million Black residents" (p. 788).

In *Emerging Influentials in State Legislatures: Women, Blacks, and Hispanics*, Albert J. Nelson (1991) examines descriptive and substantive representation in forty-five lower state legislative chambers in 1982, 1984, and 1986, though key Deep South states such as Alabama, Louisiana, and Mississippi are omitted because of their four-year terms. Descriptive representation in terms of African American presence in such leadership positions as party leaders or committee chairs actually declined nationally over this four-year time interval, which Nelson attributes to "an attempt to remove blacks from visible positions of power in order to counter the image of a black Democratic Party" (p. 98).

The extent of black power in the area of substantive representation was equally bleak. Even when African Americans occupied such party or committee leadership positions, they appeared unable to influence state spending on education, social services, and health care policies. Nelson attributes the absence of black influence over public policy to the 1980s political context of "economic stagnation and the need to reduce budget deficits, coupled with poorly organized constituencies that do not exhibit strong participatory behavior" (p. 114), as well as to "the conservative era in which we live ... opposition to taxes, human resource services, and blacks" (p. 132). It is unclear to what extent this essentially pessimistic assessment of black legislative influence can be generalized beyond the 1980s era of Ronald Reagan, or whether this national study is equally applicable to the South, where African American representation in the state legislatures has increased.

In *African American Legislators in the American States*, Kerry L. Haynie (2001) examines descriptive and substantive representation in five states (including the two Southern states of Arkansas and North Carolina) at ten-year intervals, from 1969 through 1989. Relying on economic need data and public opinion polls, Haynie defines "black interests" as legislation backing health, education, welfare, economic redistribution, and civil rights issues. Regarding descriptive representation, he finds that black legislators were overrepresented on "black interest" committees and increased their representation on "prestige" committees, suggesting a broadening of their influence. Though neither African American representation in the legislature nor representation in party or committee leadership positions helped black lawmakers pass the bills they introduced, black presence in the legislature and in leadership positions did appear to increase state health, education, and welfare expenditures. Though the number of cases analyzed was only fifteen, Haynie concludes that "The presence and growth of African American representation in government has indeed had noticeable and meaningful policy consequences" (p. 107).

The Approach of Our Representation Study

The literature yields a conflicting image of the extent to which African American interests are adequately represented in the American political system, justifying additional research into this vital question as we begin the twenty-first century. Walton (1985), Nelson (1991), and Whitby (1997) paint a fairly pessimistic portrait of African American legislative influence, citing their limited committee assignments, modest advances in enacting the bills they introduce, modest changes or improvements in civil rights bills, diminishing leadership positions, and inability to influence public policy. Swain (1993) and Haynie (2001) offer a more optimistic view of African American influence, citing black assimilation into the committee system and chairmanships, coalition building with white Democrats, a broadening of committee assignments from race specific to prestige committees, and increased influence over state social welfare expenditures. Singh (1998) provides a middle perspective, acknowledging the limited policy-making impact of African Americans but recognizing their invaluable advocacy role.

An additional justification for our study is that only half of these studies deal with state legislatures, while the other half are equally valuable works that instead examine the U.S. Congress. While tremendously wide-ranging in its scope, Walton's (1985) study examines only four state legislatures, only one of which is in the South, with data nearly thirty years old. Nelson's (1991) comprehensive analysis of forty-five state legislatures in the early-to-mid-1980s may be time-bound and tied to the Ronald Reagan era. Haynie's (2001) five-state analysis includes only two Southern states and none from the Deep South, with his informative twenty-one-year study ending just before the majority-minority redistricting controversies of the 1990s.

Our focus primarily on committee chairs to assess the adequacy of the descriptive representation of African American lawmakers is a well-established measure used in previous studies. Swain (1993), Singh (1998), and Menifield and Jones (2001) examine black representation among committee chairs in the Congress, finding African American assimilation into these leadership positions in rough proportion to their presence in the Democratic caucus. At the state legislative level, Miller (1990) points out the importance of committee chairmanships in terms of reporting out legislation favored by the Black Caucus, while Button and Hedge (1996) report on African American complaints about exclusion from the most powerful committees and find that black chairmanships are less common in the Deep South (Hedge, Button, and Spear 1996). Other legislatives studies of select Southern states prior to the decade of the 1990s examine black representation among party and chamber leadership positions in addition to committee chairmanships (Hamm, Harmel, and Thompson 1983; Nelson 1991; Haynie 2001). Our individual state chapters shall also discuss the party or chamber leadership positions (such as House Speaker Pro Tem in Mississippi) that African Americans may hold, but because of the absence of party caucuses in some overwhelmingly Democratic legislatures, we rely primarily on committee chairmanship positions that can be compared across the Southern states.

The confusion over what issues are relevant to African Americans leads to considerable variation in the literature. Feagin (1972), Nye and Bullock (1992), and Miller (1990) examined either civil rights measures or racial issues directly relevant to African Americans as a distinct group. Bullock and MacManus (1981) and Nelson (1991) relied on social welfare or health, education, and welfare measures. Walton (1985) adds crime and consumer measures to various social welfare issues. Swain (1993), Whitby (1997), Herring (1990), and Haynie (2001) examined some mix of both civil rights (or related racial issues) and economic (such as social welfare) issues. Barrett (1995) adds women's issues to minority and economic job issues in her study of black women lawmakers. Wink and Hayes (2001), Singh (1998), and Button and Hedge (1996) employ more comprehensive issue scales that include all of these types of issues, though such ideological pressure group ratings as the ADA, used in congressional studies, are not available at the state level.

Because of the diversity of issues affecting the quality of life of today's African Americans, we also examine a diverse range of such topics as education, race, and crime, among others. To assess the true impact of African American lawmakers on the South's legislative system, we focus on the most important issues that have been addressed by Southern state legislatures in the last two decades of the twentieth century. If African Americans are truly being assimilated into the political system, then they should be able to exert some influence over the key measures that shape the overall quality of life in their states. Because African Americans are more concentrated in the South than in other states, such "key bills" will also include measures that are of special importance to African Americans.

Regarding what groups should be examined in any study of coalitions in Southern state legislatures, the congressional literature is quite suggestive. Wink and Hayes (2001) and Swain (1993) focus on African American Democrats, white Democrats, and white Republicans, while Whitby (1997) subdivides the two groups of white lawmakers by region, a subdivision unnecessary in our study of only one region. Button and Hedge's (1996) national study found that in self-identification terms, black Democrats tended to be more liberal, white

Republicans more conservative, and white Democrats located somewhere in between. Our study of state legislative voting on key issues that have shaped the quality of life of the contemporary Southerner shall focus on these three critical groups—African American Democrats, white Democrats, and Republicans (nearly all of whom were white).

We examine five Southern states separately because of the importance of the concept of state political culture. The titles of state chapters of such classic Southern politics books as V. O. Key's (1949) *Southern Politics in state and Nation* and Alexander P. Lamis's (1990) *The Two-Party South* illustrate how individual states can vary in their political context. From Arkansas' "Pure One-Party Politics" to "The Delta and the Hills" in Mississippi (Key 1949), or from Georgia's "Triumph of a 'Night-and-Day' Alliance" to Florida's "Recast by Rapid Growth" (Lamis 1990), each state varies in subtle and not-so-subtle ways from its Southern neighbors. In state legislative studies, Grofman and Handley (1991) documented how Mississippi was one of the slowest states in electing African American legislators after passage of the Voting Rights Act. Harmel, Hamm, and Thompson (1983) suggested that greater interracial tolerance and cooperation existed in certain areas of some Southern states, such as urban areas in Texas and southern parts of Louisiana. With the University of Nebraska's *Politics and Governments of the American States* series, guided by founding editor Daniel J. Elazar, now including twenty-one of the states, the concept of state political culture remains an intriguing one that we shall reexamine through individual state chapters.

Our sample consists of a representative sample of Southern states, and of important issues in each year in the last two decades of the 1900s. States from both the Rim South (Arkansas, Florida, and Texas) and the Deep South (Mississippi and Georgia) are individually examined in order to assess whether the more rural, lower income, and more heavily black Deep South states produce legislative coalitions that differ from those of the Rim South states. The twenty-year time span permits us to examine change over time in the descriptive and substantive representation of African American interests, and to assess whether black lawmakers actually are assimilating into the state legislative political systems and forming governing coalitions with their white colleagues.

Finally, in the last substantive chapter, we briefly examine the remaining Southern states (Alabama, Louisiana, North Carolina, South Carolina, Tennessee, and Virginia). The growth of African American representation in each legislative chamber is plotted in five-year increments, from 1980 to 2000. In addition, committee leadership is examined for each state in 2000.

Chapter 2

African Americans in the Arkansas General Assembly: 1972–1999*

Janine A. Parry and William Miller

Scholars of Arkansas's political history have long argued that the 1957 events surrounding Little Rock's Central High School—events that came to stand for the South's stubborn insistence on the preservation of segregation—belie a history of relative racial toleration in the state. As Blair (1988) suggests, "While Arkansas had manifested all the major symbols of southern segregation and white supremacy (Jim Crow laws, a white primary, inferior public services for blacks, occasional lynchings), this racism had always been more tempered than that in some of the states in the deeper South" (p. 4). In the late 1800s, she notes, a bishop in the African Methodist Episcopal Church had declared that Arkansas was "destined to be the great Negro state of the Country. . . . The Colored people have a better start there than in any other state in the Union" (Blair 1988, p. 4). Indeed, half a century later, some of the earliest and most peaceful experiments with school integration occurred in Arkansas, most just a few years before the Little Rock crisis. In voting practices, too, there is evidence that white Arkansans were less stalwartly obstructionist than their peers in other states. Key (1949) observed, for example, that many African Americans were permitted by white poll workers to vote in local Arkansas primaries (at least those outside of the plantation-Delta counties) in the mid-twentieth century, a time when both official party policy and decades of discriminatory tradition would seem to have made it extremely unlikely (pp. 637–39).

In this chapter, we examine whether this early climate of relative racial toleration translated into meaningful participation by African Americans in Arkansas politics in the late twentieth century. Specifically, we investigate the presence and role of black Arkansans in the state's general assembly in the post–1960s era. If their prospects were indeed more promising here as compared with other Southern states in the early years of growing racial equity, then we

17

would expect that promise to have produced earlier-than-average and more substantively meaningful integration into legislative seats, committee leadership positions, and an influential voting bloc.

RESEARCH DESIGN

As this primarily is a descriptive project, our first step was to document every African American elected to the Arkansas state legislature after Reconstruction. Similar to other Southern states, the first twentieth-century Arkansas elections that included substantial African American participation did not occur until after the civil rights movement and the accompanying political reforms of the 1960s. This opened the way for greater participation in the last quarter of the century. We compiled data on African American legislators for each chamber independently, taking note of the party (all were Democrats, other than the two House terms served by Christene Brownlee, a Republican), sex, committee assignments, leadership posts, and years of service of each member.

Our second step involved looking for patterns in the legislators' voting behavior. Using two chief criteria, we selected twenty-seven policy proposals out of the tens of thousands considered by both chambers during the period in question. Our first criterion was that the proposal had to have been subjected to significant news coverage, a quality we determined by examining the pages of the two newspapers with statewide circulation (though the *Gazette* was folded into the *Democrat* in 1991). Because Arkansas remains one of only a handful of states to depend upon biennial legislative meetings, we focused on articles appearing in the week before and after the official adjournment dates in each odd-numbered year. (We also included one special session—called in the fall of 1983 to address Governor Bill Clinton's education reform plan—because of its lasting significance in the state's politics and policy.) The "session wrap-up" articles produced by the state's journalists with regularity were particularly helpful.[1] Our second criterion was to try to represent as many policy areas as possible, some of general interest to all policy makers, and some likely to be of greater interest to African Americans. These areas were education, crime, health, and abortion, race/ethnicity, economic development, and government reform.

DESCRIPTIVE REPRESENTATION IN ARKANSAS

"Integration" of Arkansas's legislative chambers arrived with little fanfare in 1972 when a handful of the eleven African Americans who had appeared on the general election ballot was elected to office. Only the four Democrats prevailed—all against black, Republican opponents—supplying African American representation in the Arkansas general assembly for the first time since 1893 and making Arkansas the last Southern state to elect a black legislator ("4 Blacks Lead" 1972; "State Second" 1973).[2] Among the four was Dr. Jerry Jewell, a Little Rock dentist and past president of the Arkansas chapter of the National Association for the Advancement of Colored People (NAACP), who was elected to serve in the state senate (and would serve as its sole African American member for more than twenty years). Jewell, who also was the first African American to serve on the Little Rock Civil Service Commission, won the post by defeating businessman Sam Sparks, who had run unsuccessfully for a senate seat just two years earlier ("Jewell Defeats" 1972). Entering the state house were Richard Mays, a partner in the state's first multi-ethnic law firm and a former prosecuting attorney, Dr. William Townsend, an optometrist and a veteran civil rights activist[3], and Professor Henry Wilkins III, a political science professor at the University of Arkansas at Pine Bluff (the state's historically black college), who had been the only African American member of the state's 1969 constitutional convention. Mays and Townsend both were elected to serve the multi-member and majority-black Third District of eastern and central Little Rock, while Wilkins scraped out a narrow victory to represent the northern region of Pine Bluff, a city just southeast of the capital with a large African American population ("Two Blacks" 1972).

The proportion of African American members in the Arkansas general assembly held fast at just 3% of each chamber (1 of 35 in the senate and 3 of 100 in the house) through the 1970s, rendering the prospect of future diversification less than promising. One longtime political observer and pollster, Jim Ranchino, observed in 1977 that if "you want to run for office in the state and lose, then simply be a woman, a black, a Jew, or a Republican—in that order" (Ranchino 1977, p. 42). Indeed, by 1989, the percentage of African American house members had inched up to just 5%, while Senator Jewell continued to be the only African American member of the senate. Growth was accelerated, however, by a court ruling later the same year (*Jeffers v. Clinton*) declaring that past legislative redistricting plans (a process completed in Arkansas by the governor, the secretary of state, and the attorney general sitting together as the Board of Apportionment) had violated the national Voting Rights Act. The remedy ordered was the creation of black-majority legislative districts, a directive the board met by creating—and maintaining, despite further court challenge—thirteen such house districts and three such senate districts (Moser 1995). The action was smaller in scale than many black activists preferred but

TABLE 2.1
African American Legislators in the Arkansas House of Representatives

1981–1982	1983–1984	1985–1986	1987–1988	1989–1990
Brown	Brown	Brown	Brown	Brown
Richardson	Richardson	Hunter	Townsend	McGee
Townsend	Townsend	Townsend	Wm. Walker	Townsend
Wilkins, III	Wilkins, III	Wilkins, III	Wilkins, III	Wm. Walker
				Wilkins, III
4 members	4 members	4 members	4 members	5 members
4% of house	4% of house	4% of house	4% of house	5% of house

1991–1992	1993–1994	1995–1996	1997–1998	1999–2000
Brown	Bennett	Bennett	Bennett	Booker
Brownlee	Brown	Booker	Booker	Eason
McGee	Brownlee	Brown	Brown	Harris
Roberts	McGee	Harris	Harris	Johnson
Smith	Roberts	McGee	McGee	Jones
Townsend	Smith	Roberts	Roberts	Lewellen
Wm. Walker	Townsend	Smith	Smith	Steele
Wilkins, III	Wm. Walker	Townsend	W. Walker	Thomas
Wilson	J. Wilkins	J. Wilkins	J. Wilkins	W. Walker
	Wilson	Wilson	Wilson	White
				Wilkins, IV
				Willis
9 members	10 members	10 members	10 members	12 members
9% of house	10% of house	10% of house	10% of house	12% of house

Note: The last two rows indicate the total number of African Americans in the state house and their % of the total chamber membership of 100 members. The complete names of African American members in the twentieth century are: M. Dee Bennett, Michael D. Booker, Irma Hunter Brown, Christene Brownlee (the sole African American Republican legislator during the period under study), John Eason, Joe Harris Jr., Clarence Hunter, Calvin Johnson, Steve Jones, John Lewellen, Ben McGee, Richard L. Mays, Grover C. Richardson, Jacqueline Roberts, Judy Seriale Smith, Tracy Steele, Lindbergh Thomas, William Townsend, William Walker, Wilma Walker, Robert White, Henry Wilkins III, Henry "Hank" Wilkins IV, Josetta E. Wilkins, Arnett Willis, and Jimmie L. Wilson. Of these twenty-six total individuals, six (23%) are female.

Source: Various legislative guides, Arkansas History Commission; photograph collection, Arkansas Black History Advisory Committee.

spurred a new wave of African American representation in Arkansas politics nonetheless (Oswald 1980).

The resulting forward thrust of African Americans being elected to the state legislature was marked (see Tables 2.1 and 2.2). Specifically, the 1990 election brought the number of black representatives to nine, while two additional African American members joined Dr. Jewell in the senate. Two years later, the house proportion grew to 10%, and the senate held steady at 9% until the 1998 election, when the house increased by still two more African

TABLE 2.2
African American Legislators in the Arkansas Senate

1981–1982	1983–1984	1985–1986	1987–1988	1989–1990
Jewell	Jewell	Jewell	Jewell	Jewell
1 member	1 member	1 member	1 member	1 member
3% of senate	3% of senate	3% of senate	3% of senate	3% of senate

1991–1992	1993–1994	1995–1996	1997–1998	1999–2000
Edwards	Edwards	Edwards	Edwards	Edwards
Jewell	Jewell	Lewellen	Lewellen	Wm. Walker
Lewellen	Lewellen	Wm. Walker	Wm. Walker	
3 members	3 members	3 members	3 members	2 members
9% of senate	9% of senate	9% of senate	9% of senate	6% of senate

Note: The last two rows indicate the total number of African Americans in the state senate and their % of the total chamber membership of thirty-five members. The complete names of African American members in the twentieth century are: Jean C. Edwards, Jerry D. Jewell, Roy C. "Bill" Lewellen, and William L. "Bill" Walker.

Source: Various legislative guides, Arkansas History Commission; photograph collection, Arkansas Black History Advisory Committee.

American members, though the senate dropped back by one member. Given his extended term of service, it is worth noting that Jewell was not among the state senators around to usher in a new century. An African American opponent (Representative Bill Walker) had defeated him in the primary election of 1994. After a bitter battle, the twenty two-year veteran legislator confided, "It was hell being here . . . alone" (Oman 1994; Caldwell and O'Neal 1994b). Heading into the 2000 election cycle, then, the number of African Americans in the Arkansas general assembly stood at two senators and twelve representatives, a grand total of fourteen—or 10.4%—of 135 state legislators. This was an improvement but still fell short of the approximately 16% of the state's population composed of African Americans.

The general assembly's small number of black members did not easily acquire leadership positions once elected. Ethnicity, however, was not the major obstacle. Until the implementation of term limits in 1998, Arkansas manifested a low legislative turnover rate compared to other states. According to the National Conference of State Legislatures, for example, while the average turnover nationally among state senators between 1987 and 1997 was 72%, Arkansas's was just 57%, making it the fourth most stable in membership. As leadership opportunities for newcomers were unlikely in such a context, the early African American members of the general assembly generally were appointed as rank-and-file members mainly of the Education, Legislative Affairs, and Judiciary

TABLE 2.3
African American Committee Chairs in the Arkansas House of Representatives

1981–1982	1983–1984	1985–1986	1987–1988	1989–1990
None	None	None	None	None
0 chairs of 16 total committees 0% of total	0 chairs of 17 total committees 0% of total	0 chairs of 17 total committees 0% of total	0 chairs of 16 total committees 0% of total	0 chairs of 18 total committees 0% of total

1991–1992	1993–1994	1995–1996	1997–1998	1999–2000
None	Townsend – Aging and Legislative Affairs	Townsend – Aging and Legislative Affairs	McGee – Public Transportation	Harris – Public Transportation
0 chairs of 18 total committees 0% of total	1 chair of 18 total committees 6% of total	1 chair of 18 total committees 6% of total	1 chair of 17 total committees 6% of total	1 chair of 17 total committees 6% of total

Note: The last three rows indicate the total number of African American committee chairs, the total number of committees in the state house (including select committees), and the % of committees chaired by African Americans.

Source: *Arkansas Legislative Digest*, Arkansas General Assembly.

Committees. Yet by 1979, both Representative Townsend and Senator Jewell had been elevated to committee vice chairs, and by the mid-1980s, Jewell was chairing the Senate Committee on Agriculture and Economic Development.

The 1990s found additional African Americans serving as committee vice chairs, including the elevation of Representative Irma Hunter Brown (D-Little Rock), the first African American woman to serve in the Arkansas general assembly, to second in command on the House Revenue and Taxation Committee (Blomley 2002b). Of perhaps greater significance, at least symbolically, was Senator Jewell's election as the president pro tempore of the senate in 1993, a post traditionally held by the member with the most seniority who had not previously served in the position (O'Neal 1995). Representative Townsend was elevated to chair of the House Aging and Legislative Affairs Committee in the same year and continued in that post through the 1995 session. In the last half of the decade, Senators Jean Edwards (D-Sherrill) and Roy C. "Bill" Lewellen (D-Marianna) chaired the upper chamber's Committees on City, County, and Local Affairs and Aging and Legislative Affairs, respectively, while Representatives Ben McGee (D-Marion) and Joe Harris Jr. (D-Osceola) each served a term heading up the house's Public Transportation Committee. A time line of African American committee chairs in both chambers is presented in Tables 2.3 and 2.4.

TABLE 2.4
African American Committee Chairs in the Arkansas Senate

1981–1982	1983–1984	1985–1986	1987–1988	1989–1990
None	Jewell – Agriculture & Economic Developm't	Jewell – Agriculture & Economic Developm't	Jewell – Agriculture & Economic Developm't	Jewell – Agriculture & Economic Developm't
0 chairs of 18 total committees 0% of total	1 chair of 17 total committees 6% of total	1 chair of 17 total committees 6% of total	1 chair of 17 total committees 6% of total	1 chair of 18 total committees 6% of total

1991–1992	1993–1994	1995–1996	1997–1998	1999–2000
Jewell – Joint, Retirement and Social Security	Jewell – Education Jewell – also President Pro Tempore	Lewellen – Aging and Legislative Affairs	Edwards – City, County, and Local Affairs	Edwards – City, County, and Local Affairs
1 chair of 19 total committees 5% of total	1 chair of 19 total committees 5% of total	1 chair of 19 total committees 5% of total	1 chair of 18 total committees 6% of total	1 chair of 17 total committees 6% of total

Note: The last three rows indicate the total number of African American committee chairs, the total number of committees (including select committees) in the state senate, and the % of committees chaired by African Americans.

Source: Arkansas Legislative Digest, Arkansas General Assembly.

THE LEGISLATIVE BLACK CAUCUS IN ARKANSAS

Though it had existed as an unofficial network for many years, the Arkansas Legislative Black Caucus was officially incorporated in 1989. Instrumental to its establishment was Representative Henry Wilkins III (Arkansas Legislative Black Caucus 2002). The caucus' official mission "is to provide a major forum primarily for African American state legislators interested in improving the quality of life for African American and other disadvantaged people in Arkansas; to provide an organizational framework for the passage of legislation; to oversee a more beneficial operation of state agencies; and to provide an additional channel for constituent input" (Arkansas Legislative Black Caucus 2002).

In keeping with a key tenet of the organization's objectives, caucus members formulated an official list of shared legislative priorities for the 2001 legislative session. Increased teacher salaries and other investments in education topped the list (Thompson 2001). Further signs of the unit's greater "institutionalization" are found in the weekly meetings held by the caucus, regular gatherings in the "off season," and sustained collaborations with an organization of significantly wider membership (i.e., not simply current state legislators), the Democratic Black Caucus (Steele 2002). The latter is an official auxiliary organization of the Democratic Party of Arkansas (Democratic Party of Arkansas 2002). Such developments no doubt play a role in Haynie's (2001) report that the Arkansas legislature has experienced a dramatic increase in the political incorporation of African Americans in recent years.[4]

Of course the caucus has not been free of criticism. When a prominent civil rights lawyer entered the race for state senator in 2002 against caucus chair Representative Tracy Steele, he sharply criticized the caucus for failing to "raise issues and make advocacy" on behalf of the state's African American population. Caucus members responded by pointing to recent policy successes, including changes to the state's plans for a large tobacco settlement and setting aside a day to honor a prominent civil rights activist (Blomley 2002a). Additional evidence of the caucus's growing significance in the Arkansas political environment lies in the fact that the support of its members was actively courted by both U.S. Senate candidates in a close election in 2002 (Pennington 2002).

SUBSTANTIVE REPRESENTATION IN ARKANSAS

Though widely examined to answer innumerable questions in the political science literature, roll-call votes possess many obvious limitations. The two most significant we encountered were: (1) the overwhelming propensity of legislators to vote with unanimity by the time measures come to a floor vote, and (2) the tendency of members to be absent or to vote "present" when a consensus emerges on a controversial issue and they find themselves on the losing side of that consensus. Future research stands to fill in the gaps left by such practices. Still, several patterns emerged, and we discuss them below.

Tables 2.5 through 2.9 provide a summary of twenty-seven roll-call votes on key pieces of Arkansas legislation between 1973 and 1999. The tables are divided by the issue areas noted earlier: education, crime, health, and abortion, race/ethnicity, economic development, and government reform. What is perhaps most striking about the data at first glance is the degree of relative consensus in the African American vote across both time and issue area. Black delegates diverged from one another on thirteen measures (or 48% of the time), and five of these were inter-chamber-only disputes in which intra-chamber voting was unanimous among African Americans. While not insubstantial, such cumulative discord is far less than the twenty-one measures (or 78% of the time) in which white Democrats cast ballots in opposition to other white Democrats. Also worth noting is that disagreement among African American legislators increased as their numbers increased; 62% of the measures in which a split is evident, for example, occurred during the last ten years of the study (1989–1999).

We turn now to a more in-depth look at the five issue areas in our analysis. With regard first to the seven education measures examined in Table 2.5, the 1983 Teacher Testing bill represents well the intense debate surrounding the state's most significant education reforms to date, as well as the multifaceted position of the state's black leadership on education matters. A special session was called in the fall of that year to address a public education system widely considered to be in crisis. A 1978 study on school finance commissioned by the legislature had concluded, for example, that "the average child in Arkansas would be much better off attending the public schools of almost any other state in the country" (Alexander and Hale 1978, p. 11). Buoyed by this report, by an ad hoc Education Standards Committee (chaired by Hillary Clinton), and by a state supreme court decision declaring the state's school funding system unconstitutionally inequitable (*Dupree v. Alma School District* 1983), Governor Clinton pitched a wide-ranging package of reforms to the special session. These proposals included raising teacher salaries, establishing a more rigorous core curriculum, mandating smaller class sizes, implementing a longer school day and a longer school year, elevating standards for high school graduation, and requiring kindergarten statewide (Osborne 1990). Three major varieties of tax increases served as the companion bills to fund such reforms; only one of them—the first one-cent hike in the state sales tax in more than twenty years—eventually passed. In exchange, the governor promised, and delivered, a comprehensive battery of teacher testing.[5]

While broadly supportive of improved public education in Arkansas, members of the Arkansas Black Caucus criticized many of the reforms, especially teacher testing. In a meeting with the caucus in early October, Clinton told the members that the one-time "inventory" of all presently certified teachers would "go a long way to restoring public confidence in what … is still the most important profession in our country" (Wells 1983, p. 4A). The governor further explained to the members that while he recognized that "there are people who have been victimized by institutional racism and institutional limitations in the past," he rejected "the notion that any group of people … have any inherent, God-imbedded limitation." He concluded that "given the proper opportunity,

TABLE 2.5
Education Issues in the Arkansas General Assembly

	House of Representatives			Senate		
	Black Dems	White Dems	Republicans	Black Dems	White Dems	Republicans
1973 Free Kindergarten Measure						
For	100%	69%	–	100%	100%	100%
Against	0	31	–	0	0	0
N = Total Voting Members	(3)	(89)	(0)	(1)	(25)	(1)
1977 School Funding Formula						
For	100%	22%	100%	100%	100%	100%
Against	0	88	0	0	0	0
N = Total Voting Members	(3)	(88)	(4)	(1)	(33)	(1)
1979 Aid to Schools						
For	100%	78%	50%	100%	76%	–
Against	0	22	50	0	24	–
N = Total Voting Members	(3)	(83)	(6)	(1)	(34)	(0)
1983 Teacher Testing						
For	0%	74%	67%	0%	65%	33%
Against	100	26	33	100	35	67
N = Total Voting Members	(4)	(76)	(6)	(1)	(31)	(3)
1985 Home Schooling						
For	100%	97%	100%	0%	72%	100%
Against	0	3	0	100	28	0
N = Total Voting Members	(2)	(71)	(9)	(1)	(29)	(4)
1989 School Choice						
For	50%	53%	82%	0%	52%	50%
Against	50	47	18	100	48	50
N = Total Voting Members	(4)	(80)	(11)	(1)	(29)	(4)
1991 School Choice						
For	17%	89%	100%	0%	56%	75%
Against	83	11	0	100%	44	25
N = Total Voting Members	(6)	(79)	(7)	(3)	(16)	(4)

Note: In the senate vote on the 1989 School Choice bill, the tie-breaking vote in favor of the measure's passage was cast by Lt. Gov. Winston Bryant, a white Democrat. One of the house Republicans voting on the 1991 School Choice bill was an African American.

Source: House and senate journals of the Arkansas general assembly, 1973–1991 volumes, secretary of state's office.

everybody can pass this test and can prove that our people are just as capable as any people in the country." Caucus members were unpacified, however, and closed the meeting with votes to oppose the examination requirement for current teachers as well as to oppose the sales tax increase unless exemptions for food and utilities were made (Wells 1983). They later made good on these resolutions with a unanimous—if futile, in light of the white majority's support for the measure—"no" vote on teacher testing during the session.

Also of particular interest among the education measures examined was the 1989 "School Choice" bill, the only education issue to evoke both "yes" and "no" votes (and one non-vote) among the African Americans in the Arkansas legislature. (This division was particularly significant because the measure passed only narrowly in both chambers.) The precise cause of the divide among the Black Caucus on the measure remains unclear, but an interview with former Representative Ben McGee, who was in his first term that session and voted "yes," revealed several related possibilities. The first was that rural legislators—black and white—were not particularly concerned with parents in their communities pulling kids out of one school to the perceived detriment of another. In most cases, McGee noted, there was not another school for many miles, so school choice "wasn't really feasible" in his district. Combine this practical reality with the fact that rural legislators often were frustrated with the cost of desegregation efforts in the central Arkansas region, and the protest of Little Rock public school advocates failed to resonate with McGee. "I was not a fan of the Little Rock district," he admitted; voting for the School Choice Act, and against the preferences of many of his urban, black colleagues, was not particularly troubling (McGee 2002). Representative Brown confirmed this analysis, identifying the divide as largely "a geographic thing," a consequence of the fact that legislators—black or white—often strive to serve the interests of constituents with markedly different demographics (Brown 2002).

With regard to the "no" votes, a successful effort to expand the School Choice Act two years later is further revealing. An element of Governor Clinton's legislative package for the 1991 session, HB 1449 promoted expansion of school choice and was raised amid concerns that it would enlarge, rather than diminish, racial and ethnic segregation in Arkansas schools (Arbanas 1991a). Many urban, black legislators were especially vocal against its passage, citing the risk of "white flight" (Reed 1989; Brown 2002). "I am unalterably opposed to this legislation because it is not progressive," noted Senator Jewell at the time. "It provides an opportunity for discrimination against white kids and black kids" (McElroy 1991). McGee countered in an interview that most of the white residents likely to flee from an integrated public school system "had already bought a house at Cabot," a small, homogenously white town northeast of Little Rock that experienced explosive growth in the 1980s (McGee 2002).

On crime, health, and abortion issues, the African American senate delegation experienced one break in their ranks while members of the house were consistently unified (Table 2.6). Of the four (of six) measures in this category on which black legislators split (either between or within chambers), a 1991 conflict over the availability of contraceptives in school-based health clinics and the adoption in 1995 of a "Two Strikes" criminal justice reform measure merit further investigation. Specifically, the former was a provision imbedded in the state health department's budget that erupted in the final days of the 1991 session. Several house members—including Gus Wingfield (D-Delight) and John Miller (D-Melbourne), both white—supported amending the budget to prevent the purchase and/or distribution of condoms in school-based health clinics, a restriction the senate refused to support (Kern and Oman 1991). While a compromise eventually emerged (the language forbade the use of only state funds for condom purchase and distribution, leaving school nurses free to use federal funds for such purposes), only six black house members (including Republican Christene Brownlee, the sponsor of a controversial anti-abortion measure in the same session) voted for it (three others abstained), and one of the three African American senators voted against it (Democrat Capitol Bureau 1991; Kern 1991).

Such division was surprising. After all, the state's black political leadership had been among the strongest supporters of sex education throughout the 1980s, and the measure's most vocal proponent was Dr. Jocelyn Elders, an African American female and director of the state health department ("Resolution Supports" 1980; Morris 1991b; Democrat Capitol Bureau 1991). Recalling the conflict in a recent interview, Dr. Elders explained the divide as a consequence of some members "voting their minister." African American legislators would not have wanted to vote "against her," she said, but they did not want to vote "against the church" either. Abstention on the controversial vote was the sensible solution (Elders 2002).

Positions virtually flipped on the 1995 criminal punishment reform measure that established a minimum prison sentence of forty years for people convicted of more than one violent crime. Backed by Democratic Governor Jim Guy Tucker, the measure received support from all three African American senators, but the seven voting house members broke with 91% of their white, Democratic colleagues to vote against it (three other black representatives abstained). McGee could not recall in a 2002 interview exactly why he was among the abstainers but suggested that his vote had been tied to some other

TABLE 2.6
Crime, Health, and Abortion Issues in the Arkansas General Assembly

	House of Representatives			Senate		
	Black Dems	White Dems	Republicans	Black Dems	White Dems	Republicans
1983 Loosened Parole						
For	0%	100%	100%	100%	100%	100%
Against	100	0	0	0	0	0
N = Total Voting Members	(2)	(64)	(6)	(1)	(20)	(3)
1985 Restricted Abortion						
For	100%	100%	100%	0%	96%	100%
Against	0	0	0	100	4	0
N = Total Voting Members	(3)	(81)	(8)	(1)	(28)	(4)
1985 Indigent Health Care						
For	100%	93%	33%	100%	100%	100%
Against	0	7	67	0	0	0
N = Total Voting Members	(4)	(72)	(6)	(1)	(30)	(4)
1991 Birth Control Clinics						
For	100%	86%	100%	67%	85%	100%
Against	0	14	0	33	15	0
N = Total Voting Members	(5)	(79)	(8)	(3)	(27)	(4)
1995 Two Strikes						
For	0%	91%	100%	100%	100%	100%
Against	100	9	0	0	0	0
N = Total Voting Members	(7)	(74)	(12)	(3)	(24)	(7)
1995 Drive-by Shooting						
For	100%	100%	100%	100%	100%	100%
Against	0	0	0	0	0	0
N = Total Voting Members	(6)	(75)	(10)	(3)	(24)	(7)

Note: One of the house Republicans voting on the 1991 Birth Control Clinics bill was an African American.

Source: House and senate journals of the Arkansas general assembly, 1983–1995 volumes, secretary of state's office.

piece of legislation. "People don't pass legislation ... because it's good policy," he said. Often they take a position based instead on the fact that somebody will owe them later, or as a show of support for a particular individual (McGee 2002). The measure's chief sponsor, Representative Lisa Ferrell, a white Democrat from

Little Rock, confirmed McGee's recollection. Specifically, she remembered that Senator Bill Walker, a member of the Black Caucus in his first term in the upper chamber, had introduced another criminal justice reform measure during the same session, one that required persons convicted of serious crimes to serve at least 70% of the time sentenced. "Some of the sentiment in the Caucus," she said, was "'we've got to support Bill Walker,' so we can't support the other bill." Noting that she did not feel the bills were mutually exclusive, she also characterized the split as "not at all rancorous" (Ferrell 2002).

Ferrell added that there likely was a more substantive consideration driving the Black Caucus's opposition: concern about the disparate impact of a "two strikes" law on African American males. Though Ferrell disputed that hers was the "harsher" measure of the two bills, she acknowledged that its effect upon black men was a clear worry among many caucus members (Ferrell 2002). This response is not surprising in light of a special session on Governor Tucker's anti-crime package the previous summer, a session that had produced several measures that allegedly "targeted young blacks" and had generated considerable concern among the assembly's African American membership (Caldwell and O'Neal 1994a, p. 1A). Representative Brown attributed her "no" vote to exactly this context. "No one condoned criminal activity by anyone—black or white," she said. But many of the "tough on crime measures," often used, in her view, to justify ballooning corrections budgets, seemed to be aimed at young African Americans, particularly those who were economically disadvantaged and lacked access to good legal representation (Brown 2002).

Our efforts uncovered only three overtly race-relevant issues that made it to a vote of the full assembly and received notable publicity in the period under study (see Table 2.7). The first two measures passed with unanimous African American support. The establishment of a Human Resources (or Civil Rights) Commission had been a failed "administration measure" of Democratic Governor David Pryor previously but was shepherded to passage by African American lawmakers in the 1977 session: Representative Henry Wilkins and Senator Jerry Jewell. During the days just prior to adjournment, three white senators spoke in opposition to the commission's establishment, all going to some length to deny that their opposition had anything to do with race. Ultimately, it was adopted by the chamber, 18–5, with twelve senators not voting (May 1977).

A 1989 vote to approve a $118 million settlement over the Little Rock school desegregation conflict—a measure Representative McGee, the first black house member from the Arkansas Delta since Reconstruction, called "an opportunity (finally) to put '57 behind us"—proved even more contentious in the chambers, though not among the African American membership (Duffy 1989a,

TABLE 2.7
Race/Ethnicity Issues in the Arkansas General Assembly

	House of Representatives			Senate		
	Black Dems	White Dems	Republicans	Black Dems	White Dems	Republicans
1977 Human Resources Comm.						
For	100%	100%	100%	100%	76%	100%
Against	0	0	0	0	24	0
N = Total Voting Members	(3)	(79)	(4)	(1)	(21)	(1)
1989 Desegregation Settlement						
For	100%	95%	90%	100%	97%	50%
Against	0	5	10	0	3	50
N = Total Voting Members	(5)	(73)	(10)	(1)	(30)	(2)
1993 Civil Rights Act						
For	100%	98%	100%	0%	100%	75%
Against	0	2	0	100	0	25
N = Total Voting Members	(7)	(66)	(8)	(3)	(27)	(4)

Note: One of the house Republicans voting on the 1993 Civil Rights Act was an African American.

Source: House and senate journals of the Arkansas general assembly, 1977–1993 volumes, secretary of state's office.

1989b). The matter stemmed from a federal court order mandating that the state help finance desegregation efforts in Little Rock's three major school districts because the state had facilitated the segregation of Pulaski County schools. The state's financial portion concentrated mainly on magnet schools and remedial programs (Knight News Service 1989). Though several white legislators balked at the steady increase of the settlement total during the session, the final vote demonstrated the eagerness of the entire assembly to put thirty years of school-related racial strife to rest.

The third overtly race-relevant measure—the Civil Rights Act of 1993—caused considerable strife among the state's African American lawmakers. The breach centered around how much to compromise in Arkansas's struggle to leave Alabama as the only state to lack an anti-discrimination statute. Senator Bill Lewellen's bill emerged early as the most stringent of the measures introduced in the 1993 session. The two primary bills circulated in the house, by Representative Bill Walker and by Representative Bob Fairchild (a white Democrat from the northwest corner of the state), lacked the Lewellen bill's public accommodation protection for gays and lesbians and its hate crimes provision. Both house measures also mandated that only businesses of fifteen or more employees would be subject to the law, rather than Lewellen's nine. With such differences still intact, all three proposals had cleared either the house or the senate by the end of February, clearing the path for an inter-chamber battle of epic proportions (Duffy 1993a).

Senator Lewellen's bill received a cold reception indeed in the house. It was immediately referred, for example, to the Public Health Committee, on which both Walker and Fairchild sat, rather than to the more hospitable Judiciary Committee (Duffy 1993b). Further, though Democratic Governor Jim Guy Tucker had endorsed Lewellen's proposal early in the session, by late March he was actively lobbying senators to accept one of the house measures. The ensuing debate was exceptionally rancorous, with both Walker and Lewellen repeatedly blocking consideration of the other's bills in their respective chambers. Members of the Black Caucus suggested—anonymously—that the standoff was a personal dispute between Walker and Lewellen. The charge was denied by both as Lewellen assured reporters that the "Black Caucus itself is making moves to compromise the two bills" (Duffy 1993c). Ultimately, however, printed news accounts placed the credit—or blame—for crafting a deal with Governor Tucker. In the closing days of the session, Tucker pushed the Walker bill through the Senate, leading Representative Jimmie Wilson, a Lewellen ally, to lash out at both the governor and fellow caucus members. The governor, he said, "led Rep. Walker down the primrose path to sponsor and encourage passage (of) legislation that would be the infamy of all African Americans ... I would hate for any African American across this nation to read our so-called civil rights law and think that was the best people of color in this state could propose" (Duffy 1993d). Despite the opposition of all three African American senators and abstentions by Representative Wilson and one other African American house member, the measure was adopted by a wide margin in both chambers.[6]

Arkansas's black legislators also experienced considerable conflict over four of the six economic development measures analyzed (see Table 2.8). The 1983 adoption of Governor Bill Clinton's "enterprise zones" sparked opposition from two African American house members; another abstained while Senator Jewell joined three-quarters of his white colleagues in approving it. Jewell likely was persuaded, as was Benjamin Hooks, executive director of the Arkansas NAACP, by the argument that the plan's tax breaks and other incentives might address depressing employment figures among African Americans (Dumas 1983). Representatives Brown and Richardson, together with *Gazette* columnist Ernie Dumas, seem to have reasoned instead that tax breaks for corporations were unlikely to improve the structural unemployment problems plaguing

TABLE 2.8
Economic Development Issues in the Arkansas General Assembly

	House of Representatives			Senate		
	Black Dems	White Dems	Republicans	Black Dems	White Dems	Republicans
1973 Tax Exemption for Poor						
For	100%	96%	–	100%	100%	100%
Against	0	4	–	0	0	0
N = Total Voting Members	(3)	(81)	(0)	(1)	(31)	(1)
1977 Minimum Wage Increase						
For	100%	100%	100%	100%	100%	100%
Against	0	0	0	0	0	0
N = Total Voting Members	(2)	(82)	(3)	(1)	(28)	(1)
1983 Enterprise Zones						
For	33%	65%	67%	100%	73%	50%
Against	67	35	33	0	27	50
N = Total Voting Members	(3)	(84)	(6)	(1)	(26)	(2)
1987 ¼ Cent Sales Tax Increase						
For	25%	27%	11%	100%	61%	0%
Against	75	73	89	0	39	100
N = Total Voting Members	(4)	(85)	(9)	(1)	(28)	(4)
1995 Five Cent Gas Tax Increase						
For	80%	79%	25%	33%	64%	100%
Against	20	21	75	67%	36	0
N = Total Voting Members	(10)	(76)	(12)	(3)	(25)	(7)
1995 Bonds for Roads						
For	100%	87%	42%	33%	68%	43%
Against	0	13	58	67	32	57
N = Total Voting Members	(8)	(75)	(12)	(3)	(25)	(7)

Source: House and senate journals of the Arkansas general assembly, 1973–1995 volumes, secretary of state's office.

the state's poor. "Education and a stronger economy," Dumas argued, "will put more blacks to work than tax subsidies" (Dumas 1983). Brown added that she was dubious about who such business incentives actually would reach. "Many of the folks that truly needed to be targeted," she said "would not have received those breaks." In particular, she recalled that the definition of "minority" was being expanded at that time to include women. "Otherwise majority businesses," she said, were putting women up front on their applications because they could then qualify for the enterprise zone incentives. The result, in her view, was great risk that the benefits would not go to people who were genuinely economically disadvantaged (Brown 2002).

A 1987 one-quarter-cent sales tax increase produced similar division, though in that case most black legislators joined a large majority of their white counterparts in defeating Clinton's plan for raising additional revenue for education and other social programs. News accounts of the marathon battle over the measure noted much concern with the impact of an increased sales tax on "blacks and poor whites" (Strickland 1987). Reacting to Governor Clinton's speech to the full legislature on the matter, however, Senator Jewell advocated the additional revenue generation as a "way to take care of our children" ("Comments Indicate" 1987, p. 9A). "Their needs are the increased funding of the schools, more efficient operation of the schools, (and) qualified teachers," he said.

Similar arguments accompanied the two 1995 measures. Both the five-cent increase in the diesel gasoline tax and the bond package were key components of Governor Tucker's large-scale road construction plan. The governor insisted that transportation upgrades were essential to economic development. Despite general support for the improvement of Arkansas highways, some Republican and African American lawmakers were concerned about a tax increase and the state's debt load. Bill Walker, the house member who had authored the winning civil rights bill two years earlier and had defeated Jerry Jewell for a state senate seat in 1994, was a leading opponent of the roads plan, voting against both measures (Tennille 1995). Despite eventual adoption by the legislature, voters resoundingly rejected the package in a special election the following year.

Finally, just one of the five government reform measures we identified appears to have been a matter of significant dispute among African Americans or white legislators (see Table 2.9). Like most such efforts in Southern states, the 1991 congressional redistricting plan for Arkansas's four U.S. House seats raised questions about the historic disenfranchisement of the black population and appropriate remedies at the congressional-district level. Representative Ben McGee (D-Marion) put forward a plan that would have put 87% of the state's African American residents into one district (the Fourth District), resulting in a district with a 42% minority population. The vast majority of the Black Caucus supported the idea, as did the state Republican Party, but it found little support elsewhere in the legislature (Stumpe 1991). Though these rather strange political bedfellows presented several versions of this "black influence district" concept during the 1991 session, white Democrats preferred a plan that would bring little change to the lines drawn ten years earlier.

TABLE 2.9
Government Reform Issues in the Arkansas General Assembly

	House of Representatives			Senate		
	Black Dems	White Dems	Republicans	Black Dems	White Dems	Republicans
1977 Freedom of Information Act Expansion						
For	100%	100%	–	100%	100%	100%
Against	0	0	–	0	0	0
N = Total Voting Members	(1)	(71)	(0)	(1)	(28)	(1)
1987 Move Primary/Super Tues.						
For	100%	99%	100%	100%	96%	100%
Against	0	1	0	0	4	0
N = Total Voting Members	(4)	(79)	(7)	(1)	(26)	(4)
1991 Congressional Redistricting						
For	20%	92%	71%	0%	96%	100%
Against	80	8	29	100	4	0
N = Total Voting Members	(5)	(72)	(7)	(2)	(27)	(4)
1995 Ethics Violations Fines						
For	100%	100%	100%	100%	100%	100%
Against	0	0	0	0	0	0
N = Total Voting Members	(10)	(76)	(12)	(3)	(25)	(7)
1995 Motor Voter						
For	100%	100%	100%	100%	100%	100%
Against	0	0	0	0	0	0
N = Total Voting Members	(10)	(73)	(12)	(3)	(25)	(7)

Note: The one African American house Republican voting on the 1991 congressional redistricting plan joined the one white house Republican in opposing the plan, while five white house Republicans favored it.

Source: House and senate journals of the Arkansas general assembly, 1977–1995 volumes, secretary of state's office.

Racial rhetoric was central to the debate. Republicans and black Democrats charged that the state Democratic Party historically had "fractured" the bulk of Arkansas's African American population among three different districts (the First, Second, and Fourth Districts), and thus diluted their voting strength (Arbanas 1991b). "They put enough blacks in those districts ... by running fingers of them" into the Delta and through the black neighborhoods of Little Rock, asserted former Representative McGee, "so a white male who says he's a Democrat could get elected" (McGee 2002). Such Democrats, in McGee's view, then pay only "lip service" to their black, Delta constituents to avoid alienating the conservative, white voters who compose the rest of the district. White Democrats parried that consolidating the African American vote in the way McGee proposed actually would reduce overall black political influence in Arkansas's congressional delegation. They added that the Black Caucus-Republican alliance was disingenuous, charging that Republicans simply desired to unseat Democratic congressional incumbents "and to create an apartheid black district under the guise of being great friends of blacks" (Oswald 1991a, p. 2B).[7] A conference committee in late March brought victory to the white Democrats in the form of the status quo, majority-backed bill, a plan that shuffled only six counties among the state's four congressional districts. The only "no" votes on the committee came from its three black members—Representative McGee and Senators Jewell and Lewellen (Oswald and Morris 1991). Importantly, not only did all but one member of the Black Caucus later vote against the redistricting plan upon final roll call in their respective chambers (though five abstained), but all except Representative Wilkins (who was ill with cancer and missed most of the 1991 legislative session) participated as plaintiffs or intervenors in a subsequent lawsuit filed by the state Republican Party (Morris 1991c). The U.S. Supreme Court, however, rejected the challenge.

It is interesting to add that a similar conflict, and an alliance between some Black Caucus members and the state Republican Party, emerged with the 2001 redistricting effort at the state legislative level. Republican Governor Mike Huckabee (who is white) put forward a redistricting plan that would have increased the number of majority-black districts in Arkansas to fifteen in the house and five in the senate, figures not far off from the NAACP's goals of seventeen and six, respectively. White Democrats Sharon Priest, secretary of state, and Mark Pryor, attorney general, preferred a plan that placed the number at thirteen in the house and four (up one) in the senate. Representative Tracy Steele (D-North Little Rock), chair of the Black Caucus, supported the Democratic plan because "Huckabee wanted more black-majority districts ... (to) dilute Democratic voting strength in other districts" (Satter 2002, p. 15A). Dale Charles, state NAACP president, countered that Steele, director of the state's Martin Luther King Jr. Commission, was "the rabid mouth of racism for the Democratic Party" (Satter 2002, p. 15A). The issue generated much controversy among African American political leaders and likely played a role in a three-way primary race among Steele, former Representative Wilma Walker, and civil rights attorney John Walker for one of the majority-black Little Rock senate seats in May 2002. Steele won with 56% of the vote, a victory that pundits attributed to his "harmony-seeking demeanor" (Murphy 2002).

CONCLUSIONS AND IMPLICATIONS

This preliminary effort to catalog and analyze the presence and behavior of African American legislators in the Arkansas general assembly produced two key findings. First, the proportion of black state legislators increased steadily following the voting rights reforms of the 1960s. This process was accelerated, significantly, by the court-ordered, race-conscious legislative redistricting of the late 1980s. Still, while a state legislative membership that is 10% black (12% of the house and 6% of the senate) may be an improvement over thirty years ago, the goal of full descriptive representation for African Americans in the Arkansas legislative process has yet to be realized. While it is true that most Southern states long have had, and continue to maintain, African American populations of at least twice the size of Arkansas's, this is not ample justification for the state's still low ratio of black legislators to black residents. If indeed Arkansas was "destined to be the great Negro state of the Country" at the dawn of the last century, such promise remains unfulfilled with regard to their descriptive representation at the dawn of the next.

That promise remains unfulfilled in terms of substantive representation as well. Specifically, our second—and most important—finding is that African Americans in the Arkansas general assembly have been unable to exercise consistent influence over policy outcomes. In part, this is because African Americans—like any demographic group—have not been wholly homogenous when it comes to policy preferences. (In fact, the greater the degree of chamber-wide contention over the policy questions included in this analysis, the greater the propensity of black legislators to take opposing positions among themselves.) But, as noted earlier in the chapter, African American members have voted together more often than not and have presented a unified front far more frequently than white Democrats.

The chief obstacle to black influence in Arkansas lies primarily in the small proportion of the total state legislative membership composed of African Americans. One senior member, a white Democrat who was influential throughout the 1980s and 1990s, indicated that the Arkansas Black Caucus was simply never big enough to "really kill anything." From time to time, he intimated, they wielded enough votes that the governor or the senior member shepherding a measure through the chamber would indeed need to court them on controversial issues. They did so, however, largely on an individual basis. This was because the Arkansas legislature was not traditionally a place in which members "caucused off"; efforts to do so were in fact seen as a bit of an "irritant" by senior members who, until the adoption of term limits in 1992, controlled the Arkansas legislative process (Blair 1988). The only measure on which the member could recall leverage exercised by black legislators as a group was on a redistricting plan for the state court of appeals debated through the mid- and late 1990s. Caucus members pressed for black-majority districts, and while "they didn't get their way," the majority did have to postpone its actions.[8]

Interviews with African American leaders active during the period of investigation confirmed that black legislators in Arkansas have been too few in number and have not occupied the necessary leadership positions to wield much observable influence. Former state health director (and later U.S. surgeon general) Dr. Elders noted, for example, that while most of the black legislators "were very proud to be there . . . representing their constituents," few of them took positions not already congruent with the white majority's preferences. The fact that the assembly was controlled by "four old, white leaders, (who, if they) couldn't get it done, it wasn't going to get done," contributed to an inhospitable environment for the Black Caucus (Elders 2002). Former state Representative McGee echoed this sentiment, noting first that with just "13 black folks in the House and 51 needed for passage, getting all the black folks wasn't going to help you" (McGee 2002). He also concurred that the lack of numbers was not the only—or even the most significant—part of the equation. Rather, a measure stood little chance during his term of service unless "kissed" by at least one of the senior members of the body. Among these was Lloyd George, a white Democrat from Danville, who, McGee reported, was ultimately responsible for the passage of the much-disputed 1993 Civil Rights Act. According to McGee, George agreed to co-sponsor the measure by Representative Bill Walker (after McGee delivered an unrelated favor and a promise that it would not apply to gays and lesbians). Suddenly, introduced and rejected at the committee level at every session for many years, the Arkansas Civil Rights Act—with the George imprimatur—"flew through the house." (McGee 2002).

Few in number and not counted among the "network of senior members," it is thus not surprising that in each of the eight times in which the majority of the Black Caucus split with the majority of white Democrats on the twenty-seven measures examined, they lost (for more on the significance of seniority, see Johnston and Storey 1983). And, by at least one measure, the future does not look much more promising. The state's African American population is small, now less than 16%. Even if the proportion of black legislators grows to match that figure, it will still play only a minor role in the vast majority of roll-call votes.

Under such circumstances, perhaps the caucus's best hope is to pursue a three-pronged strategy. First, their current numbers allow them to play the spoiler on closely divided votes such as the appellate court dispute, noted earlier, and—very nearly—the 1989 school choice measure. Representative Tracy Steele, the current chair of the Black Caucus (as well as the executive director of the Arkansas Martin Luther King Jr. Commission), offered the state's recent debate over the use of its share of the national tobacco settlement money as an additional example. "Obviously (the black membership) is not enough to pass bills, but it is (now) enough to stop them on a close vote," he said (Steele 2002). Dissatisfied with the insufficient level of attention paid to minority needs in the major tobacco settlement plan crafted in a special legislative session, they did just that in April 2000.[9] Playing this card too often of course could turn their white peers off to future cooperation, but Black Caucus members will be increasingly well positioned to successfully impede distasteful measures as the assembly's partisan balance becomes more evenly weighted between Democrats and Republicans.

African American legislators also can continue to play the "sensitizer" role identified by former Representative Brown. The election and service of people who long have been political minorities sensitizes "those who had not had to think about certain things before," she said (Brown 2002). This idea was firmly reiterated by former representative and chair of the Women's Caucus Lisa Ferrell, a white Democrat. "It helps to have folks who bring other worlds to the table," she said. In her view, this is not to suggest that other legislators purposely ignore non-majority groups. Instead, it is "a question of educating (the white, male majority) about the needs of various populations" (Ferrell 2002). The success of this role rests in part upon the Black Caucus's ability to "galvanize community support for the issues ... outside the halls of the Capitol" (Steele 2002). An important tactic of the current caucus, in fact, is to appeal to their white colleagues for cooperation by reminding them of the proportion of minorities in their districts.

Finally, Arkansas's black legislators can look toward crafting strategic alliances[10] with the major players in the general assembly, a strategy made both easier and more difficult by the full implementation of term limits with the 2002 election cycle. Senior members such as Representatives Lloyd George and John Miller have disappeared from the state's political landscape. Black legislators now must negotiate—for policy victories, committee assignments, and leadership posts—with white Democrats who have no more than four (in the house) or six (in the senate) years of experience in the respective chambers. They also must negotiate with a white, Republican governor and a much-expanded Republican legislative delegation that has benefited from both term limits and a population boom in the white, conservative business mecca of northwest Arkansas.

Their success in such an environment will depend heavily upon the elevation of African American members to legislative leadership posts, an area in which they had some success during the 2001 session. For the first time in state history, African Americans now chair the Public Health, Welfare, and Labor Committees in both chambers. Black Caucus members now serve as vice chairs for the House Education and Management Committees as well, and state Senator Bill Lewellen chairs the legislative caucus for the central Arkansas region.[11] If the state's African American legislators can aggressively retain and expand their influence in this manner, as well as continue to play the spoiler and education roles, then the Arkansas political landscape stands—finally—to be significantly transformed.

NOTES

* A version of this chapter has been accepted for publication by the *Journal of Black Studies*.

1.   News articles were inconsistent in the identification of bill (and act) numbers for both chambers. Thus before examining roll-call votes we first double-checked and/or supplemented the identification of all measures in the *Arkansas Legislative Digest* for each legislative session. Then we turned to the house and senate journals of the Arkansas general assembly to record the votes of individual members.

2.   A 1973 study by the Voter Education Project, however, reported that Arkansas trailed only Alabama in the number of African Americans elected to public office at all levels ("State Second" 1973). It retained its position, bested by only Mississippi, in the project's 1974 report, and the Arkansas Black Political Caucus hosted the second National Black Political Convention that year ("Arkansas Ranks" 1974; Chicago Tribune 1974).

3.   Townsend was nominated in 1969 by Governor Winthrop Rockefeller to serve on the state board of education; the state senate refused to confirm the appointment, however ("Two Blacks" 1972).

4.   The caucus also sponsors an internship opportunity for undergraduate students during the legislative session and a scholarship program honoring Dr. William Townsend. A $500 scholarship is awarded to one student from each district represented by a member of the Arkansas Legislative Black Caucus (Arkansas Legislative Black Caucus 2002).

5.   Long-time observer of Arkansas politics, Diane Blair, commented that "teachers felt like they were being bit by their own dog" when the Clintons backed teacher testing in exchange for the rest of the education reform package (Osborne 1990, p. 94).

6.   At the April 8 signing ceremony, Walker praised Lewellen for his role in the "tremendous scuffle to get something substantive done." Lewellen stood on the edge of the crowd, opting not to speak though invited, saying only, "It was Bill Walker's day" to a reporter covering the event (Duffy 1993e).

7.   Less overtly, Democrats and many journalists also alleged that Representative McGee's motivations were transparently self-interested: a concentration of black voters into one congressional district would be conducive to his national-level political aspirations (Oswald 1991b; Morris 1991a; Brantley 1991).

8.   The redistricting responsibility was handed off to an interim committee for resolution by 2003.

9.   A similar plan was later that year crafted into a statewide initiative, touted by Governor Mike Huckabee, and adopted by voters at the polls. The appropriations bills necessary for its implementation, however, went right back to the state legislature, at which point the Black Caucus negotiated several key concessions. These included the funding of an Addiction Studies Program at the University of Arkansas, Pine Bluff, a 15% set aside for minority-targeted prevention and cessation initiatives, and more money to a Minority Health Commission (Steele 2002).

10.   Such alliances can, and do, take colorful twists as whites battle for black support in Southern states. In Louisiana, for example, conservative lawmakers recently attempted to secure African American support for their cause by arguing that Darwin was a racist, and therefore, that evolution should be excluded from the state's textbooks (Desalte 2001).

11.   Former Representative Brown cautioned that the advent of term limits makes black members newly dependent upon the favor of their white colleagues—instead of the seniority many were finally developing by the close of the 1990s—for their election, or selection, to leadership posts (Brown 2002). Whether term limits, and the subsequent loss of seniority as the prevailing criterion for legislative power, will be an advantage or a disadvantage to the Black Caucus members in the long run remains to be seen.

Chapter 3

African Americans in the
Contemporary Florida Legislature

Steven Tauber

Although similar to other states of the former Confederacy, Florida's political culture and racial history have been unique. Since Florida was a slave state and a member of the Confederacy, African Americans could not participate politically until after the Civil War. During Reconstruction, black Floridians participated fully in the political process, and in 1868, nineteen of the seventy-six state legislators were African American (Button 1984, p. 286). At the time all black voters and elected representatives were Republicans—the party of the Great Emancipator. However, when Reconstruction ended in 1876, white Floridians disenfranchised African Americans throughout the state, thus keeping them out of the state legislature. By 1900, Florida was the least populated of the former Confederate states, and African Americans constituted 44% of the state's population. Moreover, because white Floridians were all Democrats, Florida was clearly a one-party state (Dye 1998).

Although Florida began the twentieth century as a backward frontier state, by the 1960s it had developed into a growing, prosperous, and urbanized state. During the early twentieth century, agricultural opportunities and land speculation increased its population, although the Great Depression slowed this growth. After World War II, industry and tourism stimulated immense growth. Between 1940 and 1970 northeasterners and midwesterners immigrated to the state in droves, and Florida's population increased from 1.9 million to 6.8 million. This unfettered growth resembled demographic changes occurring in southwestern states such as California and Arizona more than most other Southern states. Many of these immigrants brought their Republican attachments with them, which allowed the Republican Party to make an impression in Florida by the 1950s, a time when it was dormant in most other Southern states. The influx of Cuban refugees from the Castro regime also increased the Republican presence in Florida politics. Throughout the period 1900–1960s, however, African Americans faced economic and political discrimination, such as in voting; therefore, no African Americans were elected to the state legislature (Colburn and Scher 1984).

Beginning in the middle 1960s, however, the federal government required changes in Florida's electoral procedures, which provided African Americans with the opportunity to elect candidates to the state legislature. The Voting Rights Act of 1965 removed barriers to African American voting, such as literacy tests, and increased federal supervision over states with a history of racial discrimination in voting. Additionally, U.S. Supreme Court decisions required that state legislatures redraw district lines in order to give urban areas, where many African Americans resided, greater representation in state legislatures. Furthermore, the establishment of single-member districts in Florida in 1982 allowed areas heavily populated with African Americans to elect black candidates. Finally, the drawing of majority-minority districts after the 1992 redistricting expanded black representation.

These changes undoubtedly brought about an increase in descriptive representation for African Americans in Florida; however, it is unclear whether they have also enhanced substantive representation of African American interests. This chapter examines whether improved descriptive representation has led to improved substantive representation. First, I discuss in more detail how changes in redistricting since the late 1960s increased African American representation. Then, I explore four important aspects of Florida's African American state legislators' ability to represent African Americans' substantive interests: (1) the Black Caucus, (2) relations with the governor, (3) committee chairs, and (4) political incorporation. Finally, I examine closely the voting behavior of African American legislators to determine the extent that they are able to forge coalitions with other groups in the legislature.

A major theme of this chapter centers on the shift from Democratic to Republican control of both houses during the 1990s. From the late 1960s through the middle 1990s, Democrats overwhelmingly controlled both houses of the Florida legislature. However, since these Democrats were mainly conservative, Old South Democrats, they often allied with Republicans against progressive policies that many African American legislators advocated. During the 1980s and 1990s, the political parties polarized on key economic and social issues, including race. Although Florida had supported Republican presidential candidates during the 1950s (Eisenhower) and 1960s (Nixon), by the 1980s the anti-tax, pro-business, and religious fundamentalism message of Ronald Reagan attracted many conservative Democratic voters and politicians to the Republican Party. After the 1992 election, the forty-seat senate was split evenly between the two parties; therefore, Republican Ander Crenshaw (Jacksonville) served as senate president from 1992 to 1993, and Democrat Pat Thomas (Quincy) served as senate president from 1993 to 1994. This session marked the first time since Reconstruction that the Democrats did not control outright both houses of the state legislature. After the national Republican landslide of 1994, the Republicans wrested full control of the senate. In 1996, despite Clinton's victory in Florida in the presidential election, the Republicans took control of the house of representatives by a slim 61–59 margin. In addition to retaking the governor's mansion in 1998, the Republicans expanded their margins in both houses. Although Florida's African American legislators, virtually all of whom have been Democrats,[1] experienced difficulty during Democratic control, their influence in the legislature was sharply curtailed during the period of Republican control.

DESCRIPTIVE REPRESENTATION IN FLORIDA

Before 1980: Prior to the late 1960s, Florida's legislature was one of the least representative in the United States. Although the state became more urbanized during the twentieth century, the legislature did not redraw district boundaries, and as a result urban areas were not allotted more representatives to match their increasing population. In fact, during the 1950s, Florida's six largest counties contained more than half of the state's population, but only 20% of the seats in the house of representatives and 17% of the seats in the senate. Moreover, the smallest counties, with a combined population of less than 20% of the state, elected a majority of the house and senate (Havard and Beth 1991, p. 29). Residents of urban areas asserted that this malapportionment severely diluted their power in the legislature. Because they resided primarily in urban areas, African Americans especially felt the sting of malapportionment. Since urban areas received so few representatives for such large populations, African Americans were unable to form a voting bloc sufficient to elect a black candidate.

Redistricting reforms enacted during the late 1960s and 1970s helped African Americans win seats in the Florida house of representatives. In 1967, the U.S. Supreme Court, in the case of *Swann v. Adams*, 385 U.S. 440 (1967), mandated that Florida redraw district lines so that representatives would be apportioned on a par with population. Consequently, urban areas received more representatives, which provided black communities with more opportunity to elect a black candidate. In 1968, high school teacher Joe Kershaw became the first African American elected to the Florida legislature since Reconstruction. He was elected from the Miami-Dade region, which contained enough African Americans and liberal white voters to support his candidacy. The following election (1970), Gwen Cherry, also from Miami, became the first black female elected to the Florida legislature.

The 1972 redistricting plan apportioned the number of representatives equally; however, the legislature's decision to use multi-member districts generated a new controversy. Although the urban areas received more representatives, large geographic areas elected multiple representatives at large, meaning that the entire district voted for all of their allotted representatives. The use of multi-member districts allowed the white majority in urban areas to dominate African Americans in elections to house and senate seats. African American groups sought to carve up the larger multi-member districts into smaller, single-member districts. Because African American populations tended to cluster in certain areas, some of those single-member districts would definitely contain enough black voters to guarantee the election of more black representatives and even senators. Despite these claims, the white, Democrat-dominated legislature enacted a multi-member district plan with only twenty-one representatives and five senators elected from single-member districts, all of which represented rural areas. All others came from multi-member districts ranging from two to six representatives and two to three senators. Allied with Republicans, who were also disadvantaged in multi-member urban districts, African Americans challenged this redistricting plan in state and federal courts but were unsuccessful (Wall 1977). Despite the disadvantage of multi-member districts, African Americans did increase their representation in the Florida legislature during the 1970s. In 1976, Jacksonville dentist, Arnett Girardeau, became the first African American elected to the house from a district outside of Miami since Reconstruction. In 1978, John Thomas, who was also from Jacksonville, won a house seat, and in 1980, Republican John Plummer won a seat from Miami (see Table 3.1). No African Americans were elected to the senate. In fact, by 1981, Florida and South Carolina were the only Southern states without any black senators (Silva 1982).

The 1980s: The round of redistricting after the 1980 census provided further opportunities for African Americans to expand their representation in the Florida legislature. Fearing legal battles and reacting to increasing pressure, the Florida legislature in 1982 switched to single-member districts, many of which were dominated by African Americans. As a result, ten African Americans, twice the previous amount, were elected to the house, and for the first time

TABLE 3.1
African American Legislators in the Florida House of Representatives

1968–1970	1970–1972	1972–1974	1974–1976	1976–1978	1978–1980
Kershaw	Cherry	Cherry	Cherry	Cherry	Cherry*
	Kershaw	Kershaw	Girardeau	Girardeau	Giradeau
				Kershaw	Kershaw
					Thomas
1 member	2 members	2 members	2 members	3 members	4 members
0.8%	1.7%	1.7%#	1.7%	2.5%	3.3%

1980–1982	1982–1984	1984–1986	1986–1988	1988–1990	1990–1992
Girardeau	Brown	Brown	Brown	Brown	Brown
Kershaw	J. Burke	J. Burke	J. Burke	J. Burke	J. Burke
C. Meek	Clark	Clark	Clark	Clark	Chestnut
Plummer	Hargrett	Hargrett	Gafney	Hargrett	Clark
Thomas	Jamerson	Jamerson	Hargrett	Holzendorf	Hargrett
	Lawson	Lawson	Jamerson	Jamerson	Holzendorf
	Logan	Logan	Lawson	Lawson	Jamerson
	Reaves	Reaves	Logan	Logan	Jones
	Reddick	Reddick	Reaves	Reaves	Lawson
	Thomas	Thomas	Reddick	Reddick	Logan
					Reaves
					Reddick
5 members	10 members	10 members	10 members	10 members	12 members
4.2%	8.3%	8.3%	8.3%	8.3%	10.0%

1992–1994	1994–1996	1996–1998	1998–2000		
Bullard	Bradley	Bradley	Bradley		
B. Burke	Bullard	Bullard	Bullard		
Bush	Bush	Bush	Bush		
Chestnut	Chestnut	Chestnut	Chestnut		
Dawson	Dawson	Dawson	Dennis&		
Dennis	Dennis	Dennis	Eggelletion		
Eggelletion	Eggelletion	Eggelletion	Greene		
Greene	Greene	Greene	Hill		
Hill	Hill	Hill	Lawson		
Jamerson	Lawson	Lawson	Logan		
Lawson	Logan	Logan	Miller		
Logan	K. Meek	K. Meek	Reddick		
Miller	Miller	Miller	Roberts		
Reddick	Reddick	Reddick	Smith		
	Roberts-Burke^	Roberts-Burke	Wilson		
14 members	15 members	15 members	15 members		
11.7%	12.5%	12.5%	12.5%		

*Rep. Cherry died in 1979 and Rep. C. Meek replaced her.
#In 1972 the Florida house of representatives increased from 119 to 120 members.
^Upon marrying, Rep. B. Burke changed her last name to Roberts-Burke.
&Rep. Lee replaced Rep. Dennis in 2000.

Source: The Clerk's Manual, 1968–1970, 1970–1972, 1972–1974, 1974–1976, 1976–1978, 1978, 1980, 1980–1982, 1982–1984, 1984–1986, 1986–1988, 1988–1990, 1990–1992, 1992–1994, 1994–1996, 1996–1998, 1998–2000, the Clerk of the House of Representatives.

TABLE 3.2
African American Legislators in the Florida Senate

1980–1982	1982–1984	1984–1986	1986–1988	1988–1990
None	Girardeau C. Meek	Girardeau C. Meek	Girardeau C. Meek	Girardeau C. Meek
0 members 0.0%	2 members 5.0%	2 members 5.0%	2 members 5.0%	2 members 5.0%

1990–1992	1992–1994	1994–1996	1996–1998	1998–2000
Girardeau C. Meek	Hargrett Holzendorf Jones Meadows Turner	Hargrett Holzendorf Jones Meadows Turner	Hargrett Holzendorf Jones Meadows Turner	Dawson-White Hargrett Holzendorf Jones K. Meek
2 members 5.0%	5 members 12.5%	5 members 12.5%	5 members 12.5%	5 members 12.5%

Source: The Clerk's Manual, 1968–1970, 1970–1972, 1972–1974, 1974–1976, 1976–1978, 1978, 1980, 1980–1982, 1982–1984, 1984–1986, 1986–1988, 1988–1990, 1990–1992, 1992–1994, 1994–1996, 1996–1998, 1998–2000, the Clerk of the House of Representatives.

since Reconstruction, two African Americans were elected to the senate (see Table 3.2). Six African American house members came from majority-black districts: James Burke (107th District-Miami, 73% black population), John Thomas (16th District-Jacksonville, 62%), Willie Logan (108th District-Opa Locka, 59%), Corrine Brown (17th District-Jacksonville, 58%), James Hargrett (63rd District-Tampa, 52%), and Alzo Reddick (40th District-Orlando, 52%). The other four came from districts with sizeable black populations: Doug Jamerson (55th District-St. Petersburg, 49%), Bill Clark (91st District-Lauderdale Lakes, 45%), Jefferson Reaves (106th District-Miami, 41%), and Alfred Lawson (9th District-Tallahassee, 32%). Of the two African American senators, Carrie Meek represented a majority-black district (36th District-Miami, 65%), whereas Arnett Girardeau represented a minority, but sizeable, black district (7th District-Jacksonville, 49%) (Ammons 1991). African American strength in both houses remained constant until 1990, when two additional African Americans were elected, both from house districts that were about 30% black—Cynthia Chestnut (23rd District-Gainesville) and Daryl Jones (118th District-Miami).

The 1990s: In 1992, the controversy over race and redistricting intensified. As a result of 1982 amendments to the Voting Rights Act and Supreme Court decisions, such as *Thornburg v. Gingles*, 478 U.S. 30 (1986), minorities residing in states with a history of voting discrimination were on a strong legal footing to challenge districting plans that did not create enough majority-minority districts. Emboldened African American legislators, interest groups, and private citizens in Florida, therefore, sought the creation of more majority-minority state senate and house districts in 1992. However, this goal conflicted with white Democrats' aim to use the 1992 redistricting to protect as many Democratic incumbents as possible. Although the Democrats controlled both houses, these competing goals divided the party. Furthermore, Cuban Americans in South Florida fought for the creation of majority-Latino districts, where Republicans would most likely win. Florida Republicans, who hoped that concentrating more African American voters into majority-minority districts would increase GOP strength in the surrounding, predominately white districts, supported black and Latino challenges as well. Outnumbered white Democrats were forced to create more majority black districts. In the decade since the 1980 census, many areas that were previously majority white had become majority black. In other cases, the legislature gerrymandered to create majority black districts. Although the plan that the legislature passed in April 1992 contained more majority-minority districts, African Americans still challenged it in federal and state court. Most notably African Americans focused on the Twenty-first Senate District, which encompassed the Tampa Bay area, arguing that the district should include the largely black areas of Tampa, St. Petersburg, and Bradenton. After much wrangling among the state legislature, the U.S. Justice Department, the Florida Supreme Court, and the U.S. Supreme Court, a majority black district was established (MacManus 2002b).

By the 1992 election, thirteen house districts were majority black, and after the election twelve of those districts elected a black representative: Al Lawson (8th District-Tallahassee), Anthony Hill (14th District-Jacksonville), Willye Dennis (15th District-Jacksonville), Alzo Reddick (39th District-Orlando), Douglas Jamerson (55th District-St. Petersburg), Les Miller (59th District-Tampa), Addie Greene (84th District-Palm Beach County), Muriel Dawson (93rd District-Ft. Lauderdale), Josephus Eggelletion (94th District-Lauderdale Lakes), Willie Logan (103rd District-Opa Locka), Beryl Burke (108th District-Miami), and James Bush (109th District-Miami). Although the 104th District containing Miami and North Miami was majority black, white Democrat Elaine Gordon was reelected without facing any black opposition. In 1992, two African Americans were elected to the house from districts with only 30% African Americans. Cynthia Chestnut was reelected from the Twenty-third District (Gainesville), and newcomer Larcenia Bullard was elected to represent the 118th District from Miami after its incumbent Daryl Jones sought (and won) a state senate seat. Consequently, after the 1992 election, African American representation increased from twelve to fourteen. In 1994, Representative Gordon retired, and African American Kendrick Meek, son of U.S. Representative Carrie Meek, won the election in the 104th District, thus bringing African American representation up to fifteen, 12.5% of the total house.

The 1992 round of redistricting also created five state senate districts with largely black populations (three of which were majority black), and after the 1992 elections, black representation in the state senate increased from two to five. Since incumbents Arnett Girardeau and Carrie Meek retired to run for the U.S. House—Meek won and Girardeau lost—all five senators were new. Three of these new senators were former house members: Betty Holzendorf (2nd District-parts of Jacksonville and Gainesville), Daryl Jones (40th District-the Florida Keys and part of Miami), and James Hargrett (21st District-parts of Tampa, St. Petersburg, and Bradenton). The two other senators were relative newcomers: Matthew Meadows (30th District-parts of Broward and Palm Beach counties) and Bill Turner (36th District-parts of Dade County).

SUBSTANTIVE REPRESENTATION: POWER IN THE LEGISLATURE

The redistricting policies of the 1980s and 1990s clearly increased African American representation in the Florida legislature; however, it is less clear whether this increased descriptive representation led to substantive improvements for African Americans. To explore this issue, I focus specifically on four aspects of substantive representation: the strength of the Florida Legislative Black Caucus, black legislators' relations with governors, the importance of African American committee chairs, and the extent that African American legislators have been incorporated into the leadership of their respective houses. I shall argue that although the increases in African American descriptive representation during the 1980s and 1990s enhanced substantive representation, the Republican takeover of both houses during the middle 1990s sharply curtailed African American legislators' influence within the legislature and Florida politics in general.

The Legislative Black Caucus: The Florida Legislative Black Caucus demonstrates how increases in descriptive representation enhance substantive representation. In 1971, African Americans in the U.S. Congress formed the Congressional Black Caucus (CBC) in order to band together to improve their ability to pass legislation they desired and prevent the passage of legislation they opposed. The CBC was premised on the notion that a cohesive unit of black legislators would present a more formidable force than if each member acted individually. Additionally, the CBC conducted research, fashioned policy proposals, and lobbied presidents on behalf of African Americans living throughout the United States (Pohlman 1990, pp. 182–83). During the 1970s, African Americans in state legislatures established their own caucuses, and in 1982, the twelve African Americans in the Florida legislature (ten representatives and two senators, see Tables 3.1 and 3.2) formed the Florida Conference of Black State Legislators, better known as the "Black Caucus". Prior to 1982, black strength in the legislature had not been sufficient to support an effective caucus. According to its official literature, the purpose of the organization is "to operate exclusively for the promotion of the political, economic, and social conditions as well as the promotion of the common good and general welfare of the various peoples of Florida." (LaMarr 2002). Although the Florida Legislative Black Caucus phrases its mission in racially neutral terms, it has always concentrated its efforts on issues important to black Floridians. Its first chair, Carrie Meek (Miami), stated clearly that she would use the caucus to ensure that "the state government would be more responsive to the needs of black people" (Silva 1982).

The establishment of the Florida Legislative Black Caucus demonstrates one way that increased descriptive representation leads to more substantive representation; however, the magnitude of its effectiveness is still ambiguous. Upon its inception, internal fighting caused problems. Jacksonville Senator Arnett Girardeau battled with Jacksonville Representative John Thomas over leadership of the caucus, and ultimately the organization selected Senator Carrie Meek (Miami) as chair (Silva 1982). Since 1982, the Florida Legislative Black Caucus has put onto the legislative agenda issues of importance to black Floridians, such as the creation of a Martin Luther King Day holiday and more funding for social programs (Miller 1993). Arguably the Florida Legislative Black Caucus's most significant contribution to legislative policy making came during the battle over the 1992 redistricting. Splitting with the state Democratic Party leadership, the Florida Legislative Black Caucus proposed its own U.S. House redistricting plan, which contained four districts with significant black populations (Jacksonville, Tampa Bay-Orlando, and two in Broward-Dade County), whereas the Democratic leadership plan contained only two. Moreover, unlike the Democratic leadership's plan, the Black Caucus plan did not focus on protecting incumbents. After much political and legal wrangling, the legislature settled on three districts with sizable black populations: Jacksonville, and two in Miami-Dade (MacManus 2002a). The Florida Legislative Black Caucus was instrumental in the creation of this additional majority black congressional district. Additionally, it fought hard for the creation of as many majority-black state house and senate districts as possible. It played a major role in the creation of the previously discussed Twenty-first Senate District in Tampa-St. Petersburg (MacManus 2002b).

Although nearly every member of the Florida Legislative Black Caucus has been a Democrat, the Republican takeover of both houses of the legislature in 1997 initiated a surprising alliance between the Black Caucus and Republican legislative leaders. Despite major political differences between the conservative Republican leaders and members of the Black Caucus, the two groups were ideologically similar on social issues, such as support for legislation banning same-sex marriages, reestablishing prayer in school, and creating school vouchers (Hollis 1997). In 1998, the Black Caucus shifted further toward the Republican majority because of a rift with white Democrats in the house. House Democrats voted to remove African American Representative Willie Logan (Opa-Locka) as their minority leader and replace him with white, moderate Democrat Anne Mackenzie (Ft. Lauderdale). The white Democrats favoring this move cited Logan's poor fund-raising skills, but black representatives, all of whom opposed Logan's ouster, viewed this action as a slight against them. Black Caucus Chair Representative Beryl Roberts-Burke even publicly indicated that she would seek to work closely with Republicans (Cox 1998). However, the reaction to Logan's ouster caused a rift within the Black Caucus. Four of the five black senators publicly split with their house counterparts over the suggested alliance with the Republicans. Black senators criticized their house counterparts for causing a "riot" (Wallsten 1998). The resulting alliance between the Black Caucus and house Republicans translated to the policy-making arena during the 1998 session, when the Black Caucus abandoned its Democratic house leaders and supported the Republicans' education budget (Wallsten and Smith 1998).

By 2000, the relationship between the state's African American population and state Republicans deteriorated in general, which in turn posed major impediments to the close relationship between the Black Caucus and Republican legislative leaders. In early 2000, the Black Caucus protested Governor Jeb Bush's executive order ending affirmative action (see discussion that follows for more details). The Black Caucus demonstrated its displeasure by boycotting a ceremonial lunch with the governor that all legislators traditionally attend (Morgan 2000). Relations between black Floridians and the Republican Party deteriorated after the 2000 election debacle. Embittered African Americans throughout the state blamed Republicans for disenfranchising minorities, failing to count black votes, and stealing the election. This acrimony spilled into the state legislature early in the 2001 session. Arguing that the state law preventing felons from voting unfairly disenfranchised African Americans, the Black Caucus sponsored a bill to restore voting rights to felons, but overwhelming Republican opposition defeated the measure (Klas 2001). Differences between the Black Caucus and white Democrats still exist, and there is no evidence yet that the Black Caucus will fully realign with Democrats. Nevertheless, it is clear that the alliance between the Black Caucus and legislative Republicans was short-lived.

The Governor: African American legislators have consistently experienced adverse relationships with governors. Although one might expect that as African American representation increased in the legislature, black legislators would increase their clout with the governor, the reality is that the two entities often conflict. Before 1982, the number of African American legislators was so small that governors could ignore them; however, after 1982, especially with the formation of the Florida Legislative Black Caucus, governors were forced to work with them. Ironically, as African Americans gained influence in the legislature during the 1990s, they conflicted more frequently with governors, who did not share their goals. Black legislators, and black Floridians as a whole, expected Democratic Governor Lawton Chiles, first elected in 1990, to be a reliable ally. However, early in his term, he alienated African American lawmakers by vetoing a 1991 civil rights bill that would have granted punitive damages to victims of racial discrimination. Chiles argued that it would only benefit plaintiffs' attorneys and do little to prevent racial discrimination, but African American lawmakers interpreted the veto as Chiles' lack of commitment to civil rights (McKinnon 1991). In 1994, the Black Caucus met with Governor Chiles and Lt. Governor Buddy McKay to enlist their support for a pending bill that would compensate victims of the 1923 massacre in Rosewood. Black Representatives Al Lawson (Tallahassee)—the bill's sponsor—and Cynthia Chestnut (Gainesville) engaged in testy exchanges with Governor Chiles, and the meeting was about to end in anger until Lt. Governor McKay mollified both sides (Dye 1998, pp. 16–17). Despite their strained relationship with Governor Chiles, black legislators actively supported him for reelection in 1994. When Chiles' Republican opponent Jeb Bush was asked what he would do for the African American community, he replied "probably nothing" (Rado 1994). In response, African American legislators actively opposed Bush's candidacy by issuing sharp rebukes to his comments and urging the state's African Americans to support Chiles (Rado 1994). Their efforts paid off, because Chiles narrowly fended off Bush's challenge by a slim 51–49 vote margin, which means that overwhelming black support contributed to Chiles' reelection (*Houston Chronicle* New Services 1994).

Although Chiles mended relations with African American legislators, a rift between Florida's black politicians and the Florida Democratic Party eroded black support for Chiles' potential successor—Democratic Lt. Governor Buddy McKay. However, the source of the division came from the legislature itself, not the actions of Chiles or McKay. In 1997, state house Democrats selected black Representative Willie Logan (Opa Locka) as their minority leader. However, in early 1998, Democratic house members voted to strip Logan of his authority and replace him with white moderate Anne MacKenzie (Ft. Lauderdale). When defending their decision, Democratic leaders cited Logan's liberal views and poor fund-raising abilities. However, outraged black legislators did not accept that explanation. Claiming that white Democrats had taken African Americans for granted, Representatives Logan, Rudy Bradley (St. Petersburg), and Senator Jim Hargrett (Tampa) endorsed Republican Jeb Bush over Democrat McKay in the 1998 gubernatorial race. Compared to his 1994 campaign, Bush in 1998 portrayed himself as being far more receptive to the concerns of black citizens (Talev 1998). After the 1998 elections, Logan became an Independent and Bradley became a Republican. However, these moves probably ended their political careers, since Logan lost a 2000 bid for a U.S. Senate seat to Democrat Bill Nelson, and Bradley lost a bid for a state senate seat to Les Miller, an African American Democrat.

Bush trounced McKay in 1998, winning 14% of the black vote (Pacenti 1998); however, he quickly alienated black legislators far more than his Democratic predecessor had. In early 2000, Bush issued his "One Florida" executive order, which ended preferences for racial minorities in state hiring, contract awarding, and admitting students to state universities. Not only did African American legislators oppose ending affirmative action, but they also resented that Bush neglected to hold public meetings before issuing the order. To protest the governor's actions, Representative Tony Hill (Jacksonville) and Senator Kendrick Meek (Miami) staged a sit-in at the governor's mansion. Eventually, a crowd of 15,000 marched on the state capitol, but it was not until a reporter leaked crude remarks that Bush made about the protestors that the governor reluctantly agreed to hold three public meetings throughout the state (Liston 2000). Nevertheless, Bush enacted "One Florida" over the vehement objections that African Americans expressed at these meetings.

The controversy over the 2000 presidential election results in Florida heightened tensions between black legislators and Governor Jeb Bush. Many black Floridians suspected that Jeb Bush and Florida's Republican Secretary of

State Katherine Harris conspired to disenfranchise African Americans during the election. African American activists argued that the poor precincts, populated largely with African Americans, were the worst equipped polling places and most prone to error. Furthermore, many African Americans charged that Florida's policy prohibiting felons from voting disproportionately affected black voters. In fact, many African Americans who were not felons were turned away at the polls because their names incorrectly appeared on lists of felons who were unable to vote. Other black Floridians reported that white highway patrol and police officers intimidated them from voting (Associated Press 2001). After the U.S. Supreme Court gave George Bush the victory in December 2000, African American state legislators in Florida continued to clash with Governor Jeb Bush. When Bush announced the formation of a panel to examine election reform, he neglected to invite any African American state legislators. Al Lawson rebuked the omission of black state lawmakers, explaining, "Voter disenfranchisement is an issue that deeply affects us, and we should have been invited. It shows a lack of sensitivity from the get-go" (Gettleman 2000). The relationship between Florida's black state legislators and Governor Bush has not improved. African American opposition to Bush was reflected in his 2002 reelection bid, where only 6% of blacks supported him, compared to 14% in 1998. However, African American turnout was lower than the overall turnout, and Bush easily defeated Democratic challenger Bill McBride (Allison 2002).

Committee Chairs: Because committee chairs exert tremendous influence over the outcome of legislation, the extent that African Americans have chaired committees in the Florida house and senate is an important substantive representation concern. Clearly, increases in African American representation have provided more opportunities to chair committees in both houses; however, black legislators have experienced difficulties chairing significant committees. Different committees provide various ways for chairs to exert power, and these differences shape African American chairs' ability to use a committee chair position on behalf of black Floridians. Some committees, such as transportation, allow the members, especially the chairs, to funnel pork barrel projects to their districts. Other committees, such as education, focus on specific policy areas in which chairs significantly affect legislation. Some policy committees are especially geared toward issues affecting African Americans. For example, community affairs and housing committees have jurisdiction over public welfare and economic development programs that are essential in minority communities. Finally, committees responsible for budgeting, appropriations, taxes, and scheduling debate (Rules Committee) are the most prestigious and influential in state legislatures. Chairing appropriations and tax committees provide considerable opportunity to fashion important policies for all Floridians and to funnel pork barrel projects into one's district. Since the Rules Committee schedules votes and amendments for all legislation, its chair also influences legislation. Therefore, if an African American chaired one of these committees, then he or she would have the ability to represent black substantive interests.

While black legislators in Florida have been selected as committee chairs, most of these committees have been geared to less consequential policy areas, and there has only been one session (1994–1996) in which an African American chaired a highly influential committee (House Finance Committee). Joe Kershaw, who was first elected in 1968, became the first black to chair a committee when he rose to the top of the House Elections Committee from 1974 through 1978. Although election regulations do not necessarily affect African American interests, Kershaw used his position to sponsor and ensure the passage of a 1978 bill that prohibited political parties from endorsing primary candidates. This bill prevented Democratic Party organizations from working against African American candidates. Moreover, Kershaw's involvement in this issue stemmed from his feud with the chair of the State Democratic Party Executive Committee, Mike Abrams (from Miami-Dade County), who had not appointed African Americans to the Florida Democratic delegation to the Electoral College in 1976 (Shaw 1978).

As Table 3.3 indicates, African American legislators chaired more committees in the house of representatives as their presence increased during the 1980s and 1990s. One important black committee chair in the house was Douglas Jamerson (St. Petersburg), who led the Education Committee during the 1990–1992 and 1992–1994 sessions. In 1991, Jamerson successfully pushed through the house a massive education reform bill known as "Blueprint 2000", which gave more decision-making autonomy to local school districts instead of the state. Despite opposition from teachers unions, Jamerson ensured passage in the house of representatives, and after two years of struggle and negotiation, the senate passed the law in 1993. Alienating conservatives in the legislature, Jamerson also worked to pass a law that enhanced multicultural education in Florida's public schools (Moss 1993). In early 1994, Betty Castor resigned as Florida's education commissioner—a cabinet position—to become president of the University of South Florida, and Governor Lawton Chiles (D) appointed Jamerson to fill out the remainder of her term. However, Republican Frank Brogan defeated Jamerson for reelection as education commissioner in November 1994. The most significant committee chair for Florida's black legislators was Willie Logan (Opa Locka), who led the House Finance Committee from 1994

TABLE 3.3
African American Committee Chairs in the Florida House of Representatives

1974–1976*	1976–1978	1978–1980	1980–1982	1982–1984
Kershaw-Elections	Kershaw-Elections	Girardeau-Corrections	None	None
1 chair of 18 comm.	1 chair of 23 comm.	1 chair of 22 comm.	0 chairs	0 chairs
5.6%	4.3%	4.5%	0.0%	0.0%

1984–1986	1986–1988	1988–1990	1990–1992
None	Jamerson-Housing Reddick-Youth	Hargrett-Pub. Transp. Jamerson-Corrections Lawson-Natural Res. Reddick-Emerg.Prep.	Jamerson-Education Hargrett-Labor Rel. Logan-Corrections Reddick-Tourism & Econ. Dev.
0 chairs	2 chairs of 27 comm.	4 chairs of 29 comm.	4 chairs of 28 comms.
0.0%	7.4%	13.8%	14.3%

1992–1994	1994–1996	1996–1998&	1998–2000
Jamerson-Education# Reddick-Tourism	Chestnut-Education. Lawson-Gov't. Ops. Logan-Finance	None	None
2 chairs of 22 comm.	3 chairs of 24 comm.	0 chairs of 7 councils^	0 chairs of 7 councils
9.1%	12.5%	0.0%	0.0%

*There were no African American committee chairs until 1974.
#Rep. Jamerson resigned from the legislature in January 1994 to serve in the cabinet as education commissioner.
&First session of Republican control.
^Republican speakers organized the house according to seven councils that report legislation to the floor instead of the usual twenty to thirty committees.

Source: The Clerk's Manual, 1968–1970, 1970–1972, 1972–1974, 1974–1976, 1976–1978, 1978, 1980, 1980–1982, 1982–1984, 1984–1986, 1986–1988, 1988–1990, 1990–1992, 1992–1994, 1994–1996, 1996–1998, 1998–2000, the Clerk of the House of Representatives.

to 1996. This committee considers all bills dealing with taxation. The fact that Logan chaired this crucial committee revealed that African American legislators had achieved a significant level of substantive representation in the house. Moreover, Logan used his authority to establish a scholarship fund for minority law students in Florida. However, his role generated controversy when his wife, Lyra Logan, was named as the fund's administrator (Rado 1995).

TABLE 3.4
African American Committee Chairs in the Florida Senate

1988–1990*	1990–1992	1992–1994
Meek-Community Aff.	Girardeau-Ethics	Hargrett-Econ. Dev. Holzendorf-Personnel
1 chair of 17 comm. 5.9%	1 chair of 20 comm. 5.0%	2 chairs of 19 comm. 10.5%

1994–1996#	1996–1998	1998–2000
None	Hargrett-Transportation	None
0 chairs 0.0%	1 chair of 16 comm. 6.3%	0 chairs 0.0%

*There were no African American committee chairs until 1988.
#First session of Republican control.

Source: The Clerk's Manual, 1968–1970, 1970–1972, 1972–1974, 1974–1976, 1976–1978, 1978, 1980, 1980–1982, 1982–1984, 1984–1986, 1986–1988, 1988–1990, 1990–1992, 1992–1994, 1994–1996, 1996–1998, 1998–2000, the Clerk of the House of Representatives.

Table 3.4 shows that black senators have been less likely than black representatives to reach the position of committee chair. In 1988, Carrie Meek was named chair of the Community Affairs Committee after six years of service in the senate. Since this committee focused on urban programs and policies, her position allowed her to increase the attention that the state paid to African Americans in urban areas. The following term Senator Arnett Girardeau chaired the Ethics Committee, which although important for the operations of the senate did not influence policies affecting Floridians in general or black Floridians in particular. During the 1992–1994 session, African American committee leadership in the senate was at its height. Senator Betty Holzendorf chaired the committee dealing with state personnel, which exerted minimal impact on policies affecting Floridians in general. However, Senator Jim Hargrett chaired the International Trade, Economic Development, and Tourism Committee, which exercises jurisdiction over issues important to the economy of the state and to African Americans. Both he and African American Representative Alzo Reddick, who chaired the House Tourism Committee, tried unsuccessfully to increase taxes on tourism and restaurant meals in order to finance a state commission to promote Florida tourism (Albright 1993).

After Republicans assumed control of the senate in 1994 and the house in 1996, opportunities for African Americans to chair committees lessened but did not vanish. When the Republicans assumed control over the house in 1996,

Speaker Daniel Webster (Orlando) consolidated his power by streamlining house organization into seven councils that possessed the authority to report legislation to the floor, and approximately thirty committees within the councils specialize in a particular area. In 1996, all seven council chair slots went to Republicans. In 1998, new Speaker John Thrasher (the position generally rotates every two years) retained the council system. However, in the 1998 election for speaker, African American Democrats Beryl Roberts and Rudy Bradley voted for the Republican Thrasher over the Democratic choice Buzz Ritchie (Pensacola); consequently, they were named chairs of the Children and Family Committee and Business Development and International Trade Committee. (Democrat Bradley became a Republican the next year, after endorsing Bush for governor.) Given the council system, however, these leadership positions were more like subcommittee chairs than committee chairs. In the senate, Majority Leader Toni Jennings (Orlando) selected African American Democrat Jim Hargrett to chair the Transportation Committee during the 1996–1998 term. However, in the 1998–2000 session, that position was given to former speaker of the Florida house and newly elected Senator Daniel Webster, although the Republican leadership selected Hargrett to chair the Transportation Subcommittee of the Budget Committee.

Political Incorporation: Examining committee chairs reveals the extent that African Americans have been incorporated into leadership positions, but it neglects important elements of legislative power, such as seniority, committee assignments, and party leadership. Haynie (2001) provides a detailed measure of a comprehensive conception of political incorporation of African Americans in state legislatures. Haynie's political incorporation index sums the following values for a particular year: (1) number of African American legislators; (2) African American percent of the Democratic Party (only if the Democratic Party is the majority party); (3) number of prestige committee assignments (budget, taxes, and rules); (4) mean African American seniority in years; and (5) two points for each leadership position (committee chairs, speaker pro tempore, assistant majority-minority leaders, and whips) and three points for each top leadership position (speaker, majority-minority leader).[2] Using information collected from the *Florida's Clerk Manual* (Clerk of the House, 1968–2000), I computed the incorporation score for each session of the Florida house and senate. Specifically, I computed the political incorporation index using data from the middle year of each session: 1969, 1971, 1973, 1975, 1977, 1979, 1981, 1983, 1985, 1987, 1989, 1991, 1993, 1995, 1997, and 1999.

The results for the incorporation scores are reported in Table 3.5. In the house of representatives, the incorporation scores were extremely low throughout

TABLE 3.5
Political Incorporation Index for African Americans
in the Florida Legislature

Year	House	Senate
1969	3.3	0.0
1971	6.5	0.0
1973	8.6	0.0
1975	13.3	0.0
1977	15.0	0.0
1979	17.5	0.0
1981	14.7	0.0
1983	25.3	9.3
1985	31.4	13.5
1987	38.9	15.0
1989	47.1	23.7
1991	58.7	22.7
1993	55.6	41.0
1995	64.7	12.0*
1997	28.9*	18.0
1999	47.8	16.6

*Republicans assumed control of chamber.

Source: See Table 3.4.

the 1970s. However, as more African Americans were elected during the 1980s, older members accrued more seniority, secured better committee assignments, and even assumed leadership positions; therefore, black political incorporation increased. During the 1988–1990 session, for example, four African Americans chaired committees, and the incorporation score for 1989 was 47.1. As did Haynie (2001, pp. 68–70), I computed incorporation scores for the states in his analysis during that same year (1989). Although significantly trailing Maryland and Illinois, Florida's score was comparable to North Carolina and far ahead of New Jersey and Arkansas. African American political incorporation continued to rise through the 1990s, reaching a peak of 64.7 in 1995, which was almost as high as Illinois and Maryland in 1989. However, when the Republicans assumed control of the house in 1996, African American political incorporation dropped precipitously. In 1999, African American political incorporation rose somewhat, because Les Miller (Tampa) became the first black representative to serve as Democratic leader, and the Republicans rewarded black representatives Bradley and Roberts's support for Jeb Bush with two committee chairs. African American political incorporation in the Florida senate remained extremely low until the 1990s, when it gradually increased as African American senators amassed more seniority, better assignments, and committee chair positions. Similar to the results in the house, when the Republicans took control of the senate in 1994, African American political incorporation fell dramatically.

These findings demonstrate two important points concerning the relationship between descriptive and substantive representation. On the one hand, it is clear that African American incorporation in the Florida house and senate increased as African Americans gained more seats after the 1982 and 1992 redistricting. Similar to Haynie (2001, p. 70), I conducted a correlation analysis between the percent of African Americans in the legislature and the incorporation score in each year. I computed two separate correlations: (1) one that focused only on the house of representatives, and (2) one that included both results from the house and the senate. The correlations between representation and incorporation were quite high ($r = 0.65$ for both houses and 0.88 for solely the house of representatives) and significant ($p < 0.01$). Despite the overall correlation, Table 3.5 demonstrates that the change in party control impacted black political incorporation. Despite African American representation remaining at its peak of 12.5% of both chambers during the late 1990s, incorporation scores fell dramatically after the Republicans took control. African Americans were no longer part of the majority party, were less likely to be assigned to prestige committees, and their chances for leadership positions, especially committee chairs, virtually disappeared.

SUBSTANTIVE REPRESENTATION IN FLORIDA: VOTING COALITIONS

Another measure of African American effectiveness focuses on voting coalitions that black legislators formed with other blocs to pass progressive legislation they favored. Browning, Marshall, and Tabb (1984, 1997) demonstrate that in order to be effective minority representatives must coalesce with progressive white legislators. Therefore, this research examines the extent that the coalition of African Americans and progressive white Democrats was able to pass progressive legislation and the extent that this progressive coalition was able to prevent the passage of conservative legislation. In order to understand these voting patterns, I preselected[3] crucial votes in a variety of issue areas: civil rights bills, economics and taxation, education, constitutional and legal issues, crime, and environment and safety. Using the *Journal of the House of Representatives* and *Journal of the Senate*, I calculated voting results for white Democrats, African American Democrats, and Republicans. I then compared these results for each bill.

TABLE 3.6
Roll Call Votes in the Florida Legislature on Abortion

	House of Representatives			Senate		
	Black Dems	White Dems	Republicans	Black Dems	White Dems	Republicans
1988 Parental Consent for Minor Abortion						
For	70.0%	68.3%	97.6%	100%	66.7%	100%
Against	30.0%	21.7%	2.4%	0%	33.3%	0%
N = Total Voting Members	(10)	(63)	(42)	(2)	(18)	(13)
1997 Late Term Abortion Ban						
For	21.4%	51.2%	100%	40.0%	45.5%	100%
Against	78.6%	48.8%	0%	60.0%	54.5%	0%
N = Total Voting Members	(14)	(43)	(61)	(5)	(11)	(23)
1999 Choose Life License Plates						
For	7.1%	33.3%	81.4%	0%	18.2%	100%
Against	92.9%	66.7%	18.8%	100%	81.8%	0%
N = Total Voting Members	(14)	(30)	(70)	(5)	(11)	(23)

Source: The Florida Legislature-Journals of the House of Representatives, 1986–1988, 1996–1998, 1998–2000, Tallahassee, FL: State of Florida. Journals of the Florida Senate, 1986–1988, 1996–1998, 1998–2000, Tallahassee, FL: State of Florida.

Tables 3.6 through 3.12 display the results of the roll-call tallies. Although there was a consensus on many bills, three types of coalitions emerge from these roll-call vote data. For many issues, the coalition of conservative white Democrats and Republicans dominated the coalition of African Americans and progressive white Democrats. This dynamic existed during the period of Democratic control, when enough conservative white Democrats combined forces with minority Republicans to pass conservative legislation. After Republicans took control, this coalition persisted, except that it contained mostly Republicans plus the few remaining conservative white Democrats. In either manifestation of this conservative coalition, the coalition of progressive white Democrats and African Americans lost many key votes. A second coalition consists of African Americans, progressive white Democrats, and enough moderate white Democrats and/or Republicans to pass meaningful, albeit not monumental, civil rights legislation and other liberal bills. In the third, least common coalition, African Americans allied with Republicans and conservative white Democrats to pass conservative social policy bills.

On abortion votes (Table 3.6), African American legislators were either part of the conservative coalition supporting an abortion restriction, or they were part of the losing progressive coalition opposing an anti-abortion law. In

1988, most African American legislators coalesced with conservative Democrats and Republicans to pass a bill requiring parental consent for minors seeking abortions. Although Republican Governor Robert Martinez signed the bill into law, the Florida Supreme Court in 1989 overturned it as a violation of the Florida Constitution, *In Re T.W., A Minor*, 551 So.2d. 1186 (1989). Most African American legislators and white, progressive Democrats unsuccessfully opposed a 1997 bill banning late-term abortions. In the house a narrow majority of white Democrats and all Republicans provided enough support for passage of the bill. In the senate a slight majority of white and black Democrats opposed the bill, yet unanimous Republican support was sufficient to gain passage. Despite passage in both houses Democratic Governor Lawton Chiles vetoed this bill because it did not provide for an exception protecting the health of the mother (Epstein 1997). Finally, in 1999, the legislature passed a bill authorizing the issue of official state license plates bearing the anti-abortion slogan "choose life." Despite the fact that a large majority of Democrats, both black and white, opposed this bill, overwhelming Republican support ensured its passage. Republican Governor Jeb Bush signed it into law, and the plates have been issued, but a challenge to the legality of the state endorsing a position on the abortion debate is still pending in state court.

On crime control bills (Table 3.7), African American legislators generally supported the more conservative "law and order" position, although there was division among African American legislators themselves on controversial bills. A 1991 bill that outlawed the possession of chemicals that are used to make designer drugs passed unanimously in both houses, and Governor Chiles signed it into law. None of the other crime bills in this study achieved such a consensus. A 1989 bill required parents to keep firearms from children and punished those parents whose failure to do so resulted in harm. Republican Representative Harry Jennings (Sarasota) had tried several times to pass this law, but opposition from the National Rifle Association blocked the bill in the conservative, Democrat-controlled legislature. However, in June 1989, six youngsters throughout the state were killed by gunshot accidents in the span of only one week; therefore, the legislature received considerable public pressure to pass this bill (Landry 1989). In the house approximately one-third of black Democrats, white Democrats, and white Republicans opposed the bill. At least 80% of white Democrats and Republicans in the senate supported the bill, but the two African American senators were split. Governor Martinez signed the bill into law. A crime bill that included a provision to reinstitute chain gangs (i.e., leg and chain shackles) for state prisoners working outdoors passed in 1995. White Democrats and Republicans in the house and senate supported this bill virtually

TABLE 3.7
Roll Call Votes in the Florida Legislature on Crime Issues

	House of Representatives			Senate		
	Black Dems	White Dems	Republicans	Black Dems	White Dems	Republicans
1989 Firearm Lockup Requirement						
For	62.5%	60.7%	70.2%	50.0%	80.0%	86.7%
Against	37.5%	39.2%	29.8%	50.0%	20.0%	13.3%
N = Total Voting Members	(8)	(56)	(47)	(2)	(15)	(15)
1991 Designer Drug						
For	100%	100%	100%	100%	100%	100%
Against	0%	0%	0%	0%	0%	0%
N = Total Voting Members	(10)	(58)	(43)	(2)	(18)	(16)
1995 Prison Reform (Chain Gang)						
For	50.0%	88.9%	100%	60.0%	100%	100%
Against	50.0%	11.1%	0%	40.0%	0%	0%
N = Total Voting Members	(14)	(45)	(58)	(5)	(14)	(20)
1999 Three Strikes						
For	40.0%	84.8%	100%	100%	100%	100%
Against	60.0%	15.2%	0%	0%	0%	0%
N = Total Voting Members	(15)	(33)	(70)	(4)	(10)	(21)

Source: The Florida Legislature-Journals of the House of Representatives, 1986–1988, 1988–1990, 1990–1992, 1994–1996, 1998–2000, Tallahassee, FL: State of Florida. Journals of the Florida Senate, 1986–1988, 1988–1990, 1990–1992, 1994–1996, 1998–2000, Tallahassee, FL: State of Florida.

unanimously, but blacks were evenly split (50–50 in the house and 60–40 in the senate). African American lawmakers who supported tougher measures on criminals approved the bill, but others, such as Rep. Beryl Roberts-Burke, opposed it. Roberts-Burke remarked, "It's very demeaning to put leg irons and chains on an individual. . . . There were things in this bill I supported. But I felt strongly enough about this issue to still vote it down" (Miller 1995). Although Governor Chiles did not sign the bill, he did not veto it either, and the bill became law without his signature (Chachere 1995). A similar dynamic occurred in 1999 over a "three-strikes" bill, which imposed a life in prison term upon conviction of a third felony. Initially the bill required three-time felons to serve 100% of their life terms, but that figure was lowered to 85%. Although 40% of black house members supported this measure, 60% opposed it. Christopher Smith (Miami) argued that the money would be better spent on prevention (Kassab 1999). Despite this opposition, the bill passed unanimously in the senate, even among African American senators, and Governor Jeb Bush signed it into law.

TABLE 3.8
Roll Call Votes in the Florida Legislature on Tax Issues

	House of Representatives			Senate		
	Black Dems	White Dems	Republicans	Black Dems	White Dems	Republicans
1983 Tax on Out-of-State and Foreign Corporate Income						
For	100%	75.0%	3.0%	100%	89.7%	12.5%
Against	0%	25.0%	97.0%	0%	10.3%	87.5%
N = Total Voting Members	(9)	(72)	(33)	(2)	(29)	(8)
1987 Allow Tax on Services						
For	88.9%	85.0%	93.0%	100%	76.7%	86.7%
Against	10.1%	15.0%	7.0%	0%	23.3%	13.3%
N = Total Voting Members	(9)	(60)	(43)	(2)	(23)	(15)
1990 Fuel and Sin Tax Increase						
For	100%	87.3%	43.2%	100%	70.6%	76.5%
Against	0%	12.7%	56.8%	0%	29.4%	23.5%
N = Total Voting Members	(8)	(55)	(44)	(1)	(17)	(17)
1998 Sales Tax Week Holiday						
For	100%	97.2%	100%	20.0%	91.7%	95.5%
Against	0%	2.8%	0%	80.0%	8.3%	4.5%
N = Total Voting Members	(15)	(36)	(65)	(5)	(12)	(22)
2000 Intangibles Tax Cut						
For	100%	90.0%	100%	100%	100%	100%
Against	0%	10.0%	0%	0%	0%	0%
N = Total Voting Members	(15)	(30)	(72)	(5)	(90)	(24)

Source: The Florida Legislature-Journals of the House of Representatives, 1982–1984, 1984–1986, 1986–1988, 1990–1992, 1996–1998, 1998–2000, Tallahassee, FL: State of Florida. Journals of the Florida Senate, 1982–1984, 1984–1986, 1986–1988, 1990–1992, 1996–1998, 1998–2000, Tallahassee, FL: State of Florida.

African American legislators were generally part of a liberal coalition on tax issues (see Table 3.8), although there is one notable exception. Moreover, this liberal coalition that favored increasing taxes to pay for infrastructure and social programs dominated during the 1980s and early 1990s, but when Republicans assumed control of both houses the emphasis switched to cutting taxes. In 1983, the legislature passed, and Governor Bob Graham (D) signed into law a bill that taxed corporate income earned outside of Florida. Previously, the state taxed corporations only for their in-state business. This tax bill earmarked the increased revenue for improving education, and it enjoyed popular support. Nevertheless, businesses lobbied heavily against it (Askari 1983). Most Democrats in the house and senate, including all African Americans, supported this bill, whereas virtually all Republicans opposed it. In 1987, the legislature passed an extremely controversial bill that enacted a sales tax on services, including legal fees, pest extermination, data processing, and advertising. Previously the services industry had been exempt from the sales tax, but the state's lack of an income tax coupled with the dwindling manufacturing sector required new sources of revenue. Republican Governor Bob Martinez's support for the tax on services helped ensure its passage (Dahl 1987), and nearly all black Democrats, white Democrats, and even Republicans strongly supported the bill. Again in 1990 the legislature passed a $1.6 billion tax increase on gasoline, cigarettes, and alcohol in order to pay for road improvements. African American legislators, who unanimously supported this bill, joined with most white Democrats and some Republicans to ensure the passage of this major tax increase, and Republican Governor Bob Martinez signed the bill into law. After Republicans assumed control, tax cuts replaced tax increases on the legislative agenda. In 1998, the legislature passed a bill creating a sales tax exemption for clothing items under fifty dollars that would be in effect for a one-week period in August. The "sales tax holiday," as it became known, occurred during the time when parents shopped for their children's "back-to-school" clothes, therefore, it benefited consumers. Practically all white Democrats and Republicans supported this bill, and although African Americans in the house voted "yes", 80% of black senators opposed it. Finally, in 2000, the legislature cut the intangibles tax on stocks and bonds investment returns, which was a major aspect of Republican Governor Jeb Bush's economic agenda. Because the Republican house and senate leaders agreed to decrease the amount of the tax cut, both houses overwhelmingly supported the bill (Becker 2000). All Republicans, all blacks, and virtually all white Democrats supported the bill.

In the area of education (see Table 3.9), African Americans were generally part of the losing progressive coalition that was unable to prevent conservative changes in the education system, although there was division, sometimes significant, among black legislators. A 1999 bill to establish a private school voucher program passed with virtually unanimous Republican support. A vast majority of white Democrats (most conservative white Democrats had vanished by this point) and African Americans opposed the bill because it would take money from financially strapped public education and violate the separation of church and state. A major supporter of the bill, Governor Bush enthusiastically signed it into law. African American legislators were more split over a 2000 bill that eliminated the State University Board of Regents and replaced it with separate boards of trustees for each state institution, with each member appointed by the governor. The losing progressive coalition (consisting of a majority of the white Democrats and African Americans in the house) unsuccessfully opposed

TABLE 3.9
Roll Call Votes in the Florida Legislature on Education Issues

	House of Representatives			Senate		
	Black Dems	White Dems	Republicans	Black Dems	White Dems	Republicans
1995 Allow Prayer at Graduation						
For	46.7%	41.7%	89.3%	33.3%	50.0%	95.2%
Against	53.3%	58.3%	10.7%	67.7%	50.0%	4.8%
N = Total Voting Members	(15)	(48)	(56)	(3)	(14)	(21)
1996 Charter Schools						
For	35.7%	76.1%	100%	40.0%	57.1%	100%
Against	64.3%	23.9%	0%	60.0%	42.9%	0%
N = Total Voting Members	(14)	(46)	(55)	(5)	(14)	(21)
1999 Private School Voucher Program						
For	15.4%	9.1%	100%	0%	20%	96.0%
Against	84.6%	90.9%	0%	100%	80%	4.0%
N = Total Voting Members	(13)	(33)	(72)	(5)	(10)	(25)
2000 Abolish Univ. Board of Regents						
For	33.3%	25.0%	98.6%	60.0%	40.0%	100%
Against	67.7%	75.0%	1.4%	40.0%	60.0%	0%
N = Total Voting Members	(14)	(31)	(71)	(5)	(10)	(24)

Source: The Florida Legislature-Journals of the House of Representatives, 1994–1996, 1996–1998, 1998–2000, Tallahassee, FL: State of Florida. Journals of the Florida Senate, 1994–1996, 1996–1998, 1998–2000, Tallahassee, FL: State of Florida.

this politicization of the state university system. However, a majority of black senators supported this bill. Many black legislators supported the bill because the Board of Regents had supported ending affirmative action for university admissions and rejected a proposed law school at the historically black Florida A & M University. Conversely, African American opponents, such as Orlando's Alzo Reddick, argued, "just because an agency doesn't do everything you want them to when you want it done doesn't mean that agency should be abolished" (Csar 2000). African Americans were split over a 1996 bill establishing charter schools, which passed by wide margins in both houses and was signed into law by Governor Chiles. Specifically the bill allowed parents, teachers, or businesses to operate public schools free of regulation. All Republicans and a majority of white Democrats supported the bill. However, a majority of African American legislators and liberal white Democrats opposed this bill, arguing that it did not adequately protect desegregation (James 1996). African American lawmakers were also split over a bill to allow student-led prayers at public school graduations

TABLE 3.10
Roll Call Votes in the Florida Legislature on Government Reform Issues

	House of Representatives			Senate		
	Black Dems	White Dems	Republicans	Black Dems	White Dems	Republicans
1992 Redistricting Plan						
For	75.0%	100%	4.7%	100%	100%	5.0%
Against	25.0%	0%	95.3%	0%	0%	95.0%
N = Total Voting Members	(12)	(62)	(43)	(2)	(18)	(20)
1997 Gay Marriage Ban						
For	86.7%	58.1%	100%	60.0%	72.7%	100%
Against	13.3%	41.9%	0%	40.0%	27.3%	0%
N = Total Voting Members	(15)	(43)	(61)	(5)	(11)	(22)

Source: The Florida Legislature-Journals of the House of Representatives, 1990–1992, 1996–1998, Tallahassee, FL: State of Florida. Journals of the Florida Senate, 1990–1992, 1996–1998, Tallahassee, FL: State of Florida.

and sporting events. Black legislators split almost 50–50 in the house and actually supported the bill more than white Democrats did. Almost 90% of Republican support ensured its passage. Black support for the bill in the senate was not as strong—one-third voted for it, and two-thirds opposed it. Although a version of this bill passed in both the house and senate, it ultimately died, because the two houses could not reconcile language insisting that prayers be nonsectarian (James 1995).

Because the two government reform bills in this study (see Table 3.10) are of a vastly different nature, there is no discernable pattern of African American vote. In 1992, most black legislators reluctantly joined with all white Democrats to support the final redistricting plan. As discussed earlier, the Black Caucus would have preferred more black districts, but most black legislators ended up supporting the Democratic plan. Virtually all Republicans opposed the bill, although Republican Senator Malcolm Beard's (Seffner) reluctant support guaranteed passage in an evenly divided senate (MacManus 2002b). Most African American legislators supported the conservative majority on a 1997 bill that banned homosexual marriages in Florida, even those performed in other states. In fact, in the house a far greater proportion of African Americans (86.7%) supported this law than did white Democrats (58.1%). A 60–40 majority of African American senators voted for this bill as well, but their support was not as strong as white Democrats or Republicans. Nevertheless, it is clear that in the area of homosexual rights, Florida's black legislators ally themselves with the dominant conservative coalition.

TABLE 3.11
Roll Call Votes in the Florida Legislature on Race Issues

	House of Representatives			Senate		
	Black Dems	White Dems	Republicans	Black Dems	White Dems	Republicans
1983 Fair Lending in Housing						
For	100%	100%	100%	100%	100%	100%
Against	0%	0%	0%	0%	0%	0%
N = Total Voting Members	(9)	(84)	(36)	(2)	(26)	(8)
1989 Hate Crimes						
For	100%	100%	100%	100%	100%	100%
Against	0%	0%	0%	0%	0%	0%
N = Total Voting Members	(9)	(61)	(45)	(2)	(21)	(17)
1991 Civil Rights Act						
For	100%	100%	87.2%	100%	100%	100%
Against	0%	0%	12.8%	0%	0%	0%
N = Total Voting Members	(10)	(62)	(39)	(1)	(20)	(15)
1994 Rosewood Compensation						
For	100%	72.4%	42.3%	100%	80.0%	45.0%
Against	0%	27.6%	57.7%	0%	20.0%	55.0%
N = Total Voting Members	(14)	(58)	(45)	(5)	(15)	(20)
1998 Pitts–Lee Compensation						
For	100%	84.6%	100%	100%	90.0%	100%
Against	0%	15.4%	0%	0%	10.0%	0%
N = Total Voting Members	(15)	(39)	(63)	(5)	(10)	(25)

Source: The Florida Legislature-Journals of the House of Representatives, 1982–1984, 1988–1990, 1990–1992, 1994–1996, 1996–1998, Tallahassee, FL: State of Florida. Journals of the Florida Senate, 1982–1984, 1990–1992, 1994–1996, 1998–1998, Tallahassee, FL: State of Florida.

Despite usually voting with the losing progressive coalition, African American legislators were able to achieve moderately important progressive civil rights victories (see Table 3.11) by securing enough white moderate Democratic and even some Republican votes. The presence of African American lawmakers is important, because they are the ones who introduced and fought for the passage of these bills, but white support ensured their passage. During the 1980s, two civil rights bills passed unanimously in both houses. A 1983 bill introduced by Senator Carrie Meek gave the state authority to enforce fair housing rules. However, in order to secure passage, Senator Meek watered down the bill so that the state only possessed authority to encourage a resolution; it could not force a solution on either party (*St. Petersburg Times* 1983). Another watered-down civil rights bill passed in 1989, allowing judges to enhance penalties for crimes committed out of prejudice. As the Black Caucus grew in strength, it ensured the passage of more meaningful bills. A 1991 civil rights bill that provided for punitive damages for victims of discrimination passed by wide margins in both houses with only a small percentage of house Republicans opposing it. However, Democratic Governor Lawton Chiles vetoed it, arguing that it benefited lawyers more than minorities (McKinnon 1991). In 1994, African American legislators achieved an important symbolic civil rights victory by securing the passage of black Representative Al Lawson's (D-Tallahassee) Rosewood Compensation bill. The state officially apologized to and compensated the victims of the 1923 massacre of black residents in the town of Rosewood. Although a majority of Republicans opposed the bill, the coalition of African Americans and most white Democrats ensured its passage. Moreover, black legislators and progressive white Democrats prevented conservative white Democrats and Republicans from weakening the bill and convinced Governor Chiles to sign it (Bassett 1994). Four years later, when both houses were under Republican control, African American Senator Kendrick Meek (D-Miami) secured the passage of a bill that compensated Freddie Pitts and Wilbert Lee. Pitts and Lee were two black Floridians wrongly convicted of murder and sentenced to death during the early 1960s, when racial prejudice undoubtedly played a role in their mistreatment. Although Governor Askew had pardoned Pitts and Lee in 1975, this bill, which passed overwhelmingly and was signed into law, compensated them for the time they served in prison (Morgan 1998).

African Americans also split on the health-safety and welfare bills included in the study—a 1986 bill requiring seat belts and a 1995 welfare reform bill (see Table 3.12). In fact, all three groups were noticeably split on the seat belt bill, which fined violators an additional twenty dollars if they were pulled over for another violation and not wearing a safety belt. Supporters argued that the bill would save lives, prevent injuries, and lower health care costs, whereas opponents argued that the law was unenforceable and stifled individual liberty. African Americans also split over a 1995 welfare reform bill, though whites of both parties overwhelmingly backed the bill. The bill required that unemployed parents receiving welfare either look for work or participate in a job-training program. The house, including black and white Democrats, overwhelmingly approved the bill, but it passed more narrowly in the senate. Most blacks and a small minority of white Democrat senators objected to provisions in the bill that cut benefits for additional children and penalized welfare recipients whose children did not regularly attend school (Metz 1995). Governor Chiles signed the bill into law.

Steven Tauber 71

TABLE 3.12
Roll Call Votes in the Florida Legislature on Health and Welfare Issues

	House of Representatives			Senate		
	Black Dems	White Dems	Republicans	Black Dems	White Dems	Republicans
1986 Mandatory Seat Belt						
For	66.7%	54.4%	61.0%	50.0%	69.0%	22.2%
Against	33.3%	46.6%	39.0%	50.0%	31.0%	78.8%
N = Total Voting Members	(9)	(68)	(41)	(2)	(29)	(9)
1995 Welfare Reform (Payment Limits)						
For	100%	97.9%	100%	20.0%	92.3%	100%
Against	0%	2.1%	0%	80.0%	7.7%	0%
N = Total Voting Members	(12)	(47)	(46)	(5)	(13)	(21)

Source: The Florida Legislature-Journals of the House of Representatives, 1984–1986, 1994–1996, Tallahassee, FL: State of Florida. Journals of the Florida Senate, 1984–1986, 1994–1996, Tallahassee, FL: State of Florida.

CONCLUSION

Since the 1960s, reapportionment has augmented black representation in the Florida legislature. Basing urban and rural representation according to population allowed African Americans to win seats to the state house of representatives for the first time since Reconstruction. Furthermore, the switch to single-member districts in 1982 enhanced opportunities for African Americans to win seats to the Florida house and even the senate, in which African Americans had not served since Reconstruction. In 1992, the creation of more majority black districts for the house and senate increased African American representation in both houses to 12.5%. According to the U.S. Census, 14.6% of Florida's population is African American; consequently, black representation in the state legislature is almost at parity with its proportion of the state's population (U.S. Bureau of the Census 2000).

Clearly, this improvement in representation is important, but there is mixed evidence that this increased representation has yielded tangible benefits. As more African Americans were elected to the house and senate and accrued seniority, African Americans became more influential in the policy-making apparatus of the Florida legislature. Nevertheless, the Republican takeover of the Florida house and senate reduced the ability of African Americans to influence policymaking. The switch in party control, however, exerted less impact on black legislators' ability to forge progressive coalitions. When the Democrats controlled the legislature, conservative white Democrats and Republicans constituted the dominant coalition, whereas African Americans and liberal, white Democrats constituted the losing coalition. Occasionally the progressive coalition was able to secure enough votes to pass moderate civil rights, taxation, and expenditure bills. After the Republicans took over, the conservative coalition still dominated. African Americans and progressive white legislators lost many significant votes, but they were still able to pass moderately important bills, such as the Pitts–Lee compensation law. In fact, for some crime bills and social policy legislation, many, if not most, black legislators supported the conservative position.

In sum, increased descriptive representation has been a necessary condition for African American influence in the Florida legislature, but it has not been sufficient. To substantiate this conclusion, further research should explore more systematically the relevance of the Florida Legislative Black Caucus and employ a more sophisticated statistical analysis of black legislators' ability to pass desired bills and prevent the passage of bills they oppose. Moreover, after the 2002 redistricting and subsequent election, the dynamics of African Americans in the Florida legislature may significantly change.

NOTES

1.   The only non-Democrat African Americans to serve in the Florida legislature are Representatives John Plummer, a Republican who served from 1980 to 1982, Rudy Bradley, a Democrat who switched to the Republican Party in 1999 and left the house in 2000 (he lost to Democrat Les Miller for a senate seat in 2000), and Willie Logan, a Democrat who became an Independent in 1998 and left the house in 2000.

2.   This research varies slightly from Haynie's measure of incorporation in one respect. Haynie (2001) looked at the African American percent of the Democratic Party, but if the Republicans were the majority party, he assigned a score of 0. This research adopts a similar approach by looking at the African American percent of the majority party. For the most part this measure mirrors Haynie's, since it captures the African American proportion of the Democratic Party when the Democrats were the majority. Moreover, most of the time the Republicans controlled the house and senate, there were no African American Republicans, and I assigned a score of 0 for this indicator. However, in 1999, when the Republicans controlled the house, Democratic Representative Rudy Bradley (St. Petersburg) switched to the Republican Party. Therefore, an African American representative was part of the ruling party, and this fact is relevant to incorporation.

3.   I chose bills that received extensive media coverage in Florida's major newspapers: *St. Petersburg Times, Tampa Tribune, Miami Herald, Gainesville Sun, Orlando Sentinel,* and *Jacksonville Times-Union.*

Chapter 4

Black Representation in Georgia*

Peter W. Wielhouwer and Keesha M. Middlemass

The evolution of group politics in the United States has produced substantial discussion and debate about the nature of representation, and especially the relationship between descriptive and substantive representation. At one level, the United States has witnessed a massive transformation in the demographic characteristics of elected officials, from a near unity of white males to a much broader cross section of races, ethnicities, and the sexes (see, e.g., Bullock 1999). In Georgia, as with the nation and most states and cities, descriptive representation (that is, the physical presence) of black elected officeholders increased dramatically between the early 1970s and the late 1990s, and the Peach State now ranks near the top in terms of numbers of black elected officials (Bositis 2002). What remains unclear is whether changes in the election of black elected officials are associated with changes in substantive representation of Georgia's African American community. This chapter examines the descriptive and substantive representation of African Americans in Georgia.

REPRESENTATION AND RESPONSIVENESS

The growth in the number of black elected officials nationwide, but especially in the South, has precipitated a cottage industry of studies; this research has often focused on the concept of descriptive representation (e.g., Parker 1990; Bullock 1992; Handley and Grofman 1994). The accomplishment of a variety of descriptive goals led scholars to address the next logical link relating to representation, and studies focused on the relationship between descriptive and substantive representation (e.g., Swain 1993; Lublin 1997; Cameron et al. 1996). What has emerged is a debate over the relative value of descriptive representation, and whether the attainment of it is a prerequisite for substantive representation.

73

This chapter analyzes the connection between these types of representation in the broader academic debate and in the specific context of the state of Georgia. In particular, we assess representation of African Americans in the state's general assembly, and whether the dramatic increase in black legislators in Georgia has been accompanied by substantive representation in legislative activities.

Using the context of Georgia politics generally and the Georgia general assembly specifically, we study the connection between descriptive and substantive representation. Studying changes in descriptive and substantive representation of African Americans in Georgia is useful, because the state has a long history, when compared to other Southern states, of electing African Americans, and because today Georgia elects a large number of African Americans. This does not mitigate the historical fact that African Americans have had to persevere through discriminatory laws and an ugly history of race relations in the state. What we hope to assess is whether, in the last quarter of the twentieth century, larger numbers of black legislators yielded increased influence in the legislative process, especially in terms of passage of laws and policies deemed central to black interests in the state.

Specifically, we are interested in answering several questions:

1. How has the number of African Americans in the Georgia general assembly changed over time?
2. What kinds of committees are African Americans selected to chair?
3. Do black state legislators act homogeneously in each chamber? How does the Georgia Legislative Black Caucus (GLBC) vote when compared to non-black Democrats?
4. Is the voting homogeneity of black state legislators related to the types of legislation being considered?
5. Have voting homogeneity and substantive representation of African American interests changed over the course of the 1990s?

The balance of this chapter is organized as follows: First, we paint, with broad historical strokes, Georgia's political culture as it relates to elections and office holding. After describing the state legislature itself, we turn to the descriptive representation of African Americans in the general assembly, paying particular attention to gains made since the 1960s and the founding and mission of the GLBC. This section also documents leadership positions held by African Americans, including committee chairs. Finally, we consider the voting patterns of black state legislators on key pieces of legislation from each session during the 1990s, drawing comparisons with white Democrats and Republicans.

GEORGIA'S CULTURE AND POLITICS

As with so many other topics relating to Southern politics, the benchmark for studying Georgia politics is V. O. Key's (1949) analysis in *Southern Politics in State and Nation*. Key labeled Georgia politics the "Rule of the Rustics," because at that time the political faction surrounding Eugene Talmadge had at its core a power base centered in the rural counties, which dominated Georgia politics for more than a generation. Combining a distrust of federal government programs, anti-city rhetoric, and racial invective, Talmadge continued some of the tactics of the state's earlier populist movement and effectively divided Georgia's electorate into two rival factions. "Talmadge personified the politics of protest for poor rural whites frustrated by a system that had taken their land and relegated them to the status of tenants and sharecroppers and who had been taught that their white skin gave them the only sense of status they possessed" (Bass and Devries 1977, p. 137). The geography of these factions drew upon long-standing conflicts between the urban population centers and rural counties. White supremacist rhetoric further solidified the white rural base, as a disproportionate share of the black population resided in the so-called black belt—a band of rural counties stretching across the midsection of the state (see Key's [1949] Figure 1; see also Black and Black 1987, Figures 2.1 and 2.2).

The institutional mechanism allowing appeals to rural white voters to succeed was Georgia's county-unit system. This system allocated "county-unit votes" based upon population; the eight most populous counties were each given six unit votes, each of the thirty next most populous counties were given four unit votes, and the remaining 121 counties received two unit votes apiece. In statewide races, the eight largest counties, containing 30.1% of the total population (and 43.1% of the adult white population), cast fewer than 12% of the unit votes; the 121 smallest counties, containing 43.5% of the state's population (39.9% of adult whites), cast 59% of the unit votes (Key 1949, p. 119). In order to win a statewide nomination or election, a candidate had to gain a plurality of unit votes.[1]

The strategy for victory was clear. With an electoral structure in which the most populous counties were underrepresented and small counties held a commanding voice in who held statewide office, candidates campaigned and won office by focusing only on rural counties. Candidates could avoid campaigning in urban centers as there were enough "county unit-votes" in the rural counties to win statewide office. This system had a profound influence on the character of the state's political development, as power was held by a small segment of the population, and candidates pitted urban residents against rural citizens.

This dynamic is still being felt in the geographic split that currently exists in the Georgia legislature. In Key's day, the rural vote was by and large the reaction against black power and was related to the proportion of the county's population that was African American. Federal intervention to integrate public schools prompted significant white flight from the cities to the suburbs (Fleischmann and Pierannunzi 1997, pp. 32–33), and today urban areas are predominantly African American. As a consequence, it is likely that the old urban-rural split today exists in the form of an urban-suburban split, to wit: "Republican strongholds in Georgia include the suburban counties surrounding Atlanta ... [and] in areas surrounding Georgia's [other] cities" (Fleischmann and Pierannunzi 1997, p. 119).

One other aspect of Georgia's political culture that bears mention is its transition from a state in which one party—the Democrats, of course—completely dominated politics and government, to a highly competitive state, in which Republicans now constitute a significant presence. For Key, there was no Republican Party to speak of in the state. This was the same as in most other Southern states, as he wrote (1949, p. 277): The Republican Party "scarcely deserves the name of a party. It wavers somewhat between an esoteric cult on the order of a lodge and a conspiracy for plunder in accord with the accepted customs of our politics."

In the first half of the twentieth century any meaningful electoral competition took place within the Democratic Party. Political competition centered on personality factions such as that of the Talmadge family. In fact, prior to 1944, competition was clearly among only whites in the party, as one of the foundations for the party's maintaining its control was the continued social, economic, and political subjugation of the state's black residents. On the theory that political parties were purely private voluntary associations, the white Democratic primary was utilized to exclude African Americans from participation in Southern state politics, despite (perhaps because of) black progress in the voting rights arena. The U.S. Supreme Court overturned the white primary in *Smith v. Allwright*,[2] and by the 1960s, large gains were made in black voter registration across the South (Black and Black 1987, pp. 84–88).

By the 1990s, the Republican Party in Georgia had emerged from virtual obscurity to become a major player in state politics. During the 1990s, GOP gubernatorial candidates improved their electoral performance, polling an average of about 47% of the vote in the decade, while in the previous five elections the party's candidates averaged about 35% (Fleischmann and Pierannunzi 1997, p. 116). There have been several successful GOP candidates for other statewide offices and the U.S. Senate, and most of Georgia's U.S. House delegation (eight of thirteen members; four of the five Democrats are African Americans from predominantly black districts) in 2003 was Republican. Republican presidential candidates fare well in Georgia, winning the state nearly every year from 1964 on (the exceptions being 1976 and 1980, when former Georgia Governor Jimmy Carter was the Democratic candidate, and 1992, when a fellow Southerner, Bill Clinton, was on the ballot). Now competitive in statewide elections, 2002 was a watershed year for Republicans. For the first time since Reconstruction, the party's candidate was elected governor, and the party took control of the state senate (after a tight election and four Democratic party switches).

THE GEORGIA GENERAL ASSEMBLY

The bicameral Georgia general assembly[3] consists of 180 house seats and 56 senate seats. Historically, the house was the dominant chamber, because its members were eligible for reelection, while senate seats rotated among three counties. Until the 1960s, the house was the chamber of choice for candidates interested in building a political career. Now, both chambers are attractive to those with political ambitions.

As with most legislatures, most of the work takes place in standing committees in each chamber. The number of standing committees can vary, but in the 1990s, there were thirty-three in the house and twenty-three in the senate. Committee members, including chairs, are appointed by the chamber leadership (the speaker of the house and the lieutenant governor in the senate). Members may express preferences for committee assignments, but without a guarantee that their preferences will be honored; generally members retain previously held seats. Committee leadership positions tend to be reserved for the majority party, however, Pierre Howard (who served as lieutenant governor from 1990 to 1998) was known to appoint Republicans as committee chairs. Seniority within the chamber is more important than committee seniority for appointment as chair; other prominent factors in chair selection include a member's general legislative ability and loyalty to the party leadership. For example, in 1993, Howard appointed junior members to lead some important committees, and such positions found their way into the hands of senators who supported his own candidacy, while those who supported his chief rival did not do as well.

BLACK DESCRIPTIVE REPRESENTATION IN GEORGIA

The election of African American candidates in the state of Georgia, and across the South for that matter, is a result of three interconnected events: (1) the passage of the Voting Rights Act of 1965; (2) the implementation of the

Voting Rights Act by the Justice Department; and (3) the successful lawsuits brought by black plaintiffs and the voting section of the Justice Department. These measures changed the makeup of elected bodies, and over time the political agenda and issues addressed by the state legislature adapted to reflect these changes, as issues important to the African American community became integrated into the Democratic Party's agenda.

The history of black political participation and representation in the state of Georgia compares positively to other Southern states, even prior to the 1965 Voting Rights Act. For instance, in 1965, 27.4% of the black population in Georgia was registered to vote, compared to 6.7% percent in Mississippi. Georgia's black voter registration was lower, however, than that of Louisiana, Virginia, and the Carolinas (Grofman et al. 1992, pp. 23–24). Nonetheless, there were only three black elected officials in Georgia. This was dismal for a state in which African Americans technically had received the right to vote in 1867s federal Reconstruction.

During Reconstruction, Georgia held a constitutional convention and formally guaranteed African Americans the right to vote, the right to citizenship, and equal protection of the laws.[4] Nonetheless, after the withdrawal of federal troops, Georgia, much like other Southern states, successfully removed legitimately elected state legislators through the continued use of violence and the threat of violence, intended to intimidate and dissuade black residents from political activism (see Barker et al. 1999). Many blacks withdrew from political activity altogether, as white Southerners reimposed legal and illegal obstacles to black electoral participation (Cole 1976). In response to the reestablishment of white supremacy in the South, white politicians curtailed the advance of civil rights measures, such as the right to vote and hold office, by simply changing the laws (see Marable 1991). Southern states created new laws meant to exclude blacks from participating in the electoral arena (such as the white primary, discussed earlier). These laws, which included the literacy test and the poll tax, effectively disenfranchised black citizens.

There were a few examples of African American political participation making a difference prior to the 1965 Voting Rights Act, however. For instance, the Negro Voter League was active in the 1940s, laying a strong foundation for black electoral participation. In a 1946 nonpartisan special election, African Americans played a significant role in electing to Congress Helen Mankin, a liberal white women who was able to build a biracial coalition. In 1962, LeRoy Johnson was elected to Georgia's senate, the first black candidate elected to any Southern state legislature since Reconstruction, while Julian Bond was the first black candidate elected to the Georgia house, in 1965. The house refused to seat him, however, allegedly due to his outspoken opposition to the Vietnam War. Winning election to the same seat the next year, the house again refused to seat him, but the U.S. Supreme Court ruled that Bond had been denied his seat unconstitutionally (Southern Poverty Law Center 2002).

The electoral victories of African American politicians followed on the heels of the dismantling of Georgia's county-unit system coupled with the establishment of the one-person, one-vote doctrine. In 1963, in *Gray v. Sanders*,[5] the Supreme Court struck down Georgia's county-unit system for statewide office, which was followed closely by *Toombs v. Fortson*,[6] where the Court declared that Georgia's legislative districts were malapportioned and had to be reapportioned to reflect the one-person, one-vote principle established by such cases as *Reynolds v. Sims*[7] and *Wesberry v. Sanders*.[8] When the Georgia general assembly drew legislative districts to reflect the population distribution within the state, it created single-member and multi-member districts for the house. These changes provided permanent opportunities for the continued election of black politicians to the state legislature, the Atlanta City Council, and various school boards (McDonald, Binford, and Johnson 1994).

The early success of African Americans getting elected to the state legislature and city positions was due to a conscious effort by white political leaders in the urban areas to take a progressive stance on race relations. In fact, for all of Georgia's racial demagoguery, African Americans were an integral part in explaining why progressive white mayors and black officeholders were elected from the Atlanta area. The Atlanta business community in particular looked at what was happening in Little Rock, Arkansas, and New Orleans, Louisiana, and did not want to bring the same disastrous results to its city. Even governors, who used racial appeals to get elected, often backed off from using racial politics once in office. This created an environment in which black residents actively participated in the electoral process and were elected to office. Atlanta's Maynard Jackson was the first Southern black mayor elected (in 1973), and Atlanta has continuously elected black mayors for the last thirty years, due to the building of biracial coalitions, especially with the predominantly white business community (Stone 1989). In sum, by the early 1970s, black candidates were being elected to nearly every level of office, from the U.S. House of Representatives (Andrew Young) to local school boards, and they have since routinely been elected to Georgia's state and U.S. House delegations.

HOUSE AND SENATE GEORGIA LEGISLATIVE BLACK CAUCUS MEMBERSHIP PATTERNS

Table 4.1 shows that there were twenty-three African Americans in the Georgia general assembly in the period 1980–1982, representing 13% of the house membership. This number grew through the mid-1990s, when as many as forty African Americans were in the house (22% of members). The growth in the early 1990s followed the 1986 U.S. Supreme Court decision in *Thornburg v. Gingles*,[9] in which the purposeful diluting of minority voting strength was declared unconstitutional. In the post–1990 round of redistricting, Georgia interpreted the *Thornburg* decision to mean the state had to draw the maximum number of majority-minority districts. The state legislative redistricting plans drawn during a special session in 1991 were initially redrawn after *Miller v. Johnson*,[10] but Justice Department objections meant that the 1991 plan ultimately remained in place for the remainder of the decade.[11] For a variety of reasons, including the Republican tidal wave of 1994, the number of black representatives in the Georgia house dropped, and by 2000, seats held by African Americans fell to thirty-two, only 18% of the house.

The election pattern for the Georgia senate is comparable to the house (see Table 4.2). In the 1980–1982 session there were two black senators, with those numbers increasing to seven (13% of senators) by the end of the 1980s. Dramatic growth occurred in 1991, when the number of black senators nearly doubled in size, to twelve (21% of the chamber), but the tumultuous redistricting process of the 1990s left black elected officials ten seats (18% of the senate). Heading into the new millennium, membership held steady at that level.

Despite minor setbacks in the 1990s, ninety-eight African Americans have served in the Georgia general assembly since 1963. With the growth in numbers, a stable and cohesive group of black legislators emerged from the civil rights movement sharing a common set of values. As a group, they began to caucus together in 1968 to promote their agenda and called themselves the Georgia Legislative Black Caucus (GLBC). The GLBC was organized into a nonprofit and educational association whose primary purpose was to promote the general welfare of minorities and fight for equality of opportunity and equal justice under the law. The agenda was updated in the 1980s and 1990s to include issues such as health care and disparities, business and economic development, minority study commissions to address minority representation in government and leadership positions, and labor in the state of Georgia. The GLBC makes up a core vote bloc in the Democratic Party Caucus in the Georgia house and senate, and its agenda is influenced by an advisory board comprised

TABLE 4.1
African American Lawmakers in the Georgia House of Representatives, 1979–2000

1979–1982	1983–1986	1987–1990	1991–1994	1995–1998	1999–2000
Beal	R. Allen	Abernathy III	Abernathy III	Anderson	B. Allen
Benn	Benn	R. Allen	Baker	B. Allen	Anderson
Bishop	Bishop	Baker	Brooks	Baker	Brooks
Brooks	Brooks	Benn	Brown	Brooks	Dean
Canty	Brown	Bishop	Canty	Brown	Dukes
Clark	Clark	Brooks	Cummings	Canty	Heard
Daughtery	Cummings	Brown	Davis	Davis	Heckstall
D. Dean	Daughtery	Clark	Hart	Dukes	Holmes
Dent	D. Dean	Cummings	Heard	Fort	Howard
Glover	Hamilton	Davis	Hightower	Hart	Hugley
Hamilton	Holmes	Holmes	Holmes	Heard	Jackson III
Hill	Johnson	Johnson	Howard	Heckstall	James
Holmes	Lucas	Lucas	Hugley	Holmes	Jones
Lucas	J. McKinney	C. McKinney	James	Howard	Lucas
J. McKinney	Randall	J. McKinney	Johnson	Hugley	Maddox
Randall	Redding	Randall	Jones	J. McKinney	McClinton
A. Scott	Sinkfield	Redding	Lucas	James	J. McKinney
D. Scott	Smyre	Sinkfield	Mcclinton	Johnson	Mobley
Smyre	M. Thomas	Smyre	C. McKinney	Jones	Pelote
Thompson	C. Walker	Stanley	J. McKinney	Lucas	Ragas
Watkins	White	M. Thomas	Merritt	Maddox	Reed
White	Williams	Thurmond	(1991–1992)	Mcclinton	Roberts
Williams		C. Walker	Mobley	Mobley	Sinkfield
		White	Pelote	Pelote	Smyre
		Williams	Randall	Ragas	L. Stanley
			Randolph	Randall	P. Stanley
			Redding	Randolph	Taylor
			Roberts	Roberts	Teague
			Sinkfield	Smyre	Tillman
			Smyre	Stanley	Turnquest
			Stanley	Taylor	Von Epps
			Taylor	Teague	Watson
			Teague	Tillman	
			M. Thomas	Turnquest	
			N. Thomas	Von Epps	
			(1991–1992)	Watson	
			Thurmond	White	
			Tillman		
			Turnquest		
			Von Epps		
			White		
			Williams		
23 Members	22 Members	25 Members	38–40 Members	37 Members	32 Members
13% of	12% of	14% of	21–22% House	21% of	18% of
House	House	House		House	House

Source: Menifield, Shaffer, and Jones (2000); derived from various issues of Members of the General Assembly of Georgia Senate and House of Rep., 1980–1989, 1983–1986, 1987–1990, 1991–1994, and 1995–1999, and the Georgia General Assembly Web site.

TABLE 4.2
African American Lawmakers in the Georgia Senate, 1979–2000

1979–1982	1983–1986	1987–1990	1991–1994	1995–1998	1999–2000
Bond	Bond	Langford	Abernathy III	Abernathy III	Brown
Tate	Langford	Parker	R. Allen	Brown	Butler
	A. Scott	A. Scott	Bishop (1991–1992)	Griffin	Fort
	D. Scott	D. Scott	Brown	Harbison	Harbison
	Tate	Shumake	Harbison	James	James
	E. Walker	Tate	Langford	Johnson	D. Scott
		E. Walker	Parrish (1993–1994)	D. Scott	Stokes
			D. Scott	Stokes	Tate
			Shumake	Thomas	Thomas
			Tate	C. Walker	C. Walker
			Thomas		
			C. Walker		
			E. Walker		
2 Members	6 Members	7 Members	12 Members	10 Members	10 Members
4% of	11% of	13% of	21% of Senate	18% of Senate	18% of
Senate	Senate	Senate			Senate

Source: Menifield, Shaffer, and Jones (2000); derived from various issues of *Members of the General Assembly of Georgia Senate and House of Rep.*, 1980–1989, 1983–1986, 1987–1990, 1991–1994, and 1995–1999.

of state employees from various agencies. Advisory board members are chosen by the caucus chair and are selected based on their commitment to public service.

COMMITTEE MEMBERSHIP AND CHAIRS

The addition of African Americans to the Georgia house and senate led to the development of several different types of political relationships with white members of the Democratic majority. Over time and through reelection, black legislators gained seniority and expertise in several substantive policy areas. This progression led to the selection of black legislators to chair committees in increasing numbers through the middle 1990s (see Table 4.3). There were thirty-three standing committees in the house between 1980 and 1986, with only three black members chairing committees. By 1995, African Americans chaired six committees in the house, but this number fell to four at the turn of the century.

Similarly, as the number of black senators increased, so did the number of black committee chairs. There are twenty-three standing committees in the Georgia senate, and Table 4.4 indicates that African American committee chairs increased from two in the period 1980–1982 to five in the period 1999–2000.

TABLE 4.3
African American Committee Chairs in the Georgia House of Representatives, 1979–2000

1979–1982	*1983–1986*	*1987–1990*
Daughtery Special Judiciary	Clark Human Relations and Aging	Holmes Government Affairs
Dent Human Relations and Aging	Daughtery Special Judiciary	Randall Special Judiciary
Hamilton Congressional and Legislative Reapportionment	Hamilton Congressional and Legislative Reapportionment	
3 chairmanships of 33 committees	3 chairmanships of 33 committees	2 chairmanships of 33 committees
9% of total	9% of total	6% of total

1991–1994	*1995–1998*	*1999–2000*
Holmes Government Affairs	Holmes Government Affairs	Holmes Government Affairs
Lucas Human Relations and Aging	Lucas Human Relations and Aging	Lucas State Institutions and Property
Randall Special Judiciary	J. McKinney Martoc	Sinkfield Children & Youth
Smyre Industrial Relations	Randall Special Judiciary	Smyre Rules
	Sinkfield Children and Youth	
	Smyre University System of Georgia	
4 chairmanships of 33 committees	6 chairmanships of 33 committees	4 chairmanships of 33 committees
12% of total	18% of total	12% total

Source: Menifield, Shaffer, and Jones (2000); derived from various issues of *Journal of the Senate of the State of Georgia* and the *Journal of the House of the State of Georgia*, Secretary of State, and the Georgia General Assembly Web site.

One of the most significant events at this time was the 1995 selection of Senator David Scott to head the powerful Rules Committee. He was a member of the Black Caucus who had been elected to the senate in 1983 after spending eight years in the Georgia house.

In the 1999–2000 sessions, GLBC members chaired four committees in the house and five in the senate. In both chambers this included the Rules Committee. Perhaps the most powerful committee of all, it set the terms for debate and amendments on specific measures, and all legislation must pass through it before proceeding to the floor for debate. The Rules Committee chairs determine the time for debate, the number of speakers, and how many amendments can be offered on each bill. Although this committee does not

TABLE 4.4
African American Committee Chairs in the Georgia Senate, 1979–2000

1979–1982	1983–1986	1987–1990
Bond Consumer Affairs	Bond Consumer Affairs	Langford Consumer Affairs (1989–1990)
Tate Retirement	A. Scott Children and Youth Tate Retirement	E. Scott Consumer Affairs E. Walker Reapportionment
2 chairmanships of 23 committees 9% of total	3 chairmanships of 23 committees 13% of total	3 chairmanships of 23 committees 13% of total

1991–1994	1995–1998	1999–2000
R. Allen Government Operations	Abernathy III Interstate Cooperation	Fort Interstate Cooperation
Langford Consumer Affairs	Harbison Defense and Veterans Affairs	Harbison Veterans and Consumer Affairs
D. Scott Education, Youth, Aging and Human Ecology	D. Scott Rules	D. Scott Rules
C. Walker Health and Human Services	N. Thomas State and Local Government Operations	Stokes Health & Human Services
E. Walker Reapportionment		N. Thomas State and Local Government Operations
5 chairmanships of 23 committees 22% of total	4 chairmanships of 23 committees 17% of total	5 chairmanships of 23 committees 22% of total

Source: Menifield, Shaffer, and Jones (2000); derived from various issues of *Journal of the Senate of the State of Georgia* and the *Journal of the House of the State of Georgia*, Secretary of State, and the Georgia General Assembly Web site.

write legislation, it often has determinative power regarding the final outcome of legislation.

In the house, GLBC members also chair the Governmental Affairs, Children & Youth, and State Institutions & Property Committees. Two of these are particularly relevant to Georgia's black community. The Governmental Affairs Committee is actively involved in writing legislation directly related to elections, registration, and voting. Following the 2000 presidential election fiasco in Florida, and accusations that minority voters were disenfranchised, election legislation continues to be of significant interest for black residents. The State Institutions & Property Committee controls legislation related to state correctional institutions, of concern for the black community due to the disproportionate number of incarcerated minorities. This committee also oversees legislation related to parole eligibility, terms of probation, crime severity, and sentencing.

In addition to the Senate Rules Committee, Black Caucus members chair four other committees in the chamber: Interstate Cooperation, Veterans and Consumer Affairs, State & Local Government Operations, and Health & Human Services. The Health & Human Services Committee plays a vital role in the black community as it addresses issues related to day-care centers and other educational settings, health care benefits for poor families, welfare to work programs, and other state social services. The Interstate Cooperation, Veterans and Consumer Affairs and State & Local Government Operations Committees address issues broadly relevant to all Georgians, with no particular emphasis on the state's black community.

SUBSTANTIVE REPRESENTATION IN GEORGIA

In an effort to assess the connection between descriptive and substantive representation in Georgia, we analyze roll-call votes from 1992 through 1999, augmented with a discussion of a few key votes from the 1980s and several votes from the 1990s. We selected 1990s votes based upon legislative summaries in the *Georgia Legislative Review* (*GLR*), a publication of the Southern Center for Studies in Public Policy at Clark-Atlanta University, which includes for most years a chapter assessing votes important to the GLBC. The chapter in most of those years sought to assess the cohesiveness of the GLBC, including a description of the issues upon which the GLBC formulated its legislative agenda for each session (Boone 1992, 1993, 1994, 1995, 1998; Mitchell and Dillon 1996; Mitchell and Broomes 1997; Mitchell 1999). Therefore, we analyze votes considered important for the substantive representation of African Americans in the Georgia legislature, including roll-call votes on bills or amendments sponsored or co-sponsored by GLBC members, or potentially significant for black citizens in Georgia. In most cases, vote records were derived from the *Journal of the House* and *Journal of the Senate* for respective years.[12]

Political scientist and Georgia State Representative Robert Holmes (1994, 2000) suggests that the caucus was not effective early in its existence due to small numbers, low seniority, and a lack of support from the governor's office. During the 1980s, however, the caucus's influence grew as its members endorsed gubernatorial winners and gained seniority in their respective chambers. For example, bills establishing the Martin Luther King Jr. holiday repeatedly failed throughout the 1970s and early 1980s, until Governor Joe Frank Harris (whose election had been vigorously supported by most GLBC members) endorsed the effort. Key caucus priorities in the 1987–1988 session included state efforts to improve education, address illiteracy, increase funding for Aid to Families with Dependent Children (AFDC), and increase state support of historically black colleges in Atlanta. With Harris's support, progress was made in legislative action on these agenda items, though full funding was rarely obtained. Other concerns were addressed weakly or not at all, such as strengthening the monitoring of fair employment practices in the state, establishing new programs to address several social problems, and encouraging the divestment of state funds from South Africa. Overall, passage of caucus-sponsored bills in that session lagged behind white-sponsored bills in the house (32.5% versus 68.7% of proposed bills), though passage was more comparable in the senate (35.1% versus 44% of proposed bills) (Holmes 2000).

We now turn to the GLBC priorities in the 1990s and divide roll-call votes according to legislative subject. Each table compares house and senate votes, as well as the voting differences between Republicans, white Democrats, and black Democrats. We note that in a number of cases, bills were voted on by only one chamber, a result of the same (or comparable) bills being killed in committee in the other chamber, or never being proposed or passed over to the second chamber; some votes reported are not on entire bills but on amendments or other legislative maneuverings. Excluded from these tables, for ease of presentation, are votes in which 90% or more of all three groups voted in the same way.

Independent sample t-tests compare voting by white and black Democrats, allowing us to assess whether GLBC members as a whole voted independently of the white members of the Democratic Caucus. While we would expect that at times GLBC priorities would coincide with that of Democrats overall, in an ideologically and a geographically bifurcated state such as Georgia we anticipate intraparty differences in addition to expected differences between the GOP Caucus and the GLBC (as in most legislatures, we find a rather consistent pattern of difference between Democratic and Republican roll-call voting). We also assess the extent to which each chamber achieves substantive representation of black interests by comparing the result of each vote with the vote of Black Caucus members. In this comparison, we assume that the majority vote of GLBC members "represents" the interests of African American citizens of the state (of course, whether this is actually the case is a theoretical and philosophical question). Following the vote-by-vote analysis in Tables 4.5 through 4.11, we make an overall assessment of GLBC independence, of the substantive representation of African Americans through GLBC votes, and of changes over time, if any.

Table 4.5 presents roll-call votes on GLBC priorities relating to election reform and apportionment. On most votes there are major differences between

TABLE 4.5
Roll Call Votes in the Georgia General Assembly on Elections and Government Reform Bills

	House of Representatives				Senate			
	Black Dems	White Dems	Repub- licans	Total	Black Dems	White Dems	Repub- licans	Total
1992 Presidential Primary Date Change (HB196)								
For	87.0%	92.5%	9.1%	74.8%	100%	97%	0%	74.5%
Against	13.0	7.5	90.9	25.2	0.0	3.0	100.0	25.5
N = Total Voting Members	(23)	(107)	(33)	(163)	(3)	(33)	(11)	(47)
1992 Apportionment Final Passage (HB1657)								
For	28.6%	67.3%	30.3%	54.9%	100%	72.7%	50%	72%
Against	71.4	32.7	69.7	45.1***	0.0	27.3	50.0	28.0***
N = Total Voting Members	(21)	(110)	(33)	(164)	(7)	(33)	(10)	(50)
1994 Motor Voter (HB1429)								
For	100%	78.3%	27.5%	65.7%	87.5%	96.6%	37.5%	77.4%
Against	0.0	21.7	72.5	34.3***	12.5	3.4	62.5	22.6
N = Total Voting Members	(23)	(92)	(51)	(166)	(8)	(29)	(16)	(53)
1994 Make Elections Plurality without Runoff (SB680)								
For	92.3%	90.1%	1.9%	63.3%	80%	100%	0%	64.6%
Against	7.7	9.9	98.1	36.7	20.0	0.0	100.0	35.4
N = Total Voting Members	(26)	(91)	(52)	(169)	(5)	(27)	(16)	(48)
1997 Reconsider Making Absentee Voting Easier (HB543)								
For	0%	12.1%	97.2%	48.1%	–	–	–	–
Against	100.0	87.9	2.8	51.9***	–	–	–	–
N = Total Voting Members	(23)	(66)	(71)	(160)	–	–	–	–
1997 Require Picture ID at Polls (SB273)								
For	80.8%	97.2%	100%	95.8%				
Against	19.2	2.8	0	4.2*				
N = Total Voting Members	(26)	(71)	(71)	(168)				
1998 45% of Vote to Win in Primary Elections (HB1529) House: Williams Amendment; Senate: Fort Amendment								
For	33.3%	9.3%	93.2%	48.0%	18.2%	4.3%	95.2%	41.8%
Against	66.7	90.7	6.8	52.0**	81.8	95.7	4.8	58.2
N = Total Voting Members	(27)	(75)	(73)	(175)	(11)	(23)	(21)	(55)
1999 Allow Photographing of Voters at Election Polls (HB530), Davis Amendment								
For	4.3%	12.7%	91.9%	46.4%	–	–	–	–
Against	95.7	87.3	8.1	53.6	–	–	–	–
N = Total Voting Members	(23)	(55)	(62)	(140)	–	–	–	–

Note: Not listed are five votes on GLBC bills in which 90% or more of all three groups voted the same way (these votes are included in the summary tables). These votes are: 1993 HB298 (passed HR, S); 1995 HB646 (passed S); 1997 SB273 (passed S); 1998 SB459 (passed S); 1999 SB235 (passed S). The GLBC did not identify as a priority a senate vote on 1997 HB543; the senate did not vote on the Davis Amendment to 1999 HB530.

Sources: 1992–1998 Georgia house and senate journals; Mitchell (1999). Bill selection based upon Black Caucus (GLBC) positions, as identified in various issues of *Georgia Legislative Review* (Boone 1992, 1993, 1994, 1995, 1998; Mitchell and Dillon 1996; Mitchell and Broomes 1997; Mitchell 1999).

* = p ≤ .10; ** = p ≤ .05; *** = p ≤ .01; Significance tests are based on independent samples t-tests and test whether there are statistically significant differences between black and white Democrats.

the two major parties. In the votes where differences between the parties occur, Republicans were much less supportive of election reform than Democrats. In most votes in which there were significant racial differences among Democrats, GLBC members were more unified than whites in their support for electoral reform. The first example of internal Democratic divisions was in the 1992 vote on the then-final version of reapportionment creating three majority black congressional districts, for which previous versions had been rejected by the Department of Justice. On this bill, house Black Caucus members were significantly less supportive of passage because of the belief that the district lines were not favorable enough to the black community, though in the senate, GLBC members were significantly more supportive of its passage than white Democrats. We also see significant differences between white and black Democrats in the passage of Motor Voter legislation in 1994. This contentious bill, cosponsored by Black Caucus members, sought to implement the federal requirements of the National Voter Registration Act of 1993 and to extend its provisions to Georgia's state elections, including the maintenance of a unified voter registration list. Opposition among Republican legislators seemed to be based on the presumption that the law would benefit Democrats disproportionately. Democratic supporters used the threat of lawsuits, which would likely be lost by Motor Voter opponents anyway, as motivation to generate support among other reticent Democrats, many of whom continued to oppose the bill on principle and due to the cost of its implementation. In the final analysis, however, house GLBC members voted unanimously for the bill, whereas white Democrats were more divided; senate Democrats, white and black, were equally supportive of the legislation; GOP legislators remained largely opposed to the bill, though it was eventually signed into law (Fishman 1994, pp. 105–108). On all of the elections-related votes (including one house bill not shown in Table 4.5, in which 90% of all three groups voted the same way, see table notes), the house GLBC voted independently of white Democrats five out of nine times (56%), but the Black Caucus's preferred outcome was obtained in eight out of nine votes (89%). In the senate, black Democrats voted independently only one out of ten times, but the substantive results coincided with the Black Caucus's votes every time.

Education votes are shown in Table 4.6. On all three house votes indicated as GLBC priorities, caucus members voted in the same direction as white Democrats, but were significantly more unified in their votes against restricting middle-school sex education curriculum in the State Board of Education approved programs, and in favor of providing after-school sex education to middle-school children. Overall, house caucus members voted independently

TABLE 4.6

Roll Call Votes in the Georgia General Assembly on Education Bills

	House of Representatives				Senate			
	Black Dems	White Dems	Repub- licans	Total	Black Dems	White Dems	Repub- licans	Total
1995 Alcohol Education in Schools (SB68)								
For	–	–	–	–	100%	100%	61.9%	84.9%
Against	–	–	–	–	0	0	38.1	15.1
N = Total Voting Members	–	–	–	–	(8)	(24)	(21)	(53)
1997 Restrict Sex Education Curricula in Middle Schools (SB50)								
Westmoreland Amendment								
For	8%	35.3%	84.3%	52.1%	–	–	–	–
Against	92.0	64.7	15.7	47.9***	–	–	–	–
N = Total Voting Members	(25)	(68)	(70)	(163)	–	–	–	–
1997 Provide After-School Sex Education in Middle Schools (SB50)								
For	100%	91.3%	73.4%	85.1%	100%	95%	52.6%	78.3%
Against	0.0	8.7	26.6	14.9**	0.0	5.0	47.4	21.7
N = Total Voting Members	(21)	(69)	(64)	(154)	(7)	(20)	(19)	(46)
1997 Alcohol Education in Schools (SB41)								
For	–	–	–	–	100%	95.8%	55.6%	82.7%
Against	–	–	–	–	0.0	4.2	44.4	17.3
N = Total Voting Members	–	–	–	–	(10)	(24)	(18)	(52)
1998 Allow Charter Schools (HB353)								
For	–	–	–	–	87.5%	100%	95.2%	95.8%
Against	–	–	–	–	12.5	0	4.8	4.2
N = Total Voting Members	–	–	–	–	(8)	(19)	(21)	(48)

Note: Not listed is one vote on a GLBC bill in which 90% or more of all three groups voted the same way (this vote is included in the summary tables). This vote is 1998 HB353 (passed H). The GLBC did not identify as priorities house votes on 1995 SB68 or 1997 SB41, and no senate vote was held on the Westmoreland Amendment to 1997 SB50.

Sources: 1992–1998 Georgia house and senate journals; Mitchell (1999). Bill selection based upon Black Caucus (GLBC) positions, as identified in various issues of *Georgia Legislative Review* (Boone 1992, 1993, 1994, 1995, 1998; Mitchell and Dillon 1996; Mitchell and Broomes 1997; Mitchell 1999).

* = p ≤ .10; ** = p ≤ .05; *** = p ≤ .01; Significance tests are based on independent samples t-tests and test whether there are statistically significant differences between black and white Democrats.

of white Democrats in both cases, and the substantive result in one of those votes coincided with the caucus votes. Senate caucus members voted in concurrence with white Democrats in each of four votes, attaining substantive representation every time.

Table 4.7 shows votes relating to health care or health insurance. In general, GLBC members voted very similarly to white Democrats (in 7–11 house votes and 8–12 senate votes) and obtained high rates of substantive representation as

TABLE 4.7

Roll Call Votes in the Georgia General Assembly on Health Care and Health Insurance Bills

	House of Representatives				Senate			
	Black Dems	White Dems	Repub- licans	Total	Black Dems	White Dems	Repub- licans	Total
1992 Workers' Compensation Liability (HB1679)								
For	–	–	–	–	75%	94.3%	100%	92.6%
Against	–	–	–	–	25.0	5.7	0.0	7.4
N = Total Voting Members	–	–	–	–	(8)	(35)	(11)	(54)
1993 Personal Care Homes Reform (HB848)								
For	92.9%	71.6%	47.9%	68.3%	–	–	–	–
Against	7.1	28.4	52.1	31.7***	–	–	–	–
N = Total Voting Members	(28)	(88)	(48)	(164)	–	–	–	–
1994 Create Georgia Health Insurance Plan (HB1306)								
For	16.7%	75.8%	93.9%	72.6%	–	–	–	–
Against	83.3	24.2	6.1	27.4**	–	–	–	–
N = Total Voting Members	(24)	(95)	(49)	(168)	–	–	–	–
1995 Set Certain Standards for Provider Participation in Health Care Plans (SB195)								
For	–	–	–	–	100%	41.7%	11.1%	42.3%
Against	–	–	–	–	0.0	58.3	88.9	57.7***
N = Total Voting Members	–	–	–	–	(10)	(24)	(18)	(52)
1996 Establish Trust Fund for Indigent Care (HB1283)								
For	76.9%	97.4%	100%	95%	–	–	–	–
Against	23.1	2.6	0.0	5.0**	–	–	–	–
N = Total Voting Members	(26)	(76)	(59)	(161)	–	–	–	–
1996 Expand Use of Doctors Not in HMO Plans (SB647)								
For	–	–	–	–	100%	96%	73.7%	88.9%
Against	–	–	–	–	0.0	4.0	26.3	11.1
N = Total Voting Members	–	–	–	–	(10)	(25)	(19)	(54)
1997 Expand Health Ins. to Include Eye Care (SB254)								
For	–	–	–	–	100%	70%	19%	54.9%
Against	–	–	–	–	0.0	30.0	81.0	45.1***
N = Total Voting Members	–	–	–	–	(10)	(20)	(21)	(51)
1998 Require Health Ins. to Cover Chlamydia Screening (HB1565)								
For	96.2%	83.8%	19.4%	59%	100%	81%	28.6%	64.2%
Against	3.8	16.2	80.6	41.0**	0.0	19.0	71.4	35.8**
N = Total Voting Members	(26)	(68)	(67)	(161)	(11)	(21)	(21)	(53)
1998 Expand Coverage for Uninsured Children (SB410)								
For	100%	98.7%	78.4%	90.3%	100%	100%	81%	92.3%
Against	0.0	1.3	21.6	9.7	0.0	0.0	19.0	7.7
N = Total Voting Members	(27)	(75)	(74)	(176)	(10)	(21)	(21)	(52)

TABLE 4.7
(*Continued*)

	House of Representatives				Senate			
	Black Dems	White Dems	Republicans	Total	Black Dems	White Dems	Republicans	Total
1999 Require Health Insurance to Cover Contraceptive Prescriptions (HB374)								
For	96.2%	88.9%	37.1%	68.9%	100.0%	83.3%	18.8%	62.8%
Against	3.8	11.1	62.9	31.1	0.0	16.7	81.3	37.2*
N = Total Voting Members	(26)	(63)	(62)	(151)	(9)	(18)	(16)	(43)
1999 Extend Seat belt Requirements to SUVs and Pickup Trucks (HB916)								
For	82.6%	70.7%	10.2%	47.1%	–	–	–	–
Against	17.4	29.3	89.8	52.9	–	–	–	–
N = Total Voting Members	(23)	(58)	(59)	(140)	–	–	–	–

Note: Not listed are seven votes on GLBC bills in which 90% or more of all three groups voted the same way (these votes are included in the summary tables). These votes are: 1992 HB538 (passed HR, S); 1992 HB1679 (passed HR); 1996 HB1283 (passed S); 1997 SB254 (passed HR); 1998 SB55 (passed HR, S); 1999 SB195 (passed S); 1999 SB210 (passed S). The GLBC did not identify as priorities senate votes on 1993 HB848, 1994 HB1306, and 1999 HB916, or house votes on 1995 SB195 and 1996 SB647.

Sources: 1992–1998 Georgia house and senate journals; Mitchell (1999). Bill selection based upon Black Caucus (GLBC) positions, as identified in various issues of *Georgia Legislative Review* (Boone 1992, 1993, 1994, 1995, 1998; Mitchell and Dillon 1996; Mitchell and Broomes 1997; Mitchell 1999).

* = p ≤ .10; ** = p ≤ .05; *** = p ≤ .01; Significance tests are based on independent samples t-tests and test whether there are statistically significant differences between black and white Democrats.

well (vote results coincided with GLBC votes in 82% of house and 92% of senate votes). One of the most divisive votes occurred in the 1995 session. In the senate voting on the 1995 Health Plan Act, 100% of black Democrats voted to pass, 89% of Republicans voted against, and white Democrats were divided, voting 42%–58% against the bill. This bill sought to define the eligibility of health care providers for participation in health plans (including "hospital-based networks, health care provider networks, and health benefit plans" (Dillon and Mitchell 1995, p. 107). Essentially, it expanded state regulation of health plans and networks and prohibited the discriminatory exclusion of health care providers from health plans. Because of a perception that minority physicians were disproportionately excluded from participation in health plans in the state, the GLBC endorsed this bill, and its members gave it unanimous support.

Table 4.8 presents the voting patterns for social welfare legislation. The GLBC membership voted independently from its white co-partisans at a rate of 73% in the house and 63% in the senate, but in both chambers bills' final dispositions coincided with the Black Caucus vote the great majority of the time

TABLE 4.8
Roll Call Votes in the Georgia General Assembly on Social Welfare Bills

	House of Representatives				Senate			
	Black Dems	White Dems	Republicans	Total	Black Dems	White Dems	Republicans	Total
1992 Family & Medical Leave Act (SB831)								
For	100%	81%	67.7%	81.2%	100%	100%	80%	95.9%
Against	0.0	19.0	32.3	18.8***	0.0	0.0	20.0	4.1
N = Total Voting Members	(23)	(100)	(31)	(154)	(8)	(31)	(10)	(49)
1993 Female Business Enterprise Plan (HB281)								
For	100%	90.9%	11.4%	66.9%	80%	36.7%	50%	44.7%
Against	0.0	9.1	88.6	33.1***	20.0	63.3	50.0	55.3*
N = Total Voting Members	(18)	(77)	(44)	(139)	(5)	(30)	(12)	(47)
1994 Change Child Support Computation (HB642)								
For	46.2%	75.3%	73.1%	70.2%	–	–	–	–
Against	53.8	24.7	26.9	29.8**	–	–	–	–
N = Total Voting Members	(26)	(93)	(52)	(171)	–	–	–	–
1994 Est. Pilot Workfare Program (SB464)								
For	67.9%	96.8%	9.8%	66.5%	100%	100%	0%	67.9%
Against	32.1	3.2	90.2	33.5***	0.0	0.0	100.0	32.1
N = Total Voting Members	(28)	(94)	(51)	(173)	(7)	(29)	(17)	(53)
1995 AFDC Hiring Tax Credit (HB570)								
For	96.4%	80.6%	0%	52.8%	100%	87.5%	0.0%	57.7%
Against	3.6	19.4	100.0	47.2***	0.0	12.5	100.0	42.3*
N = Total Voting Members	(28)	(72)	(61)	(161)	(9)	(24)	(19)	(52)
1995 Table a Gutted Gender Affirmative Action Bill (HB358)								
For	96.2%	95.4%	3.4%	59.7%	–	–	–	–
Against	3.8	4.6	96.6	40.3	–	–	–	–
N = Total Voting Members	(26)	(65)	(58)	(149)	–	–	–	–
1996 Prosecution of Welfare Fraud (SB446)								
For	70.4%	100%	100%	95%	–	–	–	–
Against	29.6	0.0	0.0	5.0***	–	–	–	–
N = Total Voting Members	(27)	(73)	(59)	(159)	–	–	–	–
1997 Irvin Amendment Restricting TANF Payments Past 48 Months and from Minor Parents (SB104)								
For	14.3%	13.0%	94.2%	47.0%	–	–	–	–
Against	85.7	87.0	5.8	53.0	–	–	–	–
N = Total Voting Members	(28)	(69)	(69)	(166)	–	–	–	–
1997 Expand Study of Women's Issues by the GA Commission on Women (HB761)								
For	100%	95.4%	29.9%	68.6%	100%	87.5%	42.9%	73.2%
Against	0.0	4.6	70.1	31.4*	0.0	12.5	57.1	26.8*
N = Total Voting Members	(27)	(65)	(67)	(159)	(11)	(24)	(21)	(56)

TABLE 4.8
(Continued)

	House of Representatives				Senate			
	Black Dems	White Dems	Repub-licans	Total	Black Dems	White Dems	Repub-licans	Total
1998 Increase Minimum Wage (SB432)								
For	–	–	–	–	100%	27.3%	4.8%	33.3%
Against	–	–	–	–	0.0	72.7	95.2	66.7***
N = Total Voting Members	–	–	–	–	(11)	(22)	(21)	(54)
1999 Make Legal Immigrants Eligible for TANF (SB110)								
For	100.0%	86.4%	75.4%	83.9%	100.0%	82.4%	31.3%	66.7%
Against	0.0	13.6	24.6	16.1***	0.0	17.6	68.8	33.3*
N = Total Voting Members	(23)	(59)	(61)	(143)	(9)	(17)	(16)	(42)
1999 Mandate Public Housing Resident Representation in Housing Authorities (HB406)								
For	100.0%	98.4%	86.9%	94.0%	–	–	–	–
Against	0.0	1.6	13.1	6.0	–	–	–	–
N = Total Voting Members	(24)	(64)	(61)	(149)	–	–	–	–

Note: Not listed is one vote on a GLBC bill in which 90% or more of all three groups voted the same way (this vote is included in the summary tables). It is 1996 SB446 (passed S). The GLBC did not identify as priorities a house vote on 1998 SB432 or senate votes on 1994 HB642 or 1999 HB406. The vote on 1995 HB358 was a procedural vote in the Georgia house only, and no senate vote was taken on the Irvin Amendment to 1997 SB104.

Sources: 1992–1998 Georgia house and senate journals; Mitchell (1999). Bill selection based upon Black Caucus (GLBC) positions, as identified in various issues of *Georgia Legislative Review* (Boone 1992, 1993, 1994, 1995, 1998; Mitchell and Dillon 1996; Mitchell and Broomes 1997; Mitchell 1999).

* = p ≤ .10; ** = p ≤ .05; *** = p ≤ .01; Significance tests are based on independent samples t-tests and test whether there are statistically significant differences between black and white Democrats.

(91% in the house and 75% in the senate). One contentious piece of legislation related to the 1994 establishment of "workfare" in the state (Boone 1994; Edmund 1994). One of several welfare reform proposals, the "Work for Welfare Program" (SB 464) embodied the principle that receipt of public assistance established a social contract between the state and the recipient; the legislation thus required twenty hours per month of work at a nonprofit organization or governmental agency. The trigger for the work requirement was whether an AFDC recipient had received assistance in twenty-four out of thirty-six months. While one of the bill's co-sponsors in the senate was a GLBC member (Robert Brown), caucus chair Georgianna Sinkfield expressed reservations about the effectiveness of the legislation and concerns about its impact upon existing programs helping AFDC recipients obtain education and job training. Coalescing to fight off even more conservative welfare reform proposed by senate Republicans, African American women legislators pushed their caucus to support the bill. In the final votes in each chamber, house GLBC members voted 68% in favor, while senate caucus members supported it unanimously.

One example of a racial split in the senate related to the 1998 vote on increasing the state's minimum wage. At that time, the state minimum wage was $3.25 per hour for employees not covered by the federal minimum wage. One of several similar proposals from Democrats, supporters cited Georgia's wage as being meager compared to other states' and inadequate compared to data proposed by "living wage campaigns" that recommended city minimum wages between seven and eight dollars per hour (Maclachlan 1998, pp. 63–64). SB 432 proposed raising the state wage progressively from $3.25 to $3.72, then to $4.20, then to $5.15, and then to match the federal minimum wage by July 2000. Supported broadly by poverty, civil, and labor rights groups, the bill was eventually defeated in the senate 19–35, with black Democrats unanimously in favor of the bill, white Democrats divided 27%–73%, and Republicans opposed by 95%.

Table 4.9 presents roll calls directly related to racial issues, including affirmative action. On six house votes, Black Caucus members voted independently four times; in three of those cases, white and black Democrats voted in the opposite direction, and in each of those three cases, the caucus position was defeated. In the senate, caucus members voted independently of white Democrats in two out of five votes. Only in 1997's vote on restricting teaching of Ebonics was there a substantive division between the two sets of Democrats. One example of the house Black Caucus's disagreement with white Democrats was on 1999's HR 333. This resolution urged local boards of education to encourage the posting and reading of documents relating to America's political heritage. It specifically listed

> the United States Constitution, including the preamble; the Constitution of Georgia, including the preamble; the Declaration of Independence; the Mayflower Compact; the national motto, "In God We Trust"; the national anthem; the Pledge of Allegiance; the writings, speeches, documents, and proclamations of any of the signers of the Declaration of Independence, signers of the Constitution of the United States, or Presidents of the United States; Organic documents from the precolonial, colonial, revolutionary, federalist, and postfederalist eras; United States Supreme Court decisions; and Acts and debates of the United States Congress, including the published text of the *United States Congressional Record.* (Georgia House of Representatives 1999)

TABLE 4.9
Roll Call Votes in the Georgia General Assembly on Race-Related Bills

	House of Representatives				Senate			
	Black Dems	White Dems	Repub- licans	Total	Black Dems	White Dems	Repub- licans	Total
1992 Expand Minority Representation on State Boards (HB1541)								
For	92%	74.1%	45.2%	71.3%	100%	91.7%	63.6%	86.8%
Against	8.0	25.9	54.8	28.7***	0.0	8.3	36.4	13.2
N = Total Voting Members	(25)	(108)	(31)	(164)	(6)	(36)	(11)	(53)
1996 Eliminate State Merit System Affirmative Action (SB635)								
For	34.5%	86.7%	90.6	79.4%	80%	94.1%	95.2%	93%
Against	65.5	13.3	9.5	20.6***	20.0	5.9	4.8	7.0
N = Total Voting Members	(29)	(83)	(63)	(175)	(5)	(17)	(21)	(43)
1996 Eliminate Private Prison Affirmative Action (SB675)								
For	14.8%	83.5%	95.2%	76.8%	–	–	–	–
Against	85.2	16.5	4.8	23.2**	–	–	–	–
N = Total Voting Members	(27)	(79)	(62)	(168)	–	–	–	–
1997 Restrict Ebonics Curricula (SB51)								
For	–	–	–	–	30%	95.8%	89.5%	81.1%
Against	–	–	–	–	70.0	4.2	10.5	18.9***
N = Total Voting Members	–	–	–	–	(10)	(24)	(19)	(53)
1998 Hospital Regulation, Including ending Hospital Affirmative Action (HB1101)								
[House Version Diluted Affirmative Action Provision]								
For	95.7%	97%	70.8%	85.8%	0%	21.7%	0%	9.4%
Against	4.3	3.0	29.2	14.2	100.0	78.3	100.0	90.6**
N = Total Voting Members	(23)	(67)	(65)	(155)	(11)	(23)	(19)	(53)
1999 Table Amendment Adding Minority Contributions to "American Heritage" Documents for Schools (HR333)								
For	30.8%	67.8%	70.5%	62.3%	–	–	–	–
Against	69.2	32.2	29.5	37.7***	–	–	–	–
N = Total Voting Members	(26)	(59)	(61)	(146)	–	–	–	–

Note: Not listed are two votes on GLBC bills in which 90% or more of all three groups voted the same way (these votes are included in the summary tables). These votes are: 1993 HB57 (passed HR); 1996 SB675 (passed S). The GLBC did not identify as a priority a house vote on 1997 SB51, and no senate vote was taken on the house procedural motion for 1999 HR333.

Sources: 1992–1998 Georgia house and senate journals; Mitchell (1999). Bill selection based upon Black Caucus (GLBC) positions, as identified in various issues of *Georgia Legislative Review* (Boone 1992, 1993, 1994, 1995, 1998; Mitchell and Dillon 1996; Mitchell and Broomes 1997; Mitchell 1999).

* = p ≤ .10; ** = p ≤ .05; *** = p ≤ .01; Significance tests are based on independent samples t-tests and test whether there are statistically significant differences between black and white Democrats.

According to the *Georgia Legislative Review* for that year, "many minorities and progressive representatives" perceived that the list of documents, with its heavy emphasis on the U.S. founding period and writings, omitted significant contributions of nonwhites in American history. A substitute resolution was introduced that encouraged the addition of such contributions to the list of documents, and the vote identified as key by the GLBC leadership was whether to table that amendment. The Democratic caucus was heavily split on the vote, with the amendment ultimately rejected.

Votes on legislation relating to criminal justice and gun control are shown in Table 4.10. With regard to gun control legislation, in all but one vote, Black Caucus members were more supportive than white Democrats on increasing restrictions and regulations on private ownership of firearms. Overall, Black Caucus members voted independently of white Democrats in the house 64% of the time (9–14 votes) and in the senate only about 26% of the time (5–19 votes). Substantively, the senate was a friendlier venue for GLBC priorities, where substantive representation was obtained in about 95% of votes, versus only 57% of votes in the house. On crime legislation in general, GLBC members were less supportive of increasing penalties for crimes than white Democrats, especially in the house. This was the case, for example, in efforts to try juveniles as adults, passing "Two Strikes" legislation, increasing penalties for crimes against children, and reestablishing state chain gangs. Black Caucus members in the house were less supportive than white Democrats of a 1996 bill repealing mandatory life sentences for second drug offenses that also expanded the list of drugs for which dealers could be prosecuted, while senate caucus members were significantly more supportive of the bill.

Table 4.11 contains roll-call votes on GLBC priorities relating to economic development and taxes. In the house, Black Caucus members differed significantly from white Democrats in only 8% of roll calls, and there were significant differences in senate voting in only four out of twelve bills (33%). Substantive representation was the norm, with the outcome of the votes coinciding with GLBC votes in the house every time and in the senate 92% of the time.

COALITION FORMATIONS

It is often the case that legislators must strive to make the "best" decision in a complex and highly partisan process. As we have seen between 1980 and 2000, African Americans made up sizeable portions of the Democratic Party in the Georgia legislature. We should not be surprised to find that black representatives

TABLE 4.10
Roll Call Votes in the Georgia General Assembly on Crime and Gun Control Bills

	House of Representatives				Senate			
	Black Dems	White Dems	Repub- licans	Total	Black Dems	White Dems	Repub- licans	Total
1992 Gun Control, Including Penalties Related to Access by Minors (HB277)								
For	96%	47.4%	51.7%	56.4%	–	–	–	–
Against	4.0	52.6	48.3	43.6**	–	–	–	–
N = Total Voting Members	(25)	(95)	(29)	(149)	–	–	–	–
1993 Expanded Regulation of Gun Dealers (SB12)								
For	–	–	–	–	100%	56.3%	60%	64.3%
Against	–	–	–	–	0.0	43.8	40.0	35.7***
N = Total Voting Members	–	–	–	–	(9)	(32)	(15)	(56)
1993 Life without Parole (HB485)								
For	52.2%	67.7%	60%	63.4%	87.5%	96.8%	100%	96.3%
Against	47.8	32.3	40.0	36.6	12.5	3.2	0.0	3.7
N = Total Voting Members	(23)	(96)	(45)	(164)	(8)	(31)	(15)	(54)
1994 Establish Gun Purchase Waiting Period with Instant Background Check (SB12)								
For	92.6%	31.1%	17.6%	36.9%	83.3%	85.2%	47.1%	72%
Against	7.4	68.9	82.4	63.1**	16.7	14.8	52.9	28.0
N = Total Voting Members	(27)	(90)	(51)	(168)	(6)	(27)	(17)	(50)
1994 Try Juveniles As Adults for Violent Crimes (SB440)								
For	85%	100%	97.8%	97.4%	–	–	–	–
Against	15.0	0.0	2.2	2.6*	–	–	–	–
N = Total Voting Members	(20)	(88)	(45)	(153)	–	–	–	–
1994 Two Strikes (SB441)								
For	74.1%	100%	100%	96%	–	–	–	–
Against	25.9	0.0	0.0	4.0**	–	–	–	–
N = Total Voting Members	(27)	(95)	(51)	(173)	–	–	–	–
1995 Increase Jail Time for Crimes against Minors (HB377)								
For	31%	56.8%	96.7%	66.7%	–	–	–	–
Against	69.0	43.2	3.3	33.3**	–	–	–	–
N = Total Voting Members	(29)	(81)	(61)	(171)	–	–	–	–
1996 Allow Concealed Handguns (SB678)								
For	43.5%	88.6%	95.1%	84.7%	55.6%	100%	95%	89.8%
Against	56.5	11.4	4.9	15.3**	44.4	0.0	5.0	10.2**
N = Total Voting Members	(23)	(79)	(61)	(163)	(9)	(20)	(20)	(49)
1996 Reconsider Vote to Reinstate Chain Gangs (HB1193)								
For	94.7%	17.6%	1.7%	21.4%	–	–	–	–
Against	5.3	82.4	98.3	78.6**	–	–	–	–
N = Total Voting Members	(19)	(68)	(58)	(145)	–	–	–	–
1996 Change Drug Penalties, Repealing Mandatory Life Sentence for 2nd Offense (HB1555)								
For	70.8%	98.8%	100%	95.2%	100%	86.4%	47.4%	72.9%

(*Continued*)

TABLE 4.10
(*Continued*)

	House of Representatives				Senate			
	Black Dems	White Dems	Repub- licans	Total	Black Dems	White Dems	Repub- licans	Total
Against	29.2	1.3	0.0	4.8**	0.0	13.6	52.6	27.1*
N = Total Voting Members	(24)	(80)	(63)	(167)	(7)	(22)	(19)	(48)
1998 Abolish Parole for Some Crimes (SR463)								
For	–	–	–	–	90%	89.5%	23.8%	62%
Against	–	–	–	–	10.0	10.5	76.2	38.0
N = Total Voting Members	–	–	–	–	(10)	(19)	(21)	(50)
1998 Restrict Home Access to Guns for Minors (SB407)								
For	–	–	–	–	100%	71.4%	65%	74%
Against	–	–	–	–	0.0	28.6	35.0	26.0***
N = Total Voting Members	–	–	–	–	(9)	(21)	(20)	(50)
1999 Mandate that Convicted Felons Serve 90% of Sentence (SB11)								
For	–	–	–	–	0.0%	12.5%	93.75%	42.5%
Against	–	–	–	–	100	87.5	6.25	57.5
N = Total Voting Members	–	–	–	–	(8)	(16)	(16)	(40)
1999 Require Violators of "Crimes against Family Members Act" to Serve 90% of Sentence (SB113), Land Amendment								
For	–	–	–	–	0.0%	11.1%	87.5%	38.1%
Against	–	–	–	–	100.0	88.9	12.5	61.9
N = Total Voting Members	–	–	–	–	(8)	(18)	(16)	(42)
1999 Strip Municipalities of Power to Sue Gun Manufacturers (HB189)								
For	40.0%	88.5%	100.0%	85.2%	20.0%	94.7%	93.8%	77.8%
Against	60.0	11.5	0.0	14.8***	80.0	5.3	6.3	22.2***
N = Total Voting Members	(25)	(61)	(63)	(149)	(10)	(19)	(16)	(45)
1999 Prevent Cities from Collecting Criminal Processing Fees from Convicts (HB352), Burkhalter Amendment								
For	14.8%	22.0%	96.7%	51.4%	–	–	–	–
Against	85.2	78.0	3.3	48.6	–	–	–	–
N = Total Voting Members	(27)	(59)	(60)	(146)	–	–	–	–

Note: Not listed are nine votes on GLBC bills in which 90% or more of all three groups voted the same way (these votes are included in the summary tables). These votes are: 1992 HB277 (passed S); 1994 SB440 (passed S); 1994 SB441 (passed S); 1995 HB170 (passed HR, S); 1995 HB377 (passed S); 1995 SB77 (passed S); 1995 SB227 (passed S); 1997 HB183 (passed HR, S); 1998 SR477 (passed HR, S). The GLBC did not identify as priorities house votes on 1993 SB12, 1998 SR463, 1998 SB407, or 1999 SB11. No senate vote was taken on the house procedural motion for 1996 HB1193, or the Burkhalter Amendment to 1999 HB352; no house vote was taken on the Land Amendment to 1999 SB113.

Sources: 1992–1998 Georgia house and senate journals; Mitchell (1999). Bill selection based upon Black Caucus (GLBC) positions, as identified in various issues of *Georgia Legislative Review* (Boone 1992, 1993, 1994, 1995, 1998; Mitchell and Dillon 1996; Mitchell and Broomes 1997; Mitchell 1999).

* = p ≤ .10; ** = p ≤ .05; *** = p ≤ .01; Significance tests are based on independent samples t-tests and test whether there are statistically significant differences between black and white Democrats.

TABLE 4.11
Roll Call Votes in the Georgia General Assembly on Economic Development and Tax Bills

	House of Representatives				Senate			
	Black Dems	White Dems	Repub- licans	Total	Black Dems	White Dems	Repub- licans	Total
1992 Change Car/License Fees (HB1145)								
For	73.9%	72.1%	3.1%	59%	100%	91.4%	9.1%	75.9%
Against	26.1	27.9	96.9	41.0	0.0	8.6	90.9	24.1*
N = Total Voting Members	(23)	(111)	(32)	(166)	(8)	(35)	(11)	(54)
1993 Establish Maximum Home Interest Rate (SB105)								
For	–	–	–	–	100%	83.9%	60%	80%
Against	–	–	–	–	0.0	16.1	40.0	20.0**
N = Total Voting Members	–	–	–	–	(9)	(31)	(15)	(55)
1995 Prohibit Landfills within Two-Mile Radius (SB32)								
For	96.6%	76.5%	18.6%	59.8%	100%	62.5%	23.8%	54.5%
Against	3.4	23.5	81.4	40.2***	0.0	37.5	76.2	45.5***
N = Total Voting Members	(29)	(81)	(59)	(169)	(10)	(24)	(21)	(55)
1995 Business Development for Minority, Rural, or Economically Distressed Areas (SB253)								
For	100%	98.6%	81.8%	92.7%	100%	100%	22.2%	68.9%
Against	0.0	1.4	18.2	7.3	0.0	0.0	77.8	31.1
N = Total Voting Members	(27)	(69)	(55)	(151)	(8)	(19)	(18)	(45)
1995 Establish Georgia Institute for Community Business Development (SB404)								
For	96.6%	89.3%	42.6%	73.3%	100%	95%	5.6%	62.5%
Against	3.4	10.7	57.4	26.7	0.0	5.0	94.4	37.5
N = Total Voting Members	(29)	(75)	(61)	(165)	(10)	(20)	(18)	(48)
1997 Retrain State Workers Displaced By Privatization (SB262)								
For	–	–	–	–	100%	95%	30%	70%
Against	–	–	–	–	0.0	5.0	70.0	30.0
N = Total Voting Members	–	–	–	–	(10)	(20)	(20)	(50)
1998 Income Tax Bill (HB1162), Walker Amendment								
For	3.7%	5.5%	88%	40.6%	–	–	–	–
Against	96.3	94.5	12.0	59.4	–	–	–	–
N = Total Voting Members	(27)	(73)	(75)	(175)	–	–	–	–
1998 Establish Southern Dairy Compact (SB420)								
For	–	–	–	–	100%	27.3%	4.8%	33.3%
Against	–	–	–	–	0.0	72.7	95.2	66.7***
N = Total Voting Members	–	–	–	–	(11)	(22)	(21)	(54)
1999 Create Georgia Regional Transportation Authority (SB57)								
For	–	–	–	–	100.0%	94.4%	62.5%	83.3%
Against	–	–	–	–	0.0	5.6	37.5	16.7
N = Total Voting Members	–	–	–	–	(8)	(18)	(16)	(42)

(*Continued*)

TABLE 4.11
(*Continued*)

	House of Representatives				Senate			
	Black Dems	White Dems	Republicans	Total	Black Dems	White Dems	Republicans	Total
1999 Increase Due Process for State Merit System Employees (HB677)								
For	–	–	–	–	100.0%	88.9%	50.0%	75.0%
Against	–	–	–	–	0.0	11.1	50.0	25.0
N = Total Voting Members	–	–	–	–	(6)	(18)	(16)	(40)

Note: Not listed are seven votes on GLBC bills in which 90% or more of all three groups voted the same way (these votes are included in the summary tables). These votes are: 1993 HB237 (passed HR, S); 1995 HR460 (passed HR); 1996 HB265 (passed HR, S); 1997 SB262 (passed HR); 1998 HB1162 (passed S); 1999 HB585 (passed HR); and 1999 HB677 (passed HR). The GLBC did not identify as priorities house votes on 1993 SB105, 1998 SB420, or 1999 SB57. Please note that two votes were taken in the house on 1998 HB1162, one on the Walker Amendment (reported in the table) and one on final passage (omitted from table due to over-whelming vote).

Sources: 1992–1998 Georgia house and senate journals; Mitchell (1999). Bill selection based upon Black Caucus (GLBC) positions, as identified in various issues of *Georgia Legislative Review* (Boone 1992, 1993, 1994, 1995, 1998; Mitchell and Dillon 1996; Mitchell and Broomes 1997; Mitchell 1999).

* = p ≤ .10; ** = p ≤ .05; *** = p ≤ .01; Significance tests are based on independent samples t-tests and test whether there are statistically significant differences between black and white Democrats.

regularly formed coalitions with white legislators. Initially, this coalition was based upon mere partisan ties and general concurrence on substantive and legislative goals but later became central to Georgia's capital politics as African American legislators gained increasing seniority and the gavel on key committees.

The formation of biracial coalitions among Democrats in the 1980s and 1990s hinged on the fact that neither subset of the party constituted a majority in either chamber; as such, there was a need for both sets of legislators to work together to maintain the party's majority status. The growth of GOP representation made this especially important in the 1990s. Intra-party coalitions were most likely to form involving policies where there were common goals among whites and blacks, such as economic development and taxes. Between 1993 and 1999, the house GLBC voted statistically and substantively independent of white Democrats only about one-quarter of the time, and the black-white Democratic coalitions most often failed to form on issues such as social welfare, criminal justice, and gun control. In the senate, the GLBC voted independently only 8% of the time, with coalitions failing to predominate on gun control legislation (Wielhouwer and Middlemass 2002).

While inter-party coalitions were rare, one did form around an issue of importance to the GLBC in the 1990s: redistricting (see Holmes 1997). As the redistricting drama unfolded in Georgia, the Black Caucus challenged initial redistricting plans when the white Democratic leadership put forth a new state map, altering sixty-nine house districts. The new districts drastically reduced the number of majority-minority districts, benefited twenty-two white Democrats, and protected only two African American incumbents.

In response, the house GLBC formed a coalition with the Republicans to block passage of the house plan, voting unanimously against the plan. The GLBC formed a coalition with the GOP in order to gain leverage to force passage of more acceptable redistricting plans for the state legislative and, eventually, congressional plans. The biracial and bipartisan coalition held together until the Democratic leadership, after some minor revisions and alterations to the defeated plan, brought to the floor a plan that protected a small number of senior African American lawmakers. The plan, however, diluted the black vote throughout the state and dismantled several majority-minority districts. The GLBC split over these concerns, but members felt that it was necessary to vote in favor of the plan as they thought it was the best they could do under the political circumstances and time line set up by the Justice Department and governor. With some difficulty, over 80% of the GLBC in the house voted for the redrawn map and the GLBC split 5–5 in the senate, ensuring that the black vote was diluted throughout the state.

Strategically, the GLBC had hoped that the partnership with the GOP would ensure that the Democratic leadership would take the caucus's interests into consideration when redrawing the state and congressional plans, but that was not to be the case. The initial coalition with the GOP backfired on the GLBC, as a majority of its members supported a redistricting plan that diluted the black vote in the hope that the congressional map would be brought to a vote. The Democratic leadership never brought the congressional map up for a vote. The short-lived biracial and bipartisan coalition, therefore, may have succeeded on some procedural issues, but it failed to hold together for any long-term or substantive political gains due to the maneuvering of the Democratic leadership.

DISCUSSION AND CONCLUSIONS

African American descriptive representation in Georgia has made substantial progress in the last thirty years due to election reforms and redistricting, producing a state legislature that is considerably more representative of Georgia's black population than it was in 1980. At that time, only 13% of the house and 4% of the senate were African American; by the turn of the century, those percentages had increased to 18% in each chamber. While still not attaining the rate of the black population in the state as a whole (about 28.7% in 2000), descriptive representational parity is close at hand. How the redistricting decisions of the U.S. Supreme Court during the 1990s will affect that descriptive representation will likely be seen following the Georgia state legislative elections of 2002 and beyond. Republicans, emboldened by their gubernatorial victory and state senate majority in 2002, will likely seek to roll back 2001's redistricting plan and implement a plan more favorable to their own incumbents. Growth in descriptive representation of black elected officials was accompanied by increases in committee chairs obtained by members of the Black Caucus. The GOP senate leadership appointed Democrats (including two black senators) to chair four minor committees (Special Judiciary, State Institutions & Property, Natural Resources & The Environment, and Interstate Cooperation), though one African American resigned after black senators complained that they had been slighted in the appointments (Tharpe 2003a). While a possible power-sharing plan was discussed in the House in the transition after the 2002 elections, Republican efforts to defeat the leading Democratic candidate for Speaker, Terry Coleman, led to no Republican committee chairs for the 2003 session (Tharpe 2003b). Nine of thirty-six (25%) house committee chairs went to members of the Black Caucus in 2003 (see the Web site www.legis.state.ga.us), a vast improvement in their holdings over previous sessions (see Table 4.3).

We have discussed the substantive representation of the African American community by looking at GLBC priorities and roll-call voting results from 1992 to 1999. Tables 4.12 and 4.13 summarize GLBC independence and the substantive outcomes by legislative topic and by year, respectively. Table 4.12 shows that the degree to which GLBC members vote independently varies substantially across issue areas. The house GLBC is most distinctive in voting on education, social welfare, crime and gun control, and race-related legislation and matches white Democratic voting in nearly all economic and tax legislation. In the senate, Black Caucus members were modestly independent on social welfare and race-related roll calls but mostly voted the party line in other areas. On the whole, black Democrats voted independently from white Democrats in the house at a rate of 50% and in the senate at a rate of 30%. Of course, a more important question may be whether the vote outcomes coincided with the Black Caucus's positions. It may be that the Democratic position is congruent with black interests in the state, helping to explain the rather modest independence of the GLBC.

Table 4.12, therefore, shows the rate at which the votes cast on these bills and amendments coincide substantively with the votes of the GLBC membership. With some modest exceptions, substantive representation is obtained in most of the GLBC priority votes. In the house, outcomes in four of the seven issue

TABLE 4.12
Georgia Legislative Black Caucus Priority Roll Call Votes, by Topic, 1992–1999

Topic of Legislation	House of Representatives		Senate	
	GLBC Independence	Substantive Result	GLBC Independence	Substantive Result
Elections and Government Reform	55.6% (5/9)	88.9% (8/9)	10.0% (1/10)	100% (10/10)
Education	66.7% (2/3)	66.7% (2/3)	0% (0/4)	100% (4/4)
Health Care and Health Insurance	36.4% (4/11)	81.8% (9/11)	33.3% (4/12)	91.7% (11/12)
Social Welfare	72.7% (8/11)	90.9% (10/11)	62.5% (5/8)	75.0% (6/8)
Race Related	66.7% (4/6)	50.0% (3/6)	40.0% (2/5)	80.0% (4/5)
Crime and Gun Control	64.3% (9/14)	57.1% (8/14)	26.3% (5/19)	94.7% (18/19)
Economic Development and Taxes	8.3% (1/12)	100% (12/12)	33.0% (4/12)	91.7% (11/12)
Totals	50.0% (33/66)	78.8% (52/66)	30.0% (21/70)	91.4% (64/70)

Independence is measured as the percentage of GLBC priority votes where the difference between black and white Democrats was statistically significant (p ≤ .10).

Substantive Result is measured as the percentage of GLBC priority votes where the vote in the chamber as a whole achieved the same result as the votes of GLBC members.

Source: Tables 4.5–4.11, including votes in which 90% or more of all three groups voted in the same way (see table notes).

areas matched Black Caucus votes at rates greater than 80% (Elections & Government Reform, Health Care & Health Insurance, Social Welfare, Economic Development & Taxes). The caucus's desired outcome was obtained only about half of the time in the areas of crime and gun control and on race-related legislation. Overall, however, 79% of the votes cast on GLBC priority votes in the 1990s house matched the caucus's own votes. In the senate the results were even more impressive. While the caucus was not very independent of white Democrats in its votes, substantive representation was obtained in an amazing 91% of roll-call votes. We can thus confidently conclude that substantive representation of the African American community, here defined as legislative outcomes coinciding with GLBC votes, was largely attained by the Georgia general assembly during the 1990s.

Table 4.13 shows the rates of voting independence and substantive representation for each chamber, by each year studied in this analysis. There is little-to-no linear trend over time for any of the measures, suggesting that little consistent change occurred during the 1990s in either the independence of GLBC members in relation to white Democratic members of the assembly or in the substantive results produced by each chamber. With a substantive

TABLE 4.13
Georgia Legislative Black Caucus Priority Roll Call Votes, by Year, 1992–1999

| | House of Representatives | | Senate | |
Year	GLBC Independence	Substantive Result	GLBC Independence	Substantive Result
1992	50.0% (4/8)	87.5% (7/8)	25.0% (2/8)	100% (8/8)
1993	33.3% (2/6)	100% (6/6)	50.0% (3/6)	83.3% (5/6)
1994	87.5% (7/8)	62.5% (5/8)	0% (0/6)	100% (6/6)
1995	37.5% (3/8)	87.5% (7/8)	27.3% (3/11)	90.9% (10/11)
1996	87.5% (7/8)	50.0% (4/8)	25.0% (2/8)	100% (8/8)
1997	55.6% (5/9)	88.9% (8/9)	37.5% (3/8)	87.5% (7/8)
1998	22.2% (2/9)	100% (9/9)	38.5% (5/13)	84.6% (11/13)
1999	30.0% (3/10)	60.0% (6/10)	30.0% (3/10)	90.0% (9/10)
Totals	50.0% (33/66)	78.8% (52/66)	30.0% (21/70)	91.4% (64/70)

Independence is measured as the percentage of GLBC priority votes where the difference between black and white Democrats was statistically significant (p ≤ .10).
Substantive Result is measured as the percentage of GLBC priority votes where the vote in the chamber as a whole achieved the same result as the votes of GLBC members.

Source: Tables 4.5–4.11, including votes in which 90% or more of all three groups voted in the same way (see table notes).

agreement rate of over 75% in each chamber, the caucus's priorities appear to be largely met. Several explanations are possible for the substantive representation of GLBC priorities. The pattern may reflect the acknowledged legitimacy of the Black Caucus's representation of African Americans in the state and the general support for that position among the other Democrats in each chamber. The pattern may also simply reflect a general agreement on legislative goals coming out of a Democratically controlled state legislature and governor's mansion in the 1990s—a rare occurrence in the South in that time period. Since many of the GLBC votes were significantly more supportive of outcomes less strongly supported by the remaining Democrats in the legislature, GLBC votes could reflect both voting cues emanating from the caucus and a firmer commitment to Democratic Party goals by caucus members.

This research sought to assess descriptive and substantive representation of African Americans in Georgia, given that state's political and historical contexts, and the results may ameliorate concerns about black representation in the Peach State during the 1990s. Of course, the ability of the GLBC to attain its legislative priorities was very likely a function of the Democratic Party retaining its control over the general assembly. The Republican takeover of the senate for the 2003–2004 sessions means that the influence of the senate GLBC is likely to suffer the same fate as the Congressional Black Caucus in post–1994

Washington: political marginalization as a minority within a minority (Swain 1998). The outcome of power-sharing negotiations in the house and the composition and comportment of conference committees will determine the degree of substantive representation for the coming decade.

NOTES

*This research extends an analysis begun by Charles E. Jones of Georgia State University. We are grateful to him for his efforts and for him graciously allowing us to explicitly build upon his study in order to further this research agenda. This is Working Paper #102 for Regent University's Center for Grassroots Politics. We are also very grateful and appreciative to Andrew McDonald, a Master's Fellow in the center, for his data entry and detective work on the roll-call votes described in this chapter. The analysis and opinions expressed in this chapter reflect those of the authors, and do not necessarily reflect the positions of United States Joint Forces Command or General Dynamics Advanced Information Systems.

1. The county-unit system applied to candidates for U.S. senator, governor, statehouse offices, justices of the state supreme court and judges on the state court of appeals. For a more detailed discussion of the county-unit vote system, see Bernd (1972).

2. 321 U.S. 649 (1944).

3. This and the following paragraph draws heavily on Bullock (1995b) and Fleischmann and Pierannunzi (1997, chapter 6).

4. This right was constitutionally protected at the federal level with the passage of the Fifteenth Amendment, which was ratified in 1870.

5. 372 U.S. 368 (1963).

6. 384 U.S. 210 (1966).

7. 377 U.S. 533 (1964).

8. 376 U.S. 1 (1964).

9. 4798 U.S. 30 (1986).

10. *Miller v. Johnson*, 515 U.S. 900 (1995). This decision restricted the Justice Department in the absence of any violation of the Voting Rights Act from using Section Five of that law to maximize the number of majority-minority districts drawn.

11. The 1991 house plan contained forty-two majority-minority districts, and by 1996, thirty-one of them were represented by blacks. One white majority district was represented by a black state representative, and the remaining black reps were elected from influence districts (40% + black). The 1991 senate plan contained thirteen majority-black districts, nine of which were represented by black senators in 1996, while the others were elected from influence districts. For summaries of the saga of 1990s redistricting in Georgia, see Holmes (1992) and Bullock (1995b).

12. Several votes were included in the GLBC chapters from the *GLR* but were excluded from this analysis. They include three 1992 apportionment-related votes: HB1340, SB174, and SB567. Another apportionment vote included HB1657 and was on the passage of the final version on the last day of the 1992 session. HR463 (1998), eliminating parole for some crimes, had roll-call votes reported in the *GLR-1998*, but the votes could not be found in the house or senate Journals. Three other bills were identified as representing GLBC priorities but never had recorded roll-call votes, as each died in committee. They are: HB85 (1993), elimination of incremental increases in AFDC payments for additional children; SB298 (1995), a Learnfare pilot program requiring school attendance for children receiving public assistance; and HB586 (1998), relating to truancy among homeschoolers.

Chapter 5

Representation of African Americans in the Contemporary Mississippi Legislature

Stephen D. Shaffer and Charles E. Menifield

The Deep South state of Mississippi possesses a very traditionalistic political culture historically characterized by racial segregation, disfranchisement, and legislative district malapportionment designed to minimize black political power (Elazar 1984; Key 1949). As late as 1964, for instance, only 7% of voting-age African Americans in Mississippi were registered to vote, and it was not until 1967 that the first African American (since Reconstruction), Robert Clark, who constituted the lone black lawmaker until the 1975 elections (Coleman 1993; Davidson and Grofman 1994; Menifield and Antwi-Boasiako 2002), was elected to the state legislature. The enforcement of the Voting Rights Act of 1965, coupled with persistent redistricting lawsuits by black plaintiffs and Justice Department advocacy of majority-minority districting schemes, has produced a sea of change in the composition of the Mississippi state legislature. Yet to what extent have the increased numbers of African American lawmakers actually made a difference in the operation of the state legislature and the public policies that have been enacted into law? Do African Americans chair any important, policy-relevant committees, or do they head mere "housekeeping" committees? Has the Black Caucus ever exerted any real decisive impact over truly important public policies considered by the legislature?

Our primary concern is whether the Mississippi Black Caucus actually has the power to adequately represent the black community. We examine this representational question from the theoretical framework of Hanna Pitkin's (1967) book, *The Concept of Representation*. She theorizes about various forms of representation, of which we examine descriptive representation and representation as "acting for" the represented, which we term "substantive representation." We test the success of the Black Caucus in a descriptive representation sense by examining the extent to which its members chair standing legislative committees and are members of the more influential money committees. We then examine the substantive representation question of how successful black lawmakers have been in enacting important policies into law by studying their ability to form coalitions with other lawmakers, such as white Democrats. Our many years of study of Mississippi politics permit us to choose which issues are the truly important substantive ones that have significantly shaped the quality of life of Mississippians, which we then examine through roll-call analysis (Krane and Shaffer 1992; Menifield and Antwi-Boasiako 2002).

Descriptive Representation in Mississippi

Immediately after the 1965 Voting Rights Act, white lawmakers in Mississippi were quite "creative" in redrawing their district boundaries and creating multi-member districts to ensure that only one African American, Representative Robert Clark, served in a legislature consisting of 122 representatives and 52 senators. For instance, in populous Hinds County, housing the state capital of Jackson, African Americans comprised 40% of the population, so lawmakers abandoned a single-member district approach and combined all ten of the county's house seats into one multi-member district where a 60% white majority population would end up electing all ten members (Parker 1990). In the 1975 state elections, Doug Anderson, Fred Banks, and Horace Buckley joined Clark in the house, though the senate remained all white (Menifield and Antwi-Boasiako 2002). These members created an informal Mississippi Legislative Black Caucus organization that was assisted by house staff member (and later Representative) Hillman Frazier and Representative Clark's secretary, provided to him as vice chair of the Education Committee (Orey 2000).

After fourteen years of lawsuits filed by African American political activists and nine trips to the U.S. Supreme Court, the state legislature in 1979 enacted a single-member district plan that dramatically increased black representation from only four lawmakers. (In Mississippi, all lawmakers are elected for four-year terms at the same time, the year before a presidential election.) Fifteen African Americans were elected to the house and two to the senate, though African Americans still constituted only 12% of the house membership and 4% of the senate, a level of descriptive representation far below the 36% of the state's population and estimated 30% of adult population that is African American (see Tables 5.1 and 5.2). After a December 1979 workshop for the newly elected black lawmakers sponsored by the Political Science Department

TABLE 5.1
African American Legislators in the Mississippi House of Representatives

1980–1983	1984–1987	1988–1991	1992–1995	1996–1999	2000–
F. Banks	Blackmon	Blackmon	Blackmon	Bailey	Bailey
Buckley	Buckley	Buckley	Broomfield	E. Banks	E. Banks
Calhoun	Calhoun	Calhoun	Calhoun (1992)	Blackmon	Blackmon
Clark	Clark	Clark	Clark	Bozeman	Broomfield
Ellis	Clarke	Clarke	Clarke	Broomfield	Clark
Frazier	Ellerby	Ellerby	L. Coleman	Clark	Clarke
Fredericks	Ellis	Ellis	Ellis	Clarke	L. Coleman
D. Green	Frazier	Flaggs	Evans	L. Coleman	M. Coleman
C. Henderson	Fredericks	Frazier	Flaggs	M. Coleman	Dickson
Henry	D. Green	Fredericks	Frazier	Dickson	Ellis
King	C. Henderson	D. Green	(1992–1993)	Ellis	Espy
Schoby	Henry	C. Henderson	Fredericks	Evans	Evans
Shepphard	King	Henry	D. Green	Flaggs	Flaggs
Watson	Robinson	King	C. Henderson	Fredericks	Fleming
Young	Schoby	Robinson	Henry	Gibbs	Fredericks
	Shepphard	Schoby	King (1992)	D. Green	Gibbs
	Watson	Shepphard	Robinson	T. Green	D. Green
	Young	Walker	Schoby	(1996–1998)	Harrison
		Watson	Shepphard	C. Henderson	C. Henderson
		Young	Walker	L. Henderson	Holloway
			Watson	Huddleston	Huddleston
			Young	Middleton	Middleton
			Bailey (1995)	Morris	Morris
			E. Banks	Myers	Myers
			(1993–1995)	Perkins	Perkins
			Bozeman	Richardson	Robinson
			(1993–1995)	(1996–1997)	Scott
			M. Coleman	Robinson	Smith
			(1994–1995)	Schoby	Straughter
			Dickson	(1996–1997)	Thomas
			(1993–1995)	Scott	Thornton
			Gibbs	Smith	Wallace
			(1993–1995)	Straughter	Watson
			T. Green	Thornton	West
			(1993–1995)	Walker	Young
			Morris	Wallace	
			(1993–1995)	Watson	
			Perkins	Young	
			(1993–1995)	Thomas	
			Richardson	(1998–1999)	
			(1993–1995)	West	
			Scott	(1998–1999)	
			(1993–1995)	Fleming	
			Sweet	(1999)	
			(1993–1995)		

(*Continued*)

TABLE 5.1
(*Continued*)

1980–1983	1984–1987	1988–1991	1992–1995	1996–1999	2000–
			Thornton (1993–1995)		
15 members	18 members	20 members	21–31 members	35 members	35 members
12% of house	15% of house	16% of house	17–25% of house	29% of house	29% of house

Note: Values in parentheses indicate that the member served only in that year. The last two rows indicate the total number of African Americans in the state house and their percentage of the total chamber membership of 122 members.

Source: *Mississippi Official and Statistical Register*, 1980–1984, 1984–1988, 1988–1992, 1992–1996, 1996–2000, Secretary of State's Office, Web site, http://www.ls.state.mu.us/.

TABLE 5.2
African American Legislators in the Mississippi Senate

1980–1983	1984–1987	1988–1991	1992–1995	1996–1999	2000–
Anderson	Anderson	Anderson	Anderson (1992)	Blackmon	Blackmon
Kirksey	Kirksey	Harden	Blackmon	Frazier	Frazier
			Harden	Harden	Harden
			Jackson	Horhn	Horhn
			Frazier (1994–1995)	Jackson	Jackson
			Horhn (1993–1995)	Johnson	R. Johnson
			Johnson (1993–1995)	Jordan	Jordan
			Jordan (1993–1995)	Simmons	Simmons
			Simmons (1993–1995)	Turner	Turner
			Turner (1993–1995)	Walls	Walls
			Walls (1993–1995)		
2 members	2 members	2 members	4–10 members	10 members	10 members
4% of senate	4% of senate	4% of senate	8–19% of senate	19% of senate	19% of senate

Note: Values in parentheses indicate that the member served only in that year. The last two rows indicate the total number of African Americans in the state senate and their percentage of the total chamber membership of fifty-two members.

Source: *Mississippi Official and Statistical Register*, 1980–1984, 1984–1988, 1988–1992, 1992–1996, 1996–2000, Secretary of State's Office; Web site, http://www.ls.state.mu.us/.

at the historically black Jackson State University, the Mississippi Legislative Black Caucus was officially established, with Robert Clark and Fred Banks serving as the first two chairs (Orey 2000). Orey also relates how the Black Caucus is financially supported by a Political Education and Economic Development Foundation, which holds an annual banquet where the proceeds fund scholarships for students attending historically black colleges in Mississippi and pay for the holding of public forums that educate the public about political developments.

The next three elections produced a small rise in African American legislative representation. More dramatic change resulted from special legislative elections in 1992 necessitated by decennial reapportionment. Aggressive advocacy by African American lawmakers on the legislative redistricting committees led the numbers of black representatives to rise from twenty-one to thirty-one and the numbers of black senators to increase from four to ten. Some white Democratic lawmakers voluntarily retired rather than fight for renomination in a majority black district. The number of African American lawmakers remained at ten senators after the 1995 and 1999 state elections. The number of black representatives rose slightly to thirty-five after the 1995 elections and stabilized at that level after the 1999 elections. Therefore, as Mississippi enters the twenty-first century, African Americans comprise a sizable 29% of the state house and 19% of the state senate. White resistance to black legislative empowerment has declined to such an extent that even after Supreme Court decisions on other states' congressional majority-minority districting plans produced the demise of many black majority districts, nobody had filed a legal challenge to Mississippi's congressional or legislative districts that had produced historic high numbers of black lawmakers.

COMMITTEE AND LEADERSHIP ASSIGNMENTS

The increase in African American representation in the state house has been accompanied by a rise in political power within the committee system, the key source of legislation. After eight years of legislative service, Robert Clark in 1975 was named vice chair of the important House Education Committee, which has jurisdiction over all elementary and secondary public education issues. Four years later, Clark rose to chair the Education Committee, while sophomore Fred Banks became chair of the Ethics Committee (see Table 5.3). Two important breakthroughs occurred after the 1983 elections with African Americans beginning to chair such important committees as Universities and Colleges and one of the two House Judiciary Committees. The early 1990s saw Robert Clark's election by the state house to its second most important position, speaker pro tempore, which also entailed chairmanship of the critical Management Committee, which distributes perks among the members. African Americans continued to make net gains of one chairmanship after the 1995 and 1999 elections, by working with House Speaker Tim Ford, a white Democrat,

TABLE 5.3
African American Committee Chairs in the Mississippi House of Representatives

1980–1983	1984–1987	1988–1991
Clark-Education	Clark-Education	Clark-Ethics
Banks-Ethics	Banks-Judiciary B	Fredericks-Public Utilities
	Sheppard Univ. and Colleges	Young-Municipalities
		Watson-Judiciary A and Judiciary En Banc
2 chairmanships of	3 chairmanships of	4 chairmanships of
28 total com.	28 total com.	29 total com.
7% of total	11% of total	14% of total

1992–1995	1996–1999	2000–
Clark, Speaker Pro Tempore-Management	Clark, Speaker Pro Tempore-Management	Clark, Speaker Pro Tempore-Management
Blackmon-Judiciary B	Blackmon-Judiciary B	Blackmon-Judiciary B
Young-Univ. and Colleges	Young-Univ. and Colleges	Young-Univ. and Colleges
Ellis-Public Utilities	Watson-Municipalities	Watson-Judiciary A and Judiciary En Banc
Flaggs-Labor	Ellis-Public Utilities	Ellis-Public Utilities
	Flaggs-Labor	Flaggs-Juvenile Justice
		D. Green-County Affairs
5 chairmanships of	6 chairmanships of	7 chairmanships of
29 total com.	30 total com.	30 total com.
17% of total	20% of total	23% of total

Note: The last three rows indicate the total number of African American committee chairs, the total number of committees in the state house, and the percentage of committees chaired by African Americans.

Source: Mississippi Official and Statistical Register, 1980–1984, 1984–1988, 1988–1992, 1992–1996, 1996–2000, Secretary of State's Office, Web site, http://www.ls.state.mu.us/.

and requesting more of a say in the legislative process. As Mississippi enters the twenty-first century, African Americans comprise 23% of the house committee chairmanships, a level of descriptive representation only slightly below the African American presence in the full chamber.

A similar pattern of rising African American committee chairmanships is evident in the state senate, though at a slower pace. In 1983, after four years of legislative service, one of the two black senators, Doug Anderson, a former representative, was named chairman of the Universities and Colleges Committee, which is critical in exercising sole jurisdiction over the state's public higher education system. After Anderson switched to chair the Municipalities Committee after the 1991 elections, four years later another African American became chair

TABLE 5.4
African American Committee Chairs in the Mississippi Senate

1980–1983	1984–1987	1988–1991
None	Anderson-Universities and Colleges	Anderson-Universities and Colleges
0 chairmanships of 28 total committees 0% of total	1 chairmanship of 28 total committees 4% of total	1 chairmanship of 29 total committees 3% of total

1992–1995	1996–1999	2000–
Anderson-Municipalities	Frazier-Universities and Colleges	
	Horhn-Economic Development	Harden-Education
	Harden-Elections	Turner-Judiciary
	Turner-Judiciary	Jordan-Municipalities
	Jordan-Municipalities	Jackson-Public Property
	Jackson-Public Property	Walls-Juvenile Justice
	Walls-Constitution	
1 chairmanship of 30 total committees 3% of total	7 chairmanships of 31 total committees 23% of total	5 chairmanships of 30 total committees 17% of total

Note: The last three rows indicate the total number of African American committee chairs, the total number of committees in the state senate, and the percentage of committees chaired by African Americans.

Source: *Mississippi Official Statistical Register*, 1980–1984, 1984–1988, 1988–1992, 1992–1996, 1996–2000, Secretary of State's Office; Web site, http://www.ls.state.mu.us/.

of his old committee (see Table 5.4). While African American representation in the state senate increased significantly after the 1991 and special 1992 elections, the presence of a Republican lieutenant governor, Eddie Briggs, elected in the face of dissatisfaction over recession-induced budget cuts in 1991, may have hindered chairmanship gains by African Americans. (The lieutenant governor makes committee appointments in the senate, while the house speaker makes house committee assignments.) Briggs's defeat by moderate white Democrat Ronnie Musgrove in 1995 produced a dramatic increase in African American committee chairmanships. In addition to Hillman Frazier chairing the Universities and Colleges Committee, prominent African American senators were appointed by Musgrove to chair such key committees as Constitution, Judiciary (the senate has only one Judiciary Committee), and Elections, in addition to Economic Development, Municipalities, and Public Property. African American chairmanships dipped slightly after the 1999 election of Lieutenant Governor Amy Tuck, as at least one African American chair who had supported her more liberal opponent in the Democratic primary lost his chairmanship (Ammerman 2000a). Nevertheless, as we enter the twenty-first century, African American representation among the senate's committee chairs remains nearly as high as the black presence in the full chamber.

African American committee chairs have sometimes benefited politically by having white Democratic mentors and colleagues. Praised by a white Democratic chair of the Finance Committee, Hob Bryan, who was his seatmate, Bennie Turner came to the attention of Senate Education Committee chair and soon-to-be Lieutenant Governor Ronnie Musgrove. Senator Musgrove helped make Turner chair of a Select Committee on Juvenile Justice, where Turner won a Most Distinguished Legislator award after getting a quarter of the committee's legislation passed, including an $11 million bond bill for two facilities for mentally ill youths. Turner's select committee has since become a standing (permanent) committee, and Lieutenant Governor Musgrove and his successor, Amy Tuck, appointed Turner to chair the powerful Judiciary Committee (John 1996).

African American committee chairs never forget the state's history of racial discrimination, continually fight for racial justice, and have become important powers in their own right. Alice Harden, as chair of the Senate Elections Committee during the second term of conservative Republican Governor Kirk Fordice, was publicly vocal in relating how her grandfather was prevented from voting by a registrar whose literacy test included asking, "How many bubbles were in a bar of soap?" (Wagster 1999, p. 7A). She and the other members of the Black Caucus successfully convinced white Democrats to vote down Fordice's proposal to require all voters to show identification in order to vote. Black committee chairmen have fought to ensure that they receive the same deference that is owing to their leadership positions as their white colleagues receive. Senator John Horhn, chair of the Economic Development Committee in the late 1990s, refused to call a committee meeting to consider a Fordice nomination for chair of the Workers' Compensation Commission, after concerns were raised over the nominee's truthfulness and alleged irregularities in committee investigative reports on him. Despite Horhn's being blasted by the governor, a prominent white columnist, and the governor's supporters, other political observers pointed out that white chairmen periodically exercised a similar "pocket veto" power over nominees falling under their committees' jurisdiction, and the full senate in a special session called by the governor voted not to pull the nomination out of Horhn's committee (Ammerman 1999; Salter 1999; Stringfellow 1999).

An even more important illustration of the importance of African American chairmanship of key committees, given the state's continued litigation over its historically segregated higher education system, had come immediately after Fordice's reelection in 1995. Fordice promptly nominated four businessmen for twelve-year terms to the twelve-member College Board that governs and distributes funds to the state's eight public universities, and while qualified for the positions all four were white, male, and alumni of the three largest "comprehensive" (historically white) universities. Referred to the Senate Judiciary Committee for confirmation consideration, Hillman Frazier promptly appointed a subcommittee to consider the nominations consisting of three African Americans and two whites, chaired by the African American chairman of the state Democratic Party, Johnnie Walls. After the nominations died in subcommittee and the legislature adjourned, Fordice called the legislature into special session, asking that the entire membership of the state senate at least be given the opportunity to vote on his nominations. Frazier acceded to Lieutenant Governor Musgrove's request that he permit a vote in the full Judiciary Committee on the nominees, and the drama began. The full committee was very diverse, and included five African American Democrats, five white Republicans, and three white Democrats. After Frazier reportedly met privately with a white Democrat to plead for his support, the committee killed all four nominations on a 7–6 vote, with all blacks opposing Fordice's nominees, all Republicans supporting them, and the three white Democrats splitting 2–1 against the nominees. White Democrat Gray Tollison of Oxford cast the deciding vote to kill the nominees, even though his majority white district was home to the University of Mississippi (Ole Miss), and two of the four nominees were Ole Miss alumni! (Tollison was nevertheless reelected in 1999.) Fordice promptly sent a new slate of nominees to the state senate, a slate with one African American, one white woman, and two white men, which was easily confirmed by the senate ("*Senators Reject*" 1996).

Black Caucus members have expressed continuing concern over their limited influence over state spending and minimal representation on "money" committees, reflected in the persistent absence of African American chairs on the two chambers' appropriations and taxing committees and limited black membership on the critical Joint Legislative Budget Committee. Beginning in the mid-1990s, the Black Caucus annually unveiled its own proposed state budget, which tended to call for more spending on such programs as teacher pay raises, the historically black universities, and establishing a statewide public defender program (Ammerman 2000b). By the 2002 legislative session, African Americans came to comprise a sizable 24% of the membership of the House Appropriations Committee and 33% of the House Ways and Means Committee (including the vice chair position). Consistent with the fewer numbers of black senators, African Americans comprised 23% of the Senate Appropriations Committee and 15% of the Senate Finance Committee the same year. African American presence on the Legislative Budget Committee has been more limited, given that committee's requirement of including the chairs of the two other committees plus the speaker and lieutenant governor, but in 2000, Speaker Ford appointed two black representatives and Lieutenant Governor Amy Tuck one black senator to the fourteen-member joint committee, providing African Americans with 29% of the house members and 14% of the senate members of that committee.

Substantive Representation in Mississippi

African American lawmakers, all of whom are Democrats, have persistently served as the leading progressive force in the Mississippi state legislature. They have often joined with white Democrats to produce a biracial Democratic coalition that has been victorious on several key legislative issues. They have been most successful on education issues, where they have joined with white Democrats to enact landmark legislation to dramatically improve public elementary, secondary, and higher education, starting with the 1982 Education Reform Act. The state had repealed its compulsory school attendance law in the 1960s in reaction to court-ordered school desegregation, and at least one white conservative lawmaker had recently derided public kindergartens as "a babysitting service for a bunch of women who don't want to take care of their kids!" Democratic Governor William Winter's education reform plan had died in the regular 1982 session of the legislature, after House Speaker Buddie Newman, a white conservative from the elitist Mississippi Delta region, adjourned the state house on a deadline day for floor proposals to be considered. In a special legislative session later called by the governor in December 1982, over 70% of white Democrats and Republicans joined with every African American lawmaker to enact this landmark legislation (see Table 5.5). Similar consensus produced the 1989 School Equity Funding Act, which provided additional state funds to poorer school districts and required all districts to levy a minimum property tax rate to support their public elementary and secondary schools.

The advent of the conservative Republican gubernatorial administration of Kirk Fordice transformed African American lawmakers into a decisive voice on critical education issues. The 1991 economic recession had produced two successive years of painful budget cuts and no pay raises for teachers, professors, and state employees. In early 1992, some public school administrators warned that funds were so tight that they could not operate school buses for more than four days of the week, and a tight budget prompted the president of the largest public university in Mississippi to threaten to eliminate degree programs serving over 1,000 students and to fire tenured professors associated

TABLE 5.5
Roll Call Votes in the Mississippi State Legislature on Education Issues

	House of Representatives			Senate		
	Black Dems	White Dems	Republicans	Black Dems	White Dems	Republicans
1982 Education Reform Act						
For	100%	77%	75%	100%	71%	100%
Against	0%	23%	25%	0%	29%	0%
N = Total Voting Members	(15)	(100)	(4)	(1)	(45)	(4)
1989 School Equity Funding						
For	95%	79%	62%	100%	91%	71%
Against	5%	21%	38%	0%	9%	29%
N = Total Voting Members	(20)	(91)	(8)	(2)	(43)	(7)
1992 Veto Override of Sales Tax Hike for Education						
For	85%	79%	33%	100%	84%	60%
Against	15%	21%	67%	0%	16%	40%
N = Total Voting Members	(20)	(71)	(27)	(4)	(38)	(10)
1992 Veto Override of Bond Bill (including university libraries)						
For	100%	75%	22%	100%	82%	0%
Against	0%	25%	78%	0%	18%	100%
N = Total Voting Members	(21)	(71)	(27)	(4)	(38)	(10)
1997 Veto Override of Adequate Education Act						
For	97%	81%	26%	100%	91%	28%
Against	3%	19%	74%	0%	9%	72%
N = Total Voting Members	(33)	(52)	(35)	(10)	(22)	(18)
2000 Southeast Average, Teacher Pay						
For	97%	96%	58%	100%	96%	89%
Against	3%	4%	42%	0%	4%	11%
N = Total Voting Members	(35)	(52)	(31)	(10)	(24)	(18)

Source: *Mississippi Official and Statistical Register*, 1980–2000 volumes, Secretary of State's Office; *Clarion-Ledger* (Jackson), December 21, 1982, p. 12A; April 2, 1989, pp. 14A–15A; May 10, 1992, pp. G1–G2; April 13, 1997, pp. G1–G2; May 7, 2000, pp. H1–H2.

with those programs. Responding to constituent support for education, the great majority of black and white Democrats in both chambers successfully outvoted Republican lawmakers, who were more divided on this issue, and overrode Fordice's veto of a one-cent sales tax increase. The new revenue was earmarked for books, buses, and buildings for elementary and secondary education and for higher education "enhancement" funds (see Table 5.5). African Americans were especially critical in the house, where the override vote among white Democrats and Republicans was 65–33 or one short of the two-thirds margin necessary, illustrating the political power of the more unified (17–3 for override) black Democrats.

The biracial Democratic coalition also proved decisive in overriding Fordice's veto of the major bond bill of 1992, which included funds for much-needed new library buildings at each of the state's public universities. Indeed, the homogeneity of black lawmakers proved decisive in *both* chambers. With Republican lawmakers (all of whom are white) overwhelmingly backing the fiscal conservatism of their party's governor, votes by white lawmakers of both parties for overriding the veto were only 31–17 in the senate and 59–39 in the house, far short of the required two-thirds vote margin. All twenty-one African Americans in the house and four African Americans in the senate backed the override and were decisive in enacting this landmark bond bill. A similar pattern of homogeneity among African Americans in coalition with the great majority of white Democrats proved decisive in overturning Fordice's veto of the 1997 Adequate Education Bill, which significantly increased state support for school districts with a limited property base, thereby preventing lawsuits challenging the existing school funding system that had led to great disparities across districts. As white lawmakers split in favor of the override 51–36 in the house and 25–15 in favor in the senate, a support margin short of the two-thirds needed to override a veto, black legislators voted 32–1 in the house and 10–0 in the senate to enact this expensive landmark bill, which entailed a multi-year funding increase commitment.

More recently, the election of a moderate white Democrat as governor, Ronnie Musgrove, who has been a longtime advocate of public education, has led to bipartisan support for landmark education legislation long fought for by the Black Caucus. Over 90% of black and white Democrats in 2000 backed Musgrove's major proposal to raise public elementary and secondary teachers' salaries to the Southeast average over a six-year period, with even a solid majority of Republicans favoring the plan despite the multi-year financial commitment required. Lieutenant Governor Amy Tuck's compromise proposal to tie the multi-year funding commitment to economic growth convinced many recalcitrant senate conservatives to support the plan, and newspaper and public support for education was so high that despite a recession Tuck reversed her position the next year, and in a special session the legislature voted to make the multi-year commitment permanent, regardless of economic growth. Particularly important to the Black Caucus was the legislature's backing for a final settlement of the Ayers case, a higher education desegregation lawsuit that had first been filed by African American plaintiffs in 1975. Despite a recession that produced painful budget cuts to public higher education and no college pay raises for two successive years, Governor Musgrove backed a settlement agreed to in 2002 by key African American plaintiffs, such as Congressman Bennie Thompson, that will provide $503 million of additional funding over a seventeen-year period solely to the three historically black public universities (Kanengiser 2002).

While education issues illustrate how African Americans can be victorious by being unified and by joining with white Democrats in a biracial coalition on popular issues that transcend race, the issues of abortion and crime point out that African Americans cannot win without their white Democratic coalition partners. On these issues, the great majority of white Democrats in the socially conservative state of Mississippi have repeatedly abandoned their black colleagues and instead joined a coalition with Republican lawmakers to enact "tough-on-crime" and pro-life measures. Compounding the problem for black lawmakers was their absence of homogeneity on some of these issues, suggesting some differences of opinion in the black community and signaling to white Democrats that these were not vital issues that would endanger the biracial coalition of their party's electoral base.

With the importance of religion to the black community, the issue of abortion has been a particularly divisive one within the Black Caucus. With both black senators backing a 1986 parental consent for minors' abortion measure along with one-fourth of house African Americans, white lawmakers easily enacted this restriction on abortions (see Table 5.6). In 1991, after

TABLE 5.6
Abortion Issues in the Mississippi State Legislature

	House of Representatives			Senate		
	Black Dems	White Dems	Republicans	Black Dems	White Dems	Republicans
1986 Parental Consent for Abortion						
For	25%	74%	83%	100%	98%	100%
Against	75%	26%	17%	0%	2%	0%
N = Total Voting Members	(16)	(95)	(6)	(2)	(46)	(4)
1991 Veto Override of Abortion Waiting Period						
For	28%	86%	100%	0%	90%	100%
Against	72%	14%	0%	100%	10%	0%
N = Total Voting Members	(18)	(86)	(11)	(2)	(40)	(8)
1997 Outlaw Partial-Birth Abortion						
For	48%	98%	100%	67%	100%	100%
Against	52%	2%	0%	33%	0%	0%
N = Total Voting Members	(33)	(46)	(35)	(9)	(24)	(18)

Source: Mississippi Official and Statistical Register, 1980–2000 volumes, Secretary of State's Office; Clarion-Ledger (Jackson), April 13, 1986, pp. H1–H2; April 17, 1991, pp. H1–H2; April 13, 1997, pp. G1–G2.

Democratic Governor Ray Mabus vetoed a waiting period for abortions, over one-fourth of house African Americans joined with overwhelming numbers of whites of both parties to enact the waiting period over his veto. In 1997, two-thirds of African American senators and nearly half of black representatives voted to outlaw partial-birth abortions, joining nearly every white lawmaker.

African Americans have also lacked unity on some important crime measures, though white legislators of both parties have been so unified behind tough anti-crime measures that it is doubtful that black unity would have made much difference. Every white lawmaker, along with over one-third of African Americans, backed the 1996 Streetgang Act, which provided for the confiscation of property owned by gangs (see Table 5.7). Every white legislator, except for two in the house, voted in 1994 to crack down on school violence by getting tough with students bringing drugs or weapons to school, and while most black legislators once again opposed this anti-crime measure, over one-fourth in the house defected from their black colleagues. Similarly, despite some concern over whether African American students might be targeted, two-thirds of African American senators voted along with the great majority of white lawmakers in both chambers for the 2001 School Safety Act, which permitted the expulsion of any student age thirteen or older after three documented disruptive acts in the classroom.

The evolution of the truth in sentencing issue illustrates how by compromising, working with their white Democratic colleagues, and reframing the terms of the debate into a more conservative direction, the Black Caucus can convert an initial defeat into at least a partial victory. In 1995, most African Americans found themselves on the losing side of a conservative measure to require that all felons (even nonviolent offenders) serve at least 85% of their prison time, as the vast majority of white legislators of both parties backed this truth in sentencing measure (see Table 5.7). As prison construction costs rose with the bulging prison populations, African American lawmakers decried this financial drain on the "hardworking taxpayer" and pointed out that many other states passing such increased sentencing measures had restricted their laws to violent offenders who were more of a threat to society. Despite conservative concerns that the legislature was becoming "soft on crime," in 2000, a significant majority of white Democrats joined every African American lawmaker to limit truth in sentencing to violent criminals, though the measure died in conference committee. The next year, the legislature limited an early parole measure to *first-time* nonviolent criminals and renamed it "Early Parole," and the great majority of black and white Democrats enacted it despite the opposition of over 60% of Republican lawmakers.

TABLE 5.7
Crime Issues in the Mississippi State Legislature

	House of Representatives			Senate		
	Black Dems	White Dems	Republicans	Black Dems	White Dems	Republicans
1994 School Violence Crackdown						
For	28%	97%	100%	10%	100%	100%
Against	72%	3%	0%	90%	0%	0%
N = Total Voting Members	(29)	(63)	(27)	(10)	(28)	(13)
1995 Truth in Sentencing						
For	29%	98%	100%	0%	86%	95%
Against	71%	2%	0%	100%	14%	5%
N = Total Voting Members	(31)	(56)	(32)	(10)	(22)	(19)
1996 Streetgang Act (property confiscation)						
For	34%	100%	100%	40%	100%	100%
Against	66%	0%	0%	60%	0%	0%
N = Total Voting Members	(35)	(52)	(32)	(10)	(24)	(18)
2000 Limit Truth in Sentencing to Violent Criminals						
For	100%	56%	6%	100%	78%	59%
Against	0%	44%	94%	0%	22%	41%
N = Total Voting Members	(34)	(52)	(31)	(8)	(23)	(17)
2001 First-Time, Nonviolent, Early Parole						
For	100%	62%	32%	88%	74%	39%
Against	0%	38%	68%	12%	26%	61%
N = Total Voting Members	(33)	(55)	(31)	(8)	(23)	(18)
2001 School Safety (Expulsion Act)						
For	3%	91%	87%	67%	100%	100%
Against	97%	9%	13%	33%	0%	0%
N = Total Voting Members	(33)	(52)	(31)	(9)	(24)	(18)

Source: Mississippi Official and Statistical Register, 1980–2000 volumes, Secretary of State's Office; Clarion-Ledger (Jackson), April 17, 1994, pp. G1–G2; April 9, 1995, pp. G1–G2; April 14, 1996, pp. G1–G2; May 7, 2000, pp. H1–H2; April 8, 2001, pp. I1–I2.

On many issues of special importance to African Americans, black lawmakers have been surprisingly successful given the racist history of the state. Success has been most evident when African Americans were united *and* able to attract a large majority of white Democrats to constitute a winning, biracial Democratic coalition. In 1995, Governor Fordice vetoed a telecommunications bond bill that included racial set-asides, and lawmakers and the state press shifted the focus of the debate away from a divisive battle over affirmative action. Instead, they stressed the economic development needs of the capital city of Jackson that the bond bill would promote and Fordice's inconsistency in not objecting to previous racial set-aside measures until election time. Over three-fourths of white Democrats joined every African American lawmaker to override the veto and uphold racial set-asides in state contracts (see Table 5.8). In 1998, vocal and distraught black lawmakers citing the state's racially discriminatory past were also unified and able to convince over three-fourths of white Democrats to torpedo Fordice's proposal to have voters produce picture identification at the polling places in order to vote, a measure backed by every Republican lawmaker.

TABLE 5.8
Race Related Issues in the Mississippi State Legislature

	House of Representatives			Senate		
	Black Dems	White Dems	Republicans	Black Dems	White Dems	Republicans
1988 Constitution Convention Call						
For	25%	43%	38%	0%	86%	57%
Against	75%	57%	62%	100%	14%	43%
N = Total Voting Members	(20)	(94)	(8)	(2)	(42)	(7)
1993 Hate Crimes Bill						
For	100%	54%	4%	100%	75%	17%
Against	0%	46%	96%	0%	25%	83%
N = Total Voting Members	(30)	(63)	(27)	(10)	(28)	(12)
1994 Child Care Facilities in Schools						
For	100%	56%	19%	100%	62%	25%
Against	0%	44%	81%	0%	38%	75%
N = Total Voting Members	(30)	(61)	(27)	(10)	(29)	(12)
1995 Income Tax Cut						
For	0%	60%	100%	0%	74%	100%
Against	100%	40%	0%	100%	26%	0%
N = Total Voting Members	(31)	(55)	(32)	(10)	(23)	(19)
1995 Veto Override of Racial Set-asides in Telecomm. Bond Bill						
For	100%	77%	23%	100%	83%	28%
Against	0%	23%	77%	0%	17%	72%
N = Total Voting Members	(30)	(56)	(31)	(10)	(24)	(18)
1998 Polling Place Voter Identification						
For	0%	28%	100%	0%	13%	100%
Against	100%	72%	0%	100%	87%	0%
N = Total Voting Members	(35)	(50)	(33)	(9)	(24)	(18)

Source: *Mississippi Official and Statistical Register*, 1980–2000 volumes, Secretary of State's Office; *Clarion-Ledger* (Jackson), May 8, 1988, pp. H1–H2; April 4, 1993, pp. G1–G2; April 17, 1994, pp. G1–G2; April 9, 1995, pp. G1–G2; April 1, 1995, p. 5A; April 12, 1998, pp. H1–H2.

Inability to attract overwhelming support from white Democrats has led black lawmakers to rely on compromise, key interest groups, or constitutional rules to guarantee success on issues vital to the black community. Every African American voted to override Fordice's veto in 1993 of a Hate Crimes bill that would have doubled the penalties for crimes motivated by hatred based on race, religion, or gender, but the white Democratic majority also favoring an override was insufficient to counter overwhelming Republican opposition (see Table 5.8). The next year, Fordice signed the Hate Crimes bill after legislative proponents agreed to change the bill so that juries and not judges would decide whether hate had motivated a crime. Both African American senators in 1988 opposed a call for a constitutional convention to rewrite the state's constitution, fearing any change in the political system that had helped produce black political gains in recent years. Black lawmakers also objected to district election of convention delegates that lacked any at-large delegates appointed by the governor (Democratic Governor Mabus had promised to select at-large delegates that would ensure racial diversity). With the state Farm Bureau also fearing change in the face of the decreasing numbers of farmers in Mississippi and therefore also opposing a convention, majorities of white lawmakers in the house joined with three-fourths of African Americans to torpedo the convention. Most impressive was the ability of African American lawmakers to defeat Governor Fordice's proposed income tax cut in election year 1995, even though all Republicans and about two-thirds of white Democrats backed the tax cut. Every black lawmaker, fearing program cuts, opposed the tax cut, thereby killing the measure by keeping it from meeting the 60% margin required by the state constitution for revenue bills. The tax cut's death ensured that the state would have enough revenue for such expensive forthcoming programs as the Adequate Education bill and a multi-year program to raise public school teachers' salaries to the Southeast average. African American lawmakers, however, had found themselves on the losing side of this constitutional requirement for revenue bills on a 1994 measure to provide child care facilities in the schools. Though most white Democrats joined with every African American lawmaker to support this bill, over three-fourths of Republicans opposed it, thereby preventing it from reaching the required 60% margin.

On economic development issues, African Americans have often been successful when they have been united, and when related issues such as taxes or morality have divided white legislators. In 1987, Governor Bill Allain vetoed the ambitious Highway bill to four-lane 1,000 miles of highways by 2000, preferring his more modest highway bill that did not require any increase in the gas tax. The 17–1 African American vote to override the veto in the house was

TABLE 5.9

Economic Development and Government Reform Issues in the Mississippi State Legislature

	House of Representatives			Senate		
	Black Dems	White Dems	Republicans	Black Dems	White Dems	Republicans
1987 Highway Bill, Veto Override						
For	94%	62%	67%	100%	77%	75%
Against	6%	38%	33%	0%	23%	25%
N = Total Voting Members	(18)	(97)	(6)	(1)	(44)	(4)
1990 Riverboat Gambling						
For	94%	48%	56%	100%	58%	25%
Against	6%	52%	44%	0%	42%	75%
N = Total Voting Members	(18)	(91)	(9)	(2)	(36)	(8)
1993 Tort Reform						
For	23%	97%	100%	25%	100%	100%
Against	77%	3%	0%	75%	0%	0%
N = Total Voting Members	(30)	(63)	(27)	(8)	(28)	(13)
1996 Motor Voter						
For	100%	44%	3%	100%	96%	12%
Against	0%	56%	97%	0%	4%	88%
N = Total Voting Members	(35)	(52)	(32)	(10)	(23)	(17)
1999 Campaign Finance Reform						
For	94%	96%	58%	100%	96%	61%
Against	6%	4%	42%	0%	4%	39%
N = Total Voting Members	(34)	(49)	(36)	(9)	(24)	(18)

Source: *Mississippi Official and Statistical Register*, 1980–2000 volumes, Secretary of State's Office; *Clarion-Ledger* (Jackson), March 12, 1987, p. 12A; March 13, 1987, p. 12A; April 1, 1990, pp. H1–H2; April 4, 1993, pp. G1–G2; April 14, 1996, pp. G1–G2; April 11, 1999, pp. H1–H2.

decisive, since white legislators (more fearful of raising taxes) had voted only 64–39 in favor of overriding, short of the two-thirds vote required (see Table 5.9). The 1990 vote legalizing riverboat gambling was characterized by moral concerns that split white legislators who voted 51–49 in the house against it, but an overwhelming 17–1 favorable vote by African American representatives sent the bill to Governor Mabus for his signature. The bill had originally been backed by business leaders in Natchez and other communities along the Mississippi River and the Gulf Coast who wished to attract more tourism, and it was enacted when religious conservatives became preoccupied with killing the governor's proposed statewide lottery designed to fund his education reform plan. The racial homogeneity situation was reversed when the Black Caucus lost on the 1993 Tort Reform bill, which limited punitive damages in liability lawsuits, as *only* three-fourths of African Americans opposed the business-backed measure, and all except two white legislators (in the house) voted to enact it into law.

On government reform issues, African Americans have been victorious by combining their unity with a coalition of white and black Democrats, by resorting to federal lawsuits, or by engaging in public relations campaigns. The biracial Democratic coalition was so successful in overriding Fordice's veto of a 1999 campaign finance reform measure (which required that candidates disclose more information about their donors) that not only did over 90% of Democrats of both races back the override but so too did a bare majority of Republicans. African Americans successfully resorted to the federal courts to bring Mississippi into compliance with the federal Motor Voter Act. Though every senate Democrat except one had backed the measure in 1996 over GOP opposition, Motor Voter quickly became bogged down in a House Elections Committee chaired by a Republican, and a majority of white Democrats and Republicans had refused to suspend house rules (an extraordinary move requiring a two-thirds vote) and pull the measure out of the committee. In 1994, black lawmakers had been so incensed over Fordice's backing for legislative term limits and for reducing the size of the state legislature that many walked out of his State of the State speech. The Black Caucus was victorious on both of these issues, as the legislature refused to reduce its own size after arguing that a larger legislature permitted voters to have more contact with their elected representatives, and voters themselves rejected term limits after being "educated" that the measure would not permit them to reelect someone who was doing a good job.

The Black Caucus since the mid-1990s has expanded its role from a focus on the legislative process into a more activist group that solicits constituents' views and attracts media coverage of caucus goals. It has held annual legislator retreats to discuss important legislative issues and how to increase African American membership on the "money" committees. The Black Caucus legislative issues committee has held hearings across the state where average citizens can voice their concerns over governmental policies, such as Governor Fordice's alleged failure to wisely spend federal welfare money to help welfare recipients acquire meaningful jobs, and the need for more children to have access to health care (John and Wagster 1998; Rossilli 1998). The Black Caucus even proposes annually its own "People's Budget," though its perceived liberal, high-spending nature and the enormous power of the Joint Legislative Budget Committee limit the budget's impact on the legislative process. The Political Education and Economic Development Foundation hosts an annual banquet keynoted by a nationally recognized figure, where scholarships are awarded for students to attend the state's historically black public and private universities, and where average citizens can attend workshops on such timely concerns as voter registration and welfare reform (Wagster 1998a; Bland 1998). Black Caucus goals in addition to those already discussed that have been enacted into law include the establishment of the state's CHIP (Children's Health Insurance Plan) program, designed to provide health care insurance for children in families without health insurance or with inadequate health insurance. African American lawmakers also took the lead in opposing Governor Fordice's pilot program to privatize the collection of child support payments, a program that was killed when Musgrove became governor.

The Black Caucus has suffered some notable policy setbacks on important issues. Despite Governor Musgrove's backing for changing the state flag to remove the Confederate battle flag emblem, the state legislature merely passed the buck to voters and asked them to choose between the existing state flag and one proposed by a gubernatorial commission that removed the Confederate emblem. After angry whites voiced their opinions in letters to the editor denouncing political correctness and backing the existing flag as best representing "Southern heritage," Musgrove assumed a low profile, and voters overwhelmingly refused to change the flag. The Black Caucus exerted significant influence over debate on redistricting after the 2000 census, when slow state population growth necessitated the loss of a U.S. House district. With an incumbent Democrat (white moderate Ronnie Shows) and Republican (conservative Republican Chip Pickering) thrown into any proposed combined district, the Black Caucus fought for a plan that would maximize the new district's black voting-age population. While the Black Caucus plan was rejected by the joint legislative redistricting committee by a vote along racial lines, the Democratic Party redistricting proposal adopted by a state court (after state house and senate disagreements killed any legislative action) over the Republican-sponsored plan greatly resembled the caucus plan (Sawyer 2001). Republicans had the final say, however, appealing to a federal appeals court, dominated by GOP-appointed judges, which imposed the GOP proposal that contained the smallest African American population. Also in 2002, African American lawmakers, concerned over the College Board's membership being dominated by alumni from two comprehensive, historically white universities, unsuccessfully sought to amend a bill updating the board's apportionment. Blacks failed in bids to require alumni from each of the eight public universities to be board members and to restrict any one university from having more than two alumni as board members (Coffey 2002).

The sheer size and vocal nature of the Black Caucus in Mississippi has made it a power to be reckoned with. Certainly no agency head wants the negative publicity of being called on by the Black Caucus to resign for failure to hire enough African American workers, or to have a vocal bloc of lawmakers voting against their agency's appropriations bills (Elliott 1998; Wagster and Reid 1998). Consequently, even under a conservative Republican governor such as Fordice, the African American proportion of such key state workers as administrators, professionals, and protective services significantly increased (Tucker 2000). With the largest delegation of black elected officials in the nation, Mississippi's Black Caucus members have risen to leadership positions in the National Black Caucus of State Legislators (Wagster 1998b; see also Web site, http://www.nbcsl.com/), serving in 2001 as this national group's vice president (Mary H. Coleman), parliamentarian (Hillman Frazier), an at-large leader (Francis Fredericks), and as members of important policy committees (John Horhn, Alice V. Harden). Opposition by Black Caucus members in 2002 to a conservative Republican appointee of President George W. Bush's to the federal Fifth Circuit Court of Appeals, Charles Pickering (father of Republican Congressman Chip Pickering), proved crucial in convincing the Senate Judiciary Committee to reject the nominee on a party-line vote despite Pickering's strong backing from Senate Minority Leader and Mississippian Trent Lott (Radelat 2002).

CONCLUSIONS

The Black Caucus in Mississippi, despite the challenge of being a "liberal" ideological force in a more conservative Southern state, has become a real player in state politics. Constituting 29% of the membership of the state house and 19% of the state senate, African American lawmakers chaired 23% of the standing committees of the state house and 17% of the state senate committees at the turn of the century. While none of these are the critical "money" committees, African Americans did serve as speaker pro tempore of the house and chair such important committees as Judiciary, Education, and Universities and Colleges. As committee chairs and members, African Americans have helped enact such progressive measures as a multi-year teacher pay raise and a settlement of the state's higher education desegregation lawsuit. African American committee leaders have also blocked appointments of some conservatives to key boards and commissions and killed some election measures deemed harmful to the black community.

The Black Caucus has been particularly successful on popular education measures that command biracial support, as they have formed coalitions with white Democratic lawmakers to resist conservative Republican cost-conscious measures. Three times in the 1990s, African American lawmakers, joining with most white Democrats, were decisive in enacting important education measures over a Republican governor's vetoes. African Americans successfully raised taxes for education at all levels in 1992, enacted an ambitious bond bill for university libraries, and enacted an adequate education bill that increased school financing in poorer districts. The Black Caucus has also enjoyed some successes on key economic development measures where white legislators were divided, being a decisive force in overriding a governor's veto of an ambitious highway bill and sending to the governor a bill legalizing riverboat gambling.

African American lawmakers have even been successful on several race-related issues, due to their homogeneous voting orientations, their ability to convince white Democrats to stick with them on issues of great importance to the black community, and their reliance on political tactics. Such tactics include creating coalitions with other important interest groups, gaining support from the state media, or changing the focus of the public debate toward a more popular issue. Most white Democrats stuck with their African American party colleagues to kill Governor Fordice's effort to enact voter identification measures and to override his veto of racial set-asides in a bond bill. African American unity torpedoed Fordice's effort to cut income taxes in an election year, despite most white legislators of both parties backing the tax cuts. Joining with the Farm Bureau to oppose a new state constitution and attracting media support for a Hate Crimes bill proved to be winning strategies in these political battles. Changing the focus of public debate from the divisive issue of racial set-asides to an emphasis on the economic development needs of the capital city of Jackson helped the Black Caucus enact a telecommunications bond bill despite a Republican governor's veto.

African American lawmakers have been less successful on crime and abortion issues, where white legislators, regardless of party, have tended to vote in a conservative direction, or where black lawmakers themselves have been divided. Yet even on these issues, a strategy of willingness to compromise and the tactic of changing the focus of public debate toward a more popular theme can minimize the policy harm done to the black community. After white lawmakers of both parties enacted a trust in sentencing measure over the Black Caucus's opposition, African American lawmakers and the progressive press began to "educate" the public about the great expense of building more prisons for inmates charged with merely nonviolent offenses that were not included in most states' measures to increase the length of prison sentences. Despite much legislative concern over being perceived as "soft on crime," most white Democrats finally joined with a more homogeneous Black Caucus to overcome Republican opposition to providing early parole for first-time, nonviolent offenders.

Despite needed reforms in the state's education and political system, made possible by Black Caucus members, improvements in the quality of life for all Mississippians have been slower, and many social problems remain. The poverty rate as late as 2000 remained at 15.5%, exceeded only by the poverty rates in five other states, and the infant mortality rate remained higher in 1999 than in every other state except South Carolina (*Statistical Abstract of the United States* 2002, pp. 443, 78). Yet even on such socioeconomically relevant characteristics that are very slow to change, Mississippi has made some progress over the two-decade period characterized by a significant African American presence in the state legislature. In 1980, the state's poverty rate of 24.3% had been the highest in the nation, as was the infant mortality rate (*Statistical Abstract of the United States* 1995, p. 482). And in recognizing that Mississippi continues to face serious human rights challenges, one should not discount the persisting historic effects of racial segregation and discrimination on African Americans throughout the nation. For instance, by 1999, the infant mortality rate for African American Mississippians had fallen to 14.2 deaths per 1,000 live births, slightly lower than the national average of 14.6 for African Americans, and these mortality statistics for blacks remained over twice as high as for whites in Mississippi as well as nationally (*Statistical Abstract of the United States* 2002, p. 78).

Chapter 6

Cohesiveness and Diversity among Black Members of the Texas State Legislature

Michelle G. Briscoe

When examining the roles and influence of state legislators it is important to have a clear understanding of the ways in which legislators might have an impact on the group decision-making process. A significant amount of this understanding stems from the sociopolitical environments from which state legislatures were created, developed, and maintained. When focusing on a study of Southern politics, one must take into account the effects of resolute historical exclusion of black political participation in state and local politics, and those changing environments over time.

Given the fact that nearly all black state representatives have been elected by a majority vote of black voters in majority-minority districts, it must to a large degree be assumed that these representatives seek to serve the policy preferences of black voters. Thus, this study examines black legislators in the Texas state legislature from a descriptive and substantive context during the period 1981–2000. Chamber membership, leadership roles, initiatives and policy changes, and an examination of these changes over time might help answer questions regarding the influence of black legislators.

STATE OVERVIEW

Texas, a Southern border state, has a rich sociopolitical history. Several important factors distinguish the state from the seven states originally included in the provisions of the Voting Rights of 1965.[1] One important distinction was that many white citizens refused to even inform African Americans of the Emancipation of 1863. Their noncompliance with the law led to the "delayed" liberation of many black residents in Texas. The celebration of Juneteenth, the nineteenth of June, 1865, commemorates this date in Texas history when many black citizens became aware of their "freed" status. Republican Reconstruction permitted fourteen black candidates to be elected by their peers to the state legislature in 1871—two to the senate and twelve to the house (Brewer 1935). This brief claim and exercise of electoral rights is similar to that of other Southern states. However, the exceptional event for Texas was the subsequent large and rapid immigration of white citizens from other Southern states, whereby total white Democratic rule was quickly reestablished.[2] Even though the poll tax as a voting requirement was not legislatively implemented in Texas until 1902, its use was encouraged with the specific goal of disenfranchising black voters through intensive printed pamphlet campaigns.[3] Potential black voters in Texas were effectively prevented from exercising their right to vote starting in 1883, despite the dictates of the Fifteenth Amendment. When the white primary was systematically used in conjunction with the aforementioned tactics, black residents in Texas fared no better in most cases than before Emancipation and the fifteenth Amendment.

It is important to consider the ways in which black legislators have historically had to work cooperatively with Democratic Party interests in order to achieve their common group objectives. Given their small numbers and the fact that many white legislators did not vote with the interests of black citizens in mind, black legislators often voted in unison, despite intra-group differences. However, as my research will confirm, it should be understood that in the case of Texas, as in other Southern states, the policy preferences of African Americans are not completely monolithic, particularly in the current political context. After the realization of basic voting rights and civil protections, some black legislators began to cast votes outside of the majority of their colleagues. Modern-day black legislators, though often bound by the practical need to agree, are perhaps less constrained and tend to express dissenting opinions more freely than previously. Patterns of "independent" voting are important to distinguish and will be noted in the chapter.

Another important component of this study centers on the differences in voting preferences that are bound by region. Daniel Elazar (1984) provides an extensive examination of these distinctions based on his theory of American political subcultures. The context within which Texas black state representatives operate, in this case, typically "Southern" or traditionalistic political subculture, provides an appropriate background for an analysis of voting patterns and outcomes over time. Updated interpretations of historical-social consequences will also be examined in an effort to reveal a more complete picture of the influence and effectiveness of black leadership in the Texas state legislature.

In the state of Texas, as in other Southern states, black legislators have organized themselves into caucuses as one means to enhance their ability to influence state legislative policy making. During the late 1960s and early 1970s, black voters across the country took advantage of the opportunities offered by the Voting Rights Act of 1965. The ability of many Southern black voters to elect black legislators was realized through federal identification of locality-specific problems and the elimination of these voting barriers. Additionally, the more recent changes in many Southern states from multi-member voting districts to single-member voting districts created many new black majority districts, resulting in an increase in the number of black elected officials. Subsequent legislation and enforcement of federal law at the state level suggested that full participation for all citizens was a critical factor in legitimizing American democracy. However, as a Southern border state, Texas was not originally included in the protection and enforcement of the Voting Rights Act of 1965.

Over time, the interests and agendas of most black representatives have changed from a primary focus on the enforcement of voting rights—the identification and elimination of historically discriminatory customs and policies that hampered the economic, educational, and social progress of many black Americans. Once many of these fundamental concerns had begun to be addressed, the work of many black elected representatives began to address specific economic development issues and justice in the implementation of education, criminal justice, and environmental policy.

RESEARCH DESIGN

This chapter focuses on the behavior of black members in the Texas state legislature during regular sessions from the period 1980–2001, specifically, a sample of bills drawn from the 65th session (1977), 67th session (1981), the 71st session (1989), the 75th session (1997), and the 76th session (1999). These sessions were selected for two reasons. First, it is important to examine the Texas legislature from the time that African Americans were first seated after Reconstruction, so one year prior to the period of my study is included as a baseline. Second, significant pieces of legislation were proposed and voted on in these years. Black legislators were in many cases asked to "sell" race-relevant issues to their white colleagues. This work often required the legislators to use more cooperative efforts to convince others that the concerns of their constituencies were important to the whole of the state.

These sessions are examined with the goal of understanding several questions: Has the number of African Americans in the Texas state legislature securing committee chairs increased over time? Does the holding of such chair positions enhance the ability of black representatives to obtain policy preferences for their constituencies? What kinds of tactics are used to increase the passage of preferred legislation? Can any trends be established in the voting patterns of black legislators over time? What other factors, external to the influence of black members of the Texas state legislature, should be considered? Integrating some of the previous and current research on black representation in state legislatures, minority caucuses, group influence, voting cohesiveness, and Southern state legislatures, the recorded votes of the aforementioned sessions are analyzed. The focus in this roll-call section is on quantification of voting diversity and cohesion among black legislators over time. In addition, there is an exploration of any differences in voting cohesion between black members and other members of the Democratic Party, and a comparison of Democratic and Republican Party cohesiveness in voting on selected bills. Several qualitative questions about the utility of voting solidarity for the black members of the Texas state legislature are also examined.

Finally, it is suggested how these and other data might be used to gain more insight into the influence of black members in the Texas state legislature, power associated with committee chair and vice chair positions, and outcomes in terms of achievement of policy preferences for African Americans in the state of Texas. Another area of special interest is the Texas Legislative Black Caucus (TLBC), one of two minority caucuses in Texas, the other being the Mexican American Caucus. Questions regarding similarity in voting solidarity call for an assessment of the ability of solidarity across two minority caucuses to significantly advantage both groups on legislation of importance to both groups. A brief outline of future investigations of the TLBC concludes this chapter.

DESCRIPTIVE REPRESENTATION IN THE TEXAS STATE LEGISLATURE

Three distinct periods of growth can be distinguished for black representation in the Texas state legislature. The first period, 1867–1883, is exceptional because it demonstrates the power of nation-centered federalism. After the Southern states' succession, during the Civil War and the Reconstruction period, the national government exerted significant political and physical control over much of the South.[4] During this period, many black men assumed their lawful positions as elected representatives for their states and the Congress.

The second period of growth in Texas was during the early 1970s, starting with the election of Barbara Jordan in 1966 to the Texas state senate. Jordan's unparalleled skills as an orator and her ability to elucidate the reality and necessity of law and social obligation changed not only Texas politics but also American politics.[5] The last period, beginning in 1985, is not one of numerical growth of black elected officials to the state legislature but of a marked increase in the number of black legislators assigned to "key" chair positions. However, this last period seems also to be one of little change for black elected officials in Texas.[6] Members are assigned to the same committees year after year, and without any numerical increases. The effectiveness of black legislators is still minimal and may begin to decline if more black politicians are not elected and in turn assigned to key committee positions.

As of 1999, there were a total of sixteen black members, ten men and six women. Fourteen were members of the house, and two were male senators. The total membership for 1999 was 8.8% of the legislature—9.3% of the house (150 total members) and 6.4% of the senate (thirty-one total members). Tables 6.1 and 6.2 show the membership of the Texas house and senate, respectively, for the period 1981–1999. All of the members are Democrats, and the majority

TABLE 6.1
African American Legislators in the Texas House of Representatives

1981	1985	1989	1993	1997	1999
Cary	Delco	Blair	Coleman	Coleman	Coleman
Cofer	Dutton	K. Conley	Conley	Davis	Davis
Delco	Edwards	Delco	Y. Davis	Dukes	Deshotel
Edwards	Evans	Dutton	Delco	Dutton	Dukes
Hudson	Hudson	Edwards	Dutton	Edwards	Dutton
Lee	R. Givens	Evans	Edwards	Giddings	Edwards
Price	Oliver	Hudson	H. Giddings	Hodge	Giddings
Ragsdale	Price	Larry	Hudson	Jones	Hodge
Sutton	Ragsdale	Price	J. Jones	Lewis	Jones
Thompson	Sutton	G. Thompson	Price	McClendon	Lewis
Washington	G. Thompson	S. Thompson	G. Thompson	Price	McClendon
Webber	S. Thompson	S. Turner	S. Thompson	S. Thompson	S. Thompson
Wilson	Wilson	Wilson	Turner	Turner	Turner
			Wilson	Wilson	Wilson
13 members	13 members	13 members	14 members	14 members	14 members
8.6% of	8.6% of	8.6% of	9.3% of	9.3% of	9.3% of
house	house	house	house	house	house

Note: The last two rows indicate the number of African Americans in the house and their percentage of the total membership of 150 members.

Source: Texas Legislative Reference Library.

represents some part of the major urban areas of Dallas-Fort Worth or Houston (twelve of fourteen), where black populations approach or exceed 50% (see Table 6.3). The benefits of the judicially mandated redistricting plans of 1992 and 1994 in Texas are not apparent in terms of any numerical increases in black elected

TABLE 6.2
African American Legislators in the Texas Senate

1981	1985	1989	1993	1997	1999
-0-	C. Washington	E. B. Johnson C. Washington* R. Ellis**	R. Ellis R. West	R. Ellis R. West	R. Ellis R. West
no members 0% of senate	1 member 3.2% of senate	2 members 6.4% of senate	2 members 6.4% of senate	2 members 6.4% of senate	2 members 6.4% of senate

* Resigned 1-23-1990.
** Replaced Washington on 2-13-1990.
Note: The last two rows indicate the number of African Americans in the state senate and their percentage of the total membership of thirty-one members.

Source: Texas Legislative Reference Library.

TABLE 6.3
African American House Members, Districts and Black Populations of Districts

Member Name	District	City/Portion of City/ County Represented	Black Population as Percentage of Total Pop.
Coleman, Garnet	147	Houston, part of Harris County	51.31
Davis, Yvonne	111	Part of Dallas, Glenn Heights, Cedar Hill, part of Dallas County	55.36
Deshotel, Joseph	22	Part of Beaumont and Port Arthur, part of Jefferson County	56.87
Dukes, Dawnna	50	Part of Austin, part of Travis County	32.38
Dutton, Harold	142	Part of Northern Houston, part of Harris County	55.32
Edward, Al	146	Part of South Houston, part of Harris County	54.38
Giddings, Helen	109	Lancaster, Hutchins, Desoto, part of Dallas, part of Dallas County	52.46
Hodge, Terri	100	Part of East Dallas, part of Dallas	50.12
Jones, Jesse	110	Part of East Dallas, part of Dallas County	57.45
Lewis, Glenn	95	Part of Fort Worth, part of Bexar County	57.70
McClendon, Ruth	120	Part of San Antonio, part of Bexar County	33.09
Thompson, Senfronia	141	Part of West Houston, part of Harris County	53.30
Turner, Sylvester	139	Part of Houston, part of Harris County	48.16
Wilson, Ron	131	Part of Houston, part of Harris County	53.02

Source: Texas Legislative Council, Texas Legislature Online, FYI System, March 8, 1999.

officials in the following election cycles.[7] However, when examining the districts from which black candidates are elected, it is clear that black majorities are responsible in most cases for the election of black representatives.

THE SIGNIFICANCE OF STATE LEGISLATIVE BLACK CAUCUSES

Racial caucuses have been organized within state legislatures since the mid-1970s in many Southern states and even earlier in some midwestern states such as Missouri and Ohio (Menifield 2000). The main reason for the proliferation of black state legislative caucuses is the corrections made by the Voting Rights Act of 1965. The act allowed black citizens to increase their political influence through voting, which in turn enhanced their opportunities for winning election to state legislatures, impossible for many black politicians in prior years, given the systematic and forceful negation of black political power. The purpose of forming any legislative caucus is to increase and concentrate the strength of like-minded individual legislators in order to influence policy favorable to their interests. The numerical increase in black legislators, particularly in the South, where they had not previously had access to this level, would in itself suggest that the interests of black citizens would be attended to in ways they had not been in the past. In fact, increased representation in the "Black Belt" counties of several Southern states indicates that

> black elected officials have provided their constituents with benefits in housing, employment, education, health care, police protection, and in other areas ... ensuring a more racially equitable distribution of public goods and services within existing priorities. (Barker and Jones 1994, p. 73)

However, for the most part, black elected officials have not been able to significantly change the agendas and priorities of the institutions they work within. Barker and Jones (1994, p. 73) suggest that until black state legislators are represented in greater numbers as committee chairs and vice chairs of the more powerful committees, agenda setting will not reflect the priorities of black residents.

Although a comparative examination of the effectiveness of black legislative caucuses is beyond the scope of this research, it is important to note that caucus formation has been a successful factor in negotiating policy changes that benefit black residents. Most often, agenda-building strategies are used first within the caucus (Miller 1990, 1994). Then, traditional methods of garnering support from other key non-black legislators are employed. Support is also elicited from others who, within their own regional or socioeconomic groups, have interests that intersect with the interest of the black caucus. Until numerical representation increases, these strategies will continue to be refined by racial caucuses to augment their influence in policy making. For the purpose of this study, the black representatives will be referred to as the Texas Legislative Black Caucus, or the TLBC.

The TLBC works with the Hispanic state legislative caucus on many mutually important issues. However, the Black Caucus formally decided to exclude non-black legislators from membership. Other states' racial caucuses have chosen to deal with membership requirements in a similar fashion, while some have not placed such restrictions on membership. A comparative study of states such as Texas and California, where several racial caucuses coexist, would be useful in understanding the possibilities and problems of racial caucus coalitions.

THE TEXAS LEGISLATURE

The TLBC operates within a unique organizational structure that in many ways limits the whole legislature's ability to perform its primary job of law-making. The Texas legislature is constitutionally structured whereby legislators are essentially asked to "do more with less" in all aspects of their work. For example, legislators in Texas are among the lowest paid in any state, receiving $7,260 annually plus a $90 per diem. The legislative sessions are 140 days in length, and each session convenes every other year in odd-numbered years. Special sessions called by the governor have become routinized due to the short regular sessions. Legislators are expected to deal with several thousand pieces of legislation (over 7,000 in 1997), and real competency in all of the various policy areas is impossible.

All of these factors contribute to the high turnover of members and are credited for the "amateurism" that exists in the legislature (Maxwell and Crain 1995, pp. 144–147). Amateurism describes the state legislators' inability to make reasoned and critical decisions due to the sheer number of bills introduced in the short sessions. In conjunction with power centralized within the control of the speaker, who directs the assignment of much of the legislation, the development of specialization is particularly difficult.

However, some procedural and informal mechanisms have developed to overcome these organizational constraints. For example, one useful strategy is the introduction of the same bill into both houses simultaneously. A suspension of rules requires a two-thirds vote by the senate in order for a bill to be placed on the senate calendar. This routinized suspension limits the number of bills that will be voted on. However, if a bill is able to reach the floor for senate action, then its passage is nearly guaranteed. Given this procedural quirk, legislators from both houses will introduce similar legislation with the hope that it will reach the conference committee in a form requiring little or no revision and thereby avoid getting hung up in committee (Maxwell and Crain 1995, pp. 156–161).

COMMITTEE LEADERSHIP IN THE TEXAS LEGISLATURE

Committee leadership in the Texas state legislature is, like most other state legislatures, coveted. However, committee leadership in Texas does not automatically give members more power to control the destiny of any given piece of legislation. The constitutional structure of the Texas legislature, in addition to an established centralization of power in the hands of the speaker, allows the speaker to retain significant control over which committees members are assigned to. The speaker also exercises significant discretion over referring bills to his desired committee (see the Web site http://texaspolitics.laits.utexas.edu/html/leg/0602.html).

Tables 6.4 and 6.5 show committee chairs held by black legislators in Texas in the 1981, 1985, 1989, 1993, 1997, and 1999 sessions. Most notable in the house are the assignments to key committees beginning in 1985 with Rules and Resolutions, State, Federal, and International Relations, and Judiciary. However, the overall number of committee chair assignments did not exceed four in the house and one in the senate during this period.

METHODOLOGY AND DATA USED

This examination of data is focused on two sets of data. The first set is a subset of the larger set and is an analysis of roll-call votes from the 1997 legislative session. These data are examined with the goal of comparing and contrasting any patterns of solidarity and-or dissension between and among members of the TLBC, Democrats, and Republicans as voting subgroups of the Texas legislature. The second set of data is a compilation of voting records over time. Specifically, roll-call votes are examined across legislative sessions—1977, 1981, 1989, 1997, and 1999. This second analysis provides a longitudinal review of voting behavior by the aforementioned groups over time. A brief comparison is made of the two examinations at the end of this section.

TABLE 6.4
African American Committee Chairs in the Texas House of Representatives*

1981	1985	1989	1993	1997	1999
Delco—Higher Education	Delco—Higher Education	Delco—Higher Education	Delco—Higher Education	Edwards—Rules and Resolutions	Davis—Local and Consent Calendars
Washington—Human Services	S. Thompson—Rules and Resolutions	S. Thompson—Judiciary	Edwards—Rules and Resolutions	S. Thompson—Judicial Affairs	Edwards—Rules and Resolutions
Wilson—Health Services	Ragsdale—State Federal and International Relations	Wilson—Liquor Regulation	S. Thompson—Judicial Affairs	Wilson—Licensing and Administration	S. Thompson—Judicial Affairs
			Wilson—Licensing and Administrative Procedures		Wilson—Licensing and Administrative Procedurres
3 chairmanships of 30 total committees 10% of total	3 chairmanships of 30 total committees 10% of total	3 chairmanships of 31 total committees 9.6% of total	4 chairmanships of 31 total committees 12.9% of total	3 chairmanships of 36 total committees 8.3% of total	4 chairmanships of 36 total committees 11.1% of total

*Note: There were no African Americans in the Texas house appointed to chairmanships prior to 1975.

Source: Texas Legislative Reference Library.

TABLE 6.5
African American Committee Chairs in the Texas Senate*

1981	1985	1989	1993	1995	1997	1999
				Ellis—Jurisprudence	Ellis—Jurisprudence	Ellis—Jurisprudence
-0- of 14 total committees 0% of total	-0- of 14 total committees 0% of total	-0- of 14 total committees 0% of total	-0- of 14 total committees 0% of total	1 chairmanship of 14 total committees 7.1% of total	1 chairmanship of 15 total committees 6.7% of total	1 chairmanship of 15 total committees 6.7% of total

* Note: There were no African Americans in the Texas senate from 1973 to 1983; no African Americans chaired committees after Barbara Jordan until 1995.

Source: Texas Legislative Reference Library.

The database for the first analysis originated from the roll-call votes as compiled by the house journal clerk at the end of the 1997 legislative session. The 269 motions examined here are from a total of 630 recorded roll-call votes. The majority of the other motions that were not recorded were unanimous, commemorative, and-or had a narrow local focus. These numbers are from a total of 3,610 house bills and 1,951 senate bills introduced in this session. For the measure of voting solidarity, this first subset of record votes is drawn from a variety of motions and reflects only the numerical summaries needed to assess agreement or disagreement with the caucus majority.

When the first analysis turns from a focus on Black Caucus solidarity to a comparison between Black Caucus and white Democratic and Republican voting, I focus on a second subset of data, which is reduced in size by the exclusion of non-end-stage motions. End-stage motions, for the purposes of this study, are those motions filed as "passage to engrossment" or "third and final reading." These motions are included because they are at a critical stage of forward movement from one house to the other, or for consideration by the governor.

SOLIDARITY WITHIN THE BLACK CAUCUS

The effectiveness of the Black Caucus in terms of having any specific vote resolved in the manner preferred by the caucus consensus is directly tied to the strength of the consensus within the caucus. That is, if an overwhelming majority of the TLBC members vote the same way in any given vote, then the overall vote across the entire house is highly likely to turn out in favor of the caucus majority view. When the caucus members differ strongly, the resulting overall vote could go either way.

This conclusion was reached through the following analysis. The votes of the members of the Black Caucus were recorded for the 269 motions included in this study according to the process of selection described earlier. For each of these votes, I examined the recorded votes for the caucus totals (e.g., thirteen "aye" and one "nay") and whether or not the outcome of the vote within the entire house was in agreement with the caucus majority view. Six cases involving tie votes, either in terms of caucus voting or the vote result of the entire house, were removed from consideration. The outcome of the other 263 votes is summarized in Table 6.6.

The first column, Caucus Minority, is the number of caucus members voting against what the majority of the TLBC members supported in the vote; thus the first row of data consists of what happens when the caucus votes unanimously. The second and third columns show how many votes had outcomes that were favorable and unfavorable, where favorable is defined as the majority of the entire house being "in agreement with the views of the caucus majority." The fourth column is the percentage of outcomes favoring the view of the caucus majority.

The rows corresponding to caucus minorities of at least two do not contain as much data as the first two rows, so the 83.3% favorable rate in the final row is

TABLE 6.6
Texas Legislative Black Caucus Recorded Vote Outcomes, 1997

Caucus Minority	Favorable Outcome	Unfavorable Outcome	Percent Favorable
0	137	16	89.5%
1	29	13	69.0%
2	10	10	50%
3	10	4	71.4%
4	14	10	58.3%
5	0	4	0.0%
6	5	1	83.3%
Totals	205	58	77.9%

Source: House Journal Clerk.

TABLE 6.7
Texas Legislative Black Caucus Condensed Recorded Vote Outcomes

Caucus Minority	Favorable Outcome	Unfavorable Outcome	Percent Favorable
0	137	16	89.5%
1	29	13	69.0%
At least 2	39	29	57.4%

Source: House Journal Clerk.

merely a consequence of the small number of cases where the caucus split 8–6 or 7–6 in voting. If one combines the last five rows of the table, then a more accurate picture emerges (see Table 6.7). Thus when the caucus is able to maintain solidarity, it is very successful in achieving favorable outcomes. When one considers the aforementioned table in view of the caucus's success in maintaining solidarity (voting unanimously on 153 of the 263 motions), it is sensible to conclude that the group is having a notable influence on the legislative process. In terms of descriptive statistics, $\gamma = .55$ is computed for the first table presented. Note that γ is a common measure of association in ordinal categorical data and is on a scale of -1 to 1 (a value of zero implies no association). This value of γ is sufficiently large so as to provide quantitative evidence supporting the conclusion of the connection between caucus solidarity and the achievement of favorable vote outcomes.

COMPARISON OF CAUCUS VOTING TO NON-CAUCUS DEMOCRAT VOTING

Before the conclusions of the previous section can be accepted without reservation, some further analysis is required. For example, is the caucus actually behaving differently than any randomly chosen subset of fourteen house members would behave? If so, how? In order to answer this question, voting behavior must be analyzed in greater detail. The focus is on house bills for only those votes in the final stages of the legislative vote process, as described earlier. Specifically, the votes that were either "passage to engrossment" or "third reading and final passage" were considered here. This reduced the data set to a more manageable number of forty-nine such votes. For these votes, the number of "aye" and "nay" votes by party was recorded. (Note that the caucus voting behavior for each of these votes had already been recorded.)

First, a comparison was made between the voting behavior of Democrats and Republicans. The results, as expected, demonstrated a huge difference between the parties. It was not uncommon to see one party almost unanimously voting "aye," while the other almost unanimously voted "nay." Thus, it makes sense to view caucus voting behavior in comparison to the voting behavior of non-caucus Democrats (as every caucus member is a Democrat). Two-by-two contingency tables were created to make this comparison. Votes were classified based on whether they were "aye" or "nay" and by whether they were cast by a caucus member or a non-member. This yielded forty-nine individual χ^2 values, each with one degree of freedom. Because independent χ^2 values, when added, yield another χ^2, the sum of these forty-nine values should follow a χ^2 distribution with forty-nine degrees of freedom. The resulting sum was 69.15, yielding a P-value of .03. Thus, there is sufficient evidence to conclude that caucus membership is related to voting behavior, even when only Democrat legislators are included in the analysis.

After establishing the existence of a difference between caucus members and non-caucus Democrats, the nature of the difference was investigated. One measure considered was the solidarity of the vote. Solidarity was defined as the percentage of legislators in agreement with the majority in any given vote. As previously mentioned, the caucus tends to vote in a bloc; however, without viewing this behavior in context, it was not clear whether or not this was typical of any set of fourteen Democrat house members.

Solidarity is, in fact, significantly different within the caucus than it is for non-caucus Democrats. For the forty-nine votes in question, solidarity was calculated within the caucus and among the non-caucus Democrats. In forty of these forty-nine votes, the caucus displayed greater solidarity than the other Democrats. There were also five ties in terms of solidarity, so in only four of forty-nine votes was the non-caucus solidarity higher than the caucus solidarity. This is a statistically significant result and demonstrates clearly that the caucus differs in that members are much more likely to vote together on any given bill than their non-caucus Democratic counterparts.

A LONGITUDINAL ANALYSIS OF LEGISLATIVE GROUPS AND COALITIONS

My second analysis of data centers on patterns of votes cast for or against by members of the legislature within the defined categories of house membership, race (black or white), party affiliation (Democrat or Republican), and type of bill. It is important to restate the purposes and limitations of these categories in the Texas case. First, all of the members of the TLBC are black Democrats. The previous data subset analysis demonstrated clearly that all members did not vote together on all bills. Second, in spite of their numerical disadvantage, black members were able to get legislation passed when (1) they voted together and (2) they had the vote support of white Democratic colleagues. Lastly, this study did not attempt to account for the influences of a significantly important subgroup of the Texas state legislature—Mexican Americans—and its alliances within the larger body. Given the purposes and limitations of these analyses, they nevertheless are able to provide some insight into the voting patterns and outcomes expressed by black members of the legislature.

Educational policy issues have been a dominant and divisive area in Texas for many years. The primary concerns have centered on the state's obligation to fulfill federal public education laws and the state's historical resistance to providing education to African Americans, Hispanics and the poor. The rationale for resistance has shifted from the generally racist stance of post–Civil War times to a paternalistic view of education-skills as a way for African Americans to fulfill economic niches designated by the white elite and later by middle-class, service-driven demands. Modern debates focus on two primary areas—how to correct historical and substantial imbalances in the provision of public education, and how to pay for these corrections. The weight of national public scrutiny keeps these issues in the forefront and has helped support those legislators who work for improvements in public education at all levels.

HB 136, shown in Table 6.8, the "Free Federal Breakfast Participation Bill," is a prime example of the state's historical resistance to federal mandates. The federal breakfast programs were intended to provide low-income, eligible students with a nutritious breakfast before the beginning of the school day. Proponents cited numerous studies that had proven the need for good nutrition for growing, learning children, and the fact that many poor kids did not receive adequate morning meals at home. The federal government implemented the free breakfast program and provided incentives for states to participate without undue financial outlays—new equipment, additional staff, monitors, and so on. Opponents suggested, among other things, that parental responsibility should

TABLE 6.8
Roll Call Votes in the Texas State Legislature on Education Issues

	House of Representatives			Senate		
	Black Dems	White Dems	Republicans	Black Dems	White Dems	Republicans
1977 Free Federal Breakfast Participation (HB136)						
For	100%	75%	25%	–	82%	100%
Against	0%	25%	75%	–	18%	0%
N = Total Voting Members	(13)	(120)	(8)	(0)	(22)	(3)
1981 Prairie View A&M University (SB1171)						
For	100%	91%	85%	–	100%	100%
Against	0%	9%	15%	–	0%	0%
N = Total Voting Members	(13)	(103)	(34)	(0)	(24)	(7)
1989 Aid for Students with Children (SB151)						
For	100%	99%	95%	100%	96%	75%
Against	0%	1%	5%	0%	4%	25%
N = Total Voting Members	(13)	(80)	(57)	(2)	(23)	(8)
1997 Uniform Admissions and Reporting (HB588)						
For	100%	99%	88%	100%	100%	76%
Against	0%	1%	12%	0%	0%	24%
N = Total Voting Members	(14)	(68)	(68)	(2)	(12)	(17)
1999 Parental Notice of Uncertified Teachers (HB618)						
For	100%	100%	99%	100%	100%	100%
Against	0%	0%	1%	0%	0%	0%
N = Total Voting Members	(13)	(69)	(68)	(2)	(14)	(16)

Source: Texas Legislative Library, house journals, senate journals, focus reports—"Major Issues of the 65th, 67th, 71st, 75th, and 76th Legislature Regular Session," House Research Organization.

include primary breakfast for one's own children, that children would be stigmatized for participation in the program, that the costs would be too high, and that evidence regarding poor kids not getting breakfast at home was not clear. In the end, the bill was passed by the biracial Democratic coalition, with white Republicans in the house standing out as nonsupporters.

The Prairie View and Aid for Students with Children bills both related to funding for black students and-or poor students at public institutions. Prairie View A & M is a historically underfunded black university near Houston that was established under the provisions of the Morrill Land Grant College Act in

1876. The 1981 bill related to equal funding for the school from the state's Permanent University Fund. After a long battle in the legislature, an amendment to the state constitution required the state to provide Prairie View with its fair share of the state's funding. While strong majorities of all groups backed the bill, house Republicans were less overwhelmingly supportive of it.

The Aid for Students with Children bill concerned the balance between the state's obligation to educate and the paucity of funding for public schools. The state of Texas has been notorious in its inequitable distribution of property taxes—the backbone of public school funding. This bill raised the supplementary issue of teens who have children and want to continue their educations. In the end, the legislature easily passed the bill, though Republican lawmakers were not quite as supportive as Democrats of both races.

The Uniform Admissions and Reporting bill related to noted discrepancies in acceptance of student athletes based on their high school grade point averages and SAT-ACT scores. Once this practice had been publicly verified, the legislature passed the bill to include measures to ensure consistency in standards of public college admissions with penalties for noncompliance. HB 618 passed after much controversy. The practice of hiring uncertified teachers was supported by nearly every black and white lawmaker, based on the state's need to provide education in a system that was overburdened on all levels—increasing student enrollments, poor pay for teachers, and failure to pass adequate school finance bills.

The crime and criminal justice bills are representative of the state's long record of being "tough" on crime (see Table 6.9). As in many other states, and particularly in former slave states, these policies were initiated shortly before the Civil War and implemented as legal means to control the black population.[8] State crime statistics show increases in crime in general and violent crime in particular, much of it gang related. Black males are disproportionately found to be perpetrators of these crimes. Some "get tough on crime" advocates use this information in their efforts to reduce funding for proactive measures (education, after-school programming, social support programs, etc.) that they say are clearly ineffective. The booming prison industry in Texas, with movement toward privatization, adds pressure from public and private groups that benefit from the arrest, trial, conviction, and incarceration process. Therefore, the three most recent bills in Table 6.9 enjoyed widespread support from all groups of lawmakers—white and black Democrats, as well as Republicans. Earlier measures enjoyed less legislative support with a 1977 denial of bail measure failing, as it enjoyed majority support only among the few Republicans lawmakers.

Legislation on health and families during the sessions examined centered, for the most part, on funding for low-income eligibility and funding for recipients

TABLE 6.9
Roll Call Votes in the Texas State Legislature on Crime and Criminal Justice Issues

	House of Representatives			Senate		
	Black Dems	White Dems	Republicans	Black Dems	White Dems	Republicans
1977 Denial of Bail Pending Appeal of Federal Convictions						
For	0%	16%	85%	–	12%	100%
Against	100%	84%	15%	–	88%	0%
N = Total Voting Members	(11)	(117)	(13)	(0)	(25)	(3)
1981 Redefining Public Intoxication & Penalties (HB1475)						
For	100%	51%	56%	–	55%	29%
Against	0%	49%	44	–	45%	71%
N = Total Voting Members	(10)	(101)	(34)	(0)	(22)	(7)
1989 Prison Construction Bond Bill (HB1477)						
For	100%	100%	100%	50%	100%	100%
Against	0%	0%	0%	50%	0%	0%
N = Total Voting Members	(13)	(74)	(56)	(2)	(21)	(8)
1997 Life in Prison for 2nd Time Sex Offenders (SB46)						
For	100%	98%	100%	100%	100%	100%
Against	0%	2%	0%	0%	0%	0%
N = Total Voting Members	(11)	(70)	(52)	(2)	(13)	(12)
1999 Statewide Database of Gang Information						
For	100%	90%	74%	100%	100%	100%
Against	0%	10%	26%	0%	0%	0%
N = Total Voting Members	(11)	(58)	(65)	(2)	(13)	(14)

Source: Texas Legislative Library, house journals, senate journals, focus reports—"Major Issues of the 65th, 67th, 71st, and 76th Legislature Regular Session," House Research Organization.

of state aid. The 1977 Legalization of Laetrile, HB 1574, is one exception (see Table 6.10). This bill, sponsored by black Democrat Senfronia Thompson, legalized the manufacture, sale, and use of laetrile, a controversial treatment for cancer. Texas's proximity to Mexico, where many Americans sought alternative and illegal treatment for cancer, helped Thompson's argument for legalization of the drug.

The Agent Orange bill was unique in that it passed in both houses unanimously. In 1981, much of the research on the use and affects of Agent Orange on veterans of the Vietnam War was inconclusive. However, Texas is home to

TABLE 6.10
Roll Call Votes in the Texas State Legislature on Health and Family Issues

	House of Representatives			Senate		
	Black Dems	White Dems	Republicans	Black Dems	White Dems	Republicans
1977 Legalization of Laetrile						
For	50%	72%	46%	–	56%	67%
Against	50%	28%	54%	–	44%	33%
N = Total Voting Members	(10)	(117)	(13)	(0)	(27)	(3)
1981 Agent Orange Screening						
For	100%	100%	100%	–	100%	100%
Against	0%	0%	0%	–	0%	0%
N = Total Voting Members	(13)	(97)	(29)	(0)	(24)	(7)
1989 Medicaid Eligibility & Reimbursement (HB1345)						
For	92%	80%	9%	100%	100%	100%
Against	8%	20%	91%	0%	0%	0%
N = Total Voting Members	(12)	(96)	(32)	(2)	(23)	(6)
1997 Texas Healthy Kids Corp. (HB3)						
For	100%	100%	54%	100%	100%	59%
Against	0%	0%	46%	0%	0%	41%
N = Total Voting Members	(14)	(66)	(57)	(2)	(12)	(17)
1999 Parental Notification of Abortions on Minors (SB30)						
For	100%	88%	3%	50%	50%	94%
Against	0%	12%	97%	50%	50%	6%
N = Total Voting Members	(14)	(60)	(65)	(2)	(12)	(16)

Source: Texas Legislative Library, house journals, senate journals, focus reports–"Major Issues of the 65th, 67th, 71st, 75th, and 76th Legislature Regular Session," House Research Organization.

many war veterans, and although they did not formally lobby in their interests, legislators were keenly aware of their presence and voting power and with little debate passed this legislation. Although the bill only dealt with screening procedures, standards, and utilization of facilities, the passage of this legislation in Texas was significant in the national appeal for recognition of the concerns and problems of Vietnam War veterans.

The debate over SB 30, Parental Notification of Abortions on Minors, was very contentious. This legislation required that parents be notified when a minor requested any termination of pregnancy procedure, though exceptions could be made by medical personnel if the minor could show that she was mature, or that parental notification was not in her best interests. The black members, with one exception, supported this bill. As in many Southern states, African Americans in Texas tend to have strong religious, usually Protestant, backgrounds. Although the influence of formal religion is declining among all populations in the United States, the tendency toward absolute rejection of abortion based on biblical interpretation is high among African Americans. As shown in Table 6.3, a majority of the black representatives elected in Texas come from majority black districts. In addition, many of the black representatives rely on informal church networks to assemble their campaigns, and once elected they disseminate and gather information for support of their constituencies. Black members tended to vote on this legislation based on their past records regarding this issue. Controversy for some white members centered on parental control, the age of majority, and privacy rights for minors.

The more conservative orientations of Republican lawmakers compared to Democrats of both races are evident on two health care bills focused particularly on lower-income people, a 1989 Medicaid bill and a 1997 Texas Healthy Kids bill. While over 80% of Democrats of both races backed these measures, a large majority of house Republicans opposed the Medicaid measure, and a bare majority of GOP lawmakers backed the Healthy Kids bill.

The roll-call votes examined on "Race Relevant Issues," summarized in Table 6.11, were selected based on their significance to black Texans in terms of effect. The State Funding for Full Day Kindergarten bill addressed many groups' concerns. First, the incidence of children coming into first grade without the required skills had been well noted. Second, the state was struggling with a limited budget at the same time that the legislature debated a proposal to increase public school financing. School administrators were rightly justifiably concerned about recruiting, hiring, and paying for additional teachers, transportation, and so on. This bill, sponsored by house Democrats, was eventually passed when it was proposed as an amendment to the public school finance bill. Republicans were somewhat less supportive of the measure than were Democrats, though a majority nevertheless voted to enact it.

The 1989 and 1997 bills both focused on election procedures and had implications for black and minority voters. The Temporary Absentee Polling Places bill was an attempt to standardize the setup and collection of ballots cast prior to a scheduled election day. Discrepancies in voting registration records and ballots cast at absentee polling places prompted lawmakers to consider legislation to eliminate the resulting problems that appeared to advantage white voters at the polls. Given the facts of numerous cases presented in debate,

TABLE 6.11
Roll Call Votes in the Texas State Legislature on Race Relevant Issues

	House of Representatives			Senate		
	Black Dems	White Dems	Republicans	Black Dems	White Dems	Republicans
1977 State Funding For Full-Day Kindergarten (HB750)						
For	100%	83%	82%	–	77%	67%
Against	0%	17%	18%	–	23%	33%
N = Total Voting Members	(13)	(112)	(17)	(0)	(26)	(3)
1981 Texas House Redistricting Bill (HB960)						
For	85%	96%	13%	–	83%	29%
Against	15%	4%	87%	–	17%	71%
N = Total Voting Members	(13)	(97)	(34)	(0)	(23)	(7)
1989 Temporary Absentee Polling Places						
For	100%	80%	11%	100%	90%	25%
Against	0%	20%	89%	0%	10%	75%
N = Total Voting Members	(13)	(79)	(55)	(2)	(21)	(8)
1997 Election Processes and Procedures (HB331)						
For	100%	80%	11%	100%	95%	25%
Against	0%	20%	89%	0%	5%	75%
N = Total Voting Members	(11)	(79)	(55)	(2)	(20)	(8)
1999 Hub Contracting Requirements (SB178)						
For	100%	62%	32%	100%	76%	47%
Against	0%	38%	68%	0%	24%	53%
N = Total Voting Members	(12)	(67)	(69)	(2)	(13)	(15)

Source: Texas Legislative Library, house journals, senate journals, focus reports—"Major Issues of the 65th, 67th, 71st, 75th, and 76th Legislature Regular Session," House Research Organization.

a majority of the body voted to pass this bill. The Elections Processes and Procedures bill put forward similar concerns as the 1989 bill—discrepancies in ballot collection and processing. Specifically, mail-in ballots for military personnel were considered, with supporters saying that the bill would "remedy confusing and outdated election procedures that have led to a variety of problems." Both election bills passed because of the unanimous backing of black Democrats and the support of over three-fourths of white Democrats, while majorities of Republican lawmakers in both chambers opposed the measures.

TABLE 6.12
Roll Call Votes in the Texas State Legislature on Government Regulation and
Economic Development Issues

	House of Representatives			Senate		
	Black Dems	White Dems	Republicans	Black Dems	White Dems	Republicans
1977 Higher Interest Rates on Consumer Loans						
For	25%	18%	79%	–	14%	100%
Against	75%	82%	21%	–	86%	0%
N = Total Voting Members	(12)	(120)	(14)	(0)	(28)	(3)
1981 Motor Vehicle Liability Insurance						
For	85%	95%	76%	–	79%	67%
Against	15%	5%	24%	–	21%	33%
N = Total Voting Members	(13)	(103)	(33)	(0)	(24)	(3)
1989 Children in Open Truck Beds (SB170)						
For	22%	59%	74%	–	86%	86%
Against	78%	41%	26%	–	14%	14%
N = Total Voting Members	(9)	(88)	(27)	(0)	(22)	(7)
1997 Funding Legal Services for Indigents (SB1534)						
For	100%	87%	52%	100%	100%	65%
Against	0%	13%	48%	0%	0%	35%
N = Total Voting Members	(14)	(77)	(62)	(2)	(12)	(17)
1999 Regulating Amusement Rides (HB1059)						
For	100%	95%	94%	100%	92%	36%
Against	0%	5%	6%	0%	8%	64%
N = Total Voting Members	(14)	(64)	(68)	(2)	(13)	(14)

Source: Texas Legislative Library, house journals, senate journals, focus reports—"Major Issues of the 65th, 67th, 71st, 75th, and 76th Legislature Regular Session," House Research Organization.

The issue of regulation and funding of historically underutilized businesses (HUBs) has been debated in Texas as in other states since the 1970s. The 1999 bill simply codified previous state agency provisions that were bundled together in the senate bill to assure passage. This bill sought to stem the erosion of benefits for minority business in Texas. It was backed by all black Democrats and a majority of white Democrats over the opposition of most Republicans lawmakers.

Table 6.12 summarizes the Texas legislature's voting on government regulations and economic development issues. The 1977 bill on higher interest rates was favored by most Republicans but was killed by the votes of most Democrats, who feared that socially disadvantaged persons would be hurt. The loans under consideration were the type usually sought by lower-income and lower-middle-income consumers who would not qualify for lower-interest bank loans. The 1981 bill requiring motor vehicle liability insurance was supported by most members across party lines. Although it meant an increased cost for many drivers, the concerns related to the growing number of accidents involving uninsured motorists and the associated costs were thought to be more important.

SB 170, regarding children riding in open truck beds, was initiated by citizens in response to several deaths resulting from children being thrown from truck beds in motor vehicle accidents. Part of the controversy over this bill centered on class and income. Some one-vehicle families opted for trucks over standard passenger vehicles. Rural traditions, multiple child families, urbanization, poverty, and Texas truck traditions collided with parental responsibility and public health costs, though the bill was passed.

Funding for legal services for indigents—SB 1534—was part of an ongoing debate about how much legal service poor defendants were constitutionally entitled to. Inadequate representation of defendants continues to be a real problem facing the criminal justice system in Texas. Legal aid funding had dropped nationally, and supporters of the bill noted that nearly twenty other states used court fees, as proposed in this bill, to fund the services. With limitations on class action suits and those cases that would result in fee recovery, the bill passed with the unanimous backing of black Democrats in the house and senate and white Democrats in the senate, though Republicans were more split over the bill.

The 1999 bill, Regulating Amusement Rides, was part of a national awareness of most states' lax regulation of amusement parks, specifically standards for the maintenance of equipment and liability for injuries. Texas is home to several large, corporate amusement parks and hosts scores of traveling parks. In light of highly publicized accidents and deaths, the legislature followed the leads of many states in increasing the regulation of amusement parks, though most senate Republicans opposed the bill.

Several important patterns and a few peculiarities are revealed in this longitudinal examination of roll-call votes. First, as in the analysis of the legislative session 1997, it is shown that black members tend to vote together in most cases. White Democrats also demonstrate this tendency in both the house and the senate. White Republicans in the house, on the bills surveyed here, split their votes more often than the other groups. White Republicans in the senate voted together approximately two-thirds of the time. These findings are consistent with the accepted assessments of voting patterns.

The bills in this study were loosely categorized to demonstrate patterns over time. Attempts to predict voting behavior based solely on these categorizations would be erroneous. A more comprehensive study would attempt to categorize and examine bills in more detail. For example, the initiation of bills, that is, who sponsors and promotes pieces of legislation, is very important. An examination of the perceived impact of legislation is also significant. It would also be useful to look at those pieces of legislation that appear to have a clear impact on black votes and constituencies—funding of historically black institutions of higher education, reinstatement of voting rights, and location of waste sites, for example.

CONCLUSIONS

This initial research on the TLBC indicates that the caucus does express solidarity as measured by voting cohesion. However, the number of African Americans elected since 1981 has remained very stable. In fact, the total number of black house members only increased by one member in 1999. The finding in the senate was similar. African American membership increased from zero to two.

A link between solidarity and the achievement of favorable outcomes has also been found. This finding is interesting in light of Wiggins, Hamm, and Bell's (1992) assessment of party strength in Texas. They suggest that party unity (cohesion) is quite weak in Texas. This analysis demonstrated strong voting cohesion within the caucus and highlights the need for further comparative study between the TLBC and the Texas legislature.

Despite its small numbers, the TLBC, when it votes as a bloc, does have a greater chance of success. It can then be inferred that the TLBC has enjoyed a relatively high level of success in influencing policy in the state. However, it will be necessary to examine more closely those motions connected to bills that come from the TLBC's agenda and make more comparisons between the caucus and other subgroups of the legislature to verify this supposition.

In addition, recent procedural changes force all caucuses to meet at times and places outside of the legislature. However, these same obstacles could provide additional opportunities for the caucus. For example, the long periods between sessions could be used to develop and refine an agenda for the next session. Assessments of constituency needs could be done at this time as well. The break could also be used to develop and reinforce relationships with other legislators. Given the geographic size of the state, low compensation, biennial sessions, and workloads, some incentive would likely be necessary to coordinate and implement this additional work.

Because the TLBC has not been as thoroughly considered in research as other Southern state black caucuses, there are numerous avenues for definition, comparison, and interpretation. For example, the Hispanic Caucus is more diverse, at least in terms of party. It would be useful to make comparisons of voting solidarity between its members, the TLBC, and with both groups across "race-focused" legislation. Another avenue of investigation could involve an examination of record votes to address the question of whether votes of caucus members demonstrate a similar level of solidarity found in this study when looking at individual bills or across issue areas. In addition, legislative sessions could be compared.

As advised by Jones (2000), the majority of scholarly research on legislative behavior tends to "make assumptions that do not pertain to African American state legislators" (p. 743). This lack of distinction in assessing the impact of African Americans in state legislative decision making undermines the ability to make sound comparisons and to offer reasoned suggestions that may enhance the positive impact of legislative black caucuses on their constituencies. Clearly, as more African Americans gain membership in state legislatures, more specific attention to their agenda-setting abilities, voting behavior, consensus-building efforts, and the like is increasingly important.

NOTES

1.   The Voting Rights Act of 1965 states that it is intended to redress the historical vestiges of the political disenfranchisement of African Americans that played an important part in the creation and maintenance of the United States' sociopolitical system. Specifically, the act was an attempt to end the use of literacy tests as a prerequisite for voting in six Southern states—Alabama, Georgia, Louisiana, Mississippi, South Carolina, and Virginia.

2.   See Brewer (1935). "Negro" legislators went from a high of fourteen in the state house to two in 1883, and no African Americans were reelected to the senate until Barbara Jordan in 1966.

3.   See Brewer (1935). These printed campaign pamphlets stressed the importance of the white vote while emphasizing the negative results that would come about from a majority black vote.

4.   See Brewer (1935) for a thorough description of the role of nation-centered politics in the election of black representatives in Texas.

5.   Jordan's contribution to African Americans, women and law is briefly chronicled in Barker and Jones (1994). See Jeffrey (1997) and Rogers (1998) for extensive biographical records of her contributions to Texas and U.S. politics.

6.   See Tables 6.4 and 6.5.

7.   Lamare (1998) describes the process of reapportionment in Texas and equates it to gerrymandering, which he defines as "the practice of drawing districts to improve or harm the electoral chances of certain groups" (p. 73). This definition neglects the complexities of the need to redress past inequities. Many would argue that this definition overlooks historical disadvantages associated with the disenfranchisement of African Americans and other minorities. According to Lamare, in the Texas case, Democrats were the clear winners. However, recent federal court rulings may swiftly undermine any advantage the Democrats might have had.

8.   Donald G. Nieman (1990), in "Black Political Power and Criminal Justice: Washington County, Texas, 1868–1884," provides an extensive case study of arrest, jury selection, trial, and conviction of black and white citizens. Nieman suggests that African Americans "played a prominent role on the counties juries (p. 398)," although conviction rates were higher and punishments were much more severe for African Americans.

Chapter 7

An Overview of African American Representation in Other Southern States

Charles E. Menifield, Stephen D. Shaffer, and Brandi J. Brassell

INTRODUCTION

Our case study analyses in the previous five state-focused chapters have shown quite clearly the progress that has been made regarding African American representation in some Southern states. The purpose of this chapter is to briefly overview African American representation in the remaining states that make up the South. These include Alabama, Louisiana, North Carolina, South Carolina, Tennessee, and Virginia. We will plot the growth of numbers of African Americans in both chambers of each state's legislature from 1980 to 2000, analyze committee leadership in 2000, and provide background information on the Black Caucus in each state.

ALABAMA

The state of Alabama is one of five Southern states whose black population equals or exceeds 25% of the total population (Menifield and Jones 2001). Yet it is also one of the Deep South states whose white political leadership has historically been particularly unresponsive to the interests of African Americans. In a 1980 study of state senate voting in three Deep South states, Mary Herring (1990) found that only in Alabama were the votes of white senators on issues of interest to blacks unaffected by the size of the black population in the senate district. She concluded that "In Alabama, white accommodation to black political power was much slower in coming" (p. 751).

Alabama has 140 members in its state legislature, 105 in the house and 35 in the senate. Though Democrats have continually controlled both chambers since Reconstruction, the Democratic super majority in both houses has gradually decreased since 1958 (Stanley 2003). Members of both chambers serve four-year terms. The office of legislator in Alabama is unique in that the term begins on the day after the election and expires on the day after the election four years later (see the Web site http://www.legislature.state.al.us).

As in the Deep South state of Mississippi, tremendous change has occurred in the adjacent state of Alabama. As seen in Table 7.1, the number of African Americans in the house and senate more than doubled from 1980 to 2000. The eras of the early 1980s and the early 1990s saw the greatest increases. The number of African American senators doubled, and the number of black representatives rose by nearly 50% from 1980 to 1985. After stabilizing, African American representation rose again from 1990 to 1995, increasing by 50% or more in both chambers. Since then, African American representation in the state legislature has remained steady, with black lawmakers comprising about one-fourth of each legislative chamber. Thus African American numerical strength in the Alabama state legislature by the turn of the century paralleled the percentage of African Americans in the state population.

The Alabama Legislative Black Caucus (ALBC) meets weekly. There is a house Black Caucus and a senate Black Caucus, and the ALBC chairmanship rotates each year between the two houses. In addition, the caucus maintains a treasurer.

Tremendous change has occurred in the ability of African American lawmakers to achieve leadership positions within both legislative chambers. State Senator Michael A. Figures was overwhelmingly elected president pro tempore

TABLE 7.1
African Americans in the Alabama State Legislature

	House		Senate			
	#	% of House	#	% of Senate	Total #	%
1980	13	12.4	2	5.7	15	10.7
1985	19	18.1	5	14.3	24	17.1
1990	18	17.1	5	14.3	23	16.4
1995	27	25.7	8	22.9	35	25.0
2000	27	25.7	8	22.9	35	25.0

Source: Various issues of *Black Elected Officials: A National Roster*, Joint Center for Political and Economic Studies, http://www.jointcenter.org.

of the senate in 1995 by his colleagues, briefly making him the highest-ranking African American in state government. Upon his death in 1996, his wife Vivian finished his unexpired senate term and has been reelected in her own right. To honor his memory, she established the Michael A. Figures Legacy Education Fund to assist deserving Alabama students through a Leadership Experience program for rising ninth-grade students and a scholarship program. This education fund also sponsors the Helping School Tags program, whereby Alabamians can request a special car tag whose proceeds go to fund the public schools (see the Web site http://www.helpingschoolstags.com/fund.asp). Another important African American legislative leader has been Demetrius C. Newton, who has served as speaker pro tempore of the house since 1999. An attorney for the city of Birmingham, Newton served as a past president of the Birmingham Urban League and has received the Outstanding Lawyer and Outstanding Legislator awards from prominent interest groups (see the Web site www.legislature.state.al.us).

African Americans have also acquired the power to chair notable committees in both legislative chambers, thereby shaping the nature of contemporary public policy (see Table 7.2). In 2000, black lawmakers chaired six of the twenty-four standing committees in the house, leading one-fourth of the chamber's committees, a level of representation paralleling the proportion of African Americans in the state population and in the chamber as a whole. African

TABLE 7.2

Black Committee Chairs and Vice Chairs in the Alabama Legislature, 2000

Senate Chairs	House Chairs
Clay, Health	Clark, Boards and Commissions
Figures, Local Legislation 3	Ford, Local Legislation
Figures, Education	Hilliard, State Government
Langford, Tourism and Marketing	Jackson, Agr., Forestry, & Natural Resources
McClain, Confirmations Comm.	Kennedy, Education
McClain, Local Legislation 2	Knight, Government Finance and Appropriations
Sanders, Finance and Taxation Education	
Steele, Industrial Dev't & Recruitment	
Smitherman, Judiciary	
Senate Vice Chairs	House Vice Chairs
Clay, Banking and Insurance	Bandy, Local Legislation
Clay, Tourism and Marketing	Baker, Health
Figures, Veterans & Military Affairs	Perdue, Judiciary
McClain, Health	Rogers, Education, Finance and Appropriations

Source: Legislative staff; http://www.legislature.state.al.us.

Americans also chaired nine of twenty-four standing committees in the senate, leading a very impressive 38% of state senate committees. Most notable among these assignments were the Education Committees in both houses and the Government Finance and Appropriations Committee in the house. At the turn of the century, there were eight African American vice chairs, four in each house. The opportunity for African Americans to achieve such notable legislative leadership positions is undoubtedly enhanced by the persistent Democratic Party control of the legislature.

Despite progress made by African American lawmakers in Alabama, individual legislators continue to experience some frustrations. Most Black Caucus members of the Alabama house opposed a constitutional convention to rewrite the state's 1901 constitution. As in the Mississippi case of unsuccessful constitutional reform, they feared that African Americans would not be fully involved in the convention and would lose some of the political advances made in recent decades (see the Web site http://www.constitutionalreform.org/news/bham_032202.html). One Black Caucus member, Representative Johnny Ford, became so frustrated with the legislative process that he switched to the Republican Party in 2003 after being reelected as a Democrat. Blasting the Democratic-controlled legislature as being "controlled by special interest" and by powerful committee chairs who could prevent bills from even being voted on, Ford had supported Republican Bob Riley's election as governor in 2002. Joining the "party of Abraham Lincoln," Ford promised to be a "new breed of independent Republicans" and Democrats who would cross party and racial lines to work with the Republican governor, do the "people's business," and make Alabama a "world class state" (see the Web site http://www.voternewsnetwork.com/VNN/newsletters/march403.html).

LOUISIANA

The state of Louisiana is another Deep South state that has a high percentage of African Americans, but its unique culture of a populist history (reflected in Governor Huey P. Long), a large urban population (New Orleans particularly), and a significant Catholic population introduced a more moderate tone to the strident segregation found in other Deep South states. Indeed, a study of roll-call votes in the 1977 lower chambers of Louisiana and two other Southern states found that white lawmakers were more likely to vote in agreement with African Americans in Louisiana than in South Carolina or Texas (Harmel, Hamm, and Thompson 1983). Despite some cooperation between the two races in the

Louisiana state legislature in the late 1970s, these authors found that African American lawmakers remained more distinctive than white legislators, as blacks were significantly more likely to be in agreement among themselves on roll-call votes than were whites likely to be cohesive in their own votes.

Louisiana is second only to Mississippi regarding the percentage of African Americans in the population. In 2000, 32.2% of the state's population was African American (King-Meadows and Schaller 2001). While blacks remain an important component of the state's political map, the fortunes of the party backed by the great majority of African Americans have declined somewhat. Although Democrats control both houses of the legislature by large margins, these margins have declined fairly steadily in both houses since 1968, when there were no Republicans in the legislature. In addition, the percentage of voters registering as Democrats dropped from 98.6% in 1960 to 59.9% in 2000. Similarly, residents registering as Republicans increased from 0.9% in 1960 to 22.2% in 2000 (Parent and Perry 2003). Louisiana has a thirty-nine-member senate and a 105-member house. Members in both chambers serve four-year terms and are elected in the year before a presidential election.

Ernest "Dutch" Morial, a New Orleans lawyer, was the first African American elected to serve in the house since Reconstruction. He was elected in 1968 and shortly thereafter resigned from the post to become a juvenile court judge in New Orleans. Dorothy Mae Taylor, a New Orleans community leader, was elected to fill his unexpired term in 1971. She was the first African American woman elected to serve in the Louisiana state legislature. The Louisiana Legislative Black Caucus was officially established in 1977 with ten founding members. The mission of the organization has always been to "raise the quality of life for individuals living in impoverished Louisiana communities through education and economic development initiatives" (see the Web site http://www.legis.state.la.us/llbc/history&.htm, p. 3). One of its most important accomplishments was to fight for reapportionment legislation in 1983 and 1990 that increased the number of majority black legislative districts. Recent events sponsored by the Black Caucus have included a community outreach tour in 2000, where black legislators met with constituents at schools, universities, health care centers, and churches across the state, and a 2001 Economic Development Conference, entitled "Empowering People to Do Business," where current and aspiring business owners could gain valuable information (press releases, Office of Public Information, Louisiana House of Representatives, and Louisiana Legislative Black Caucus). Currently, all thirty-one African Americans in the house and senate are members of the caucus (see the Web site http://www. legis.state.la.us/llbc/history&.htm).

TABLE 7.3
African Americans in the Louisiana State Legislature

	House		Senate			
	#	% of House	#	% of Senate	Total #	%
1980	10	9.5	2	5.1	12	8.3
1985	14	13.3	4	10.3	18	12.5
1990	15	14.3	5	12.8	20	13.9
1995	22	21.0	8	20.5	30	20.8
2000	22	21.0	9	23.1	31	21.5

Source: Various issues of Black Elected Officials, Joint Center for Political and Economic Studies, http://www.jointcenter.org.

As in other Southern states, there has been a significant increase in African American legislative representation over the past two decades. Starting from relatively modest numbers in 1980, the numbers of black lawmakers doubled in the senate and rose 40% in the house before temporarily leveling off in the late 1980s (see Table 7.3). An even more significant increase in sheer numbers occurred after 1990, when the numbers of African American lawmakers reached twenty-two in the house and eight in the senate. By 2000, African Americans comprised nearly 22% of Louisiana state legislators.

With the increase in descriptive representation in Louisiana, African American lawmakers have achieved some coveted institutional leadership positions. Louisiana's legislature elects a house speaker, a house speaker pro tempore, a senate president, and a senate president pro tempore. In 1984, Representative Joseph A. Delpit became the first African American to be elected speaker pro tempore of the Louisiana house, and in 1992, Representative Sherman N. Copelin Jr. became the second. Also in 1992, Senator Dennis Bagneris became the first African American elected president pro tempore of the Louisiana senate, a position to which he was reelected in 1996. In 1998, Bagneris was elected judge to the Fourth Circuit Court of Appeals in Louisiana (see the Web site http://www.legis.state.la.us/llbc/history&.htm). Thus began a temporary decline in African American leadership power, reflected in white males (of both political parties) occupying these four positions in 2003. After the 2003 elections, the Democratic-controlled legislature elected Democrats to all four positions, including two African American females to the pro tempore positions. Diana Bajoie, a state senator since 1991 and a state representative the previous fifteen years, was elected senate president pro tempore, and Sharon Weston Broome, a state representative since 1991, was elected house speaker pro tempore (see the

TABLE 7.4
Black Committee Chairs and Vice Chairs in the Louisiana Legislature, 2000

Senate Chairs	*House Chairs*
Bajoie, Joint Leg. Comm. on	Broome, Commerce
the Budget	Guillory, Health & Welfare
Tarver, Judiciary C	Pierre, House Executive Committee
Senate Vice Chairs	*House Vice Chairs*
None	Baylor, Insurance
	Curtis, Education
	Green, Civil Law & Procedure
	Hudson, Agriculture
	Hunter, Legislative Budgetary Control Council
	Murray, House Executive Committee
	Quezaire, Municipal, Parochial & Cultural Affairs
	Welch, Appropriations

Source: Louisiana Legislative Black Caucus: 2003 House and Senate Committees Fact Sheet, http://www.legis.state.la.us/llbc/history&.htm.

Web site http://www.legis.state.la.us). They were elected to these key posts after newly elected Democratic Governor Kathleen Blanco threw her support to them. Speaking at a Black Legislative Caucus breakfast before a football game between two historically black universities, the first female governor of Louisiana in history argued that "Diana and Sharon are skilled legislators who are widely admired and respected by their colleagues. I know that they will be effective advocates for the kind of change the voters endorsed on November 15" (Associated Press 2003).

African Americans who chaired committees in the Louisiana house and senate were few and far between compared to their counterparts in other Southern states. In 2000, African Americans chaired only two of the seventeen committees in the senate and did not serve as vice chairs of any committees. African Americans had slightly more representation in house committee leadership positions, chairing three of the chamber's seventeen committees and serving as vice chairs of several committees (see Table 7.4). After the 2003 elections, committees chaired by African Americans rose to four in each chamber, though none of these were major committees. In the senate, African Americans now chaired the Labor and Industrial Relations, Retirement, Local and Municipal Affairs, and Senate and Governmental Affairs Committees. In the house, African Americans chaired the Labor and Industrial Relations, the Municipal, Parochial, and Cultural Affairs, the Natural Resources, and the Transportation Committees (see the Web site http://www.legis.state.la.us).

NORTH CAROLINA

North Carolina is a more urbanized Rim South state, with approximately 8 million residents in 2000. Though not having as high of a percentage of African Americans as in the historically more race-obsessed Deep South states, a substantial 22% of the state population is African American. In the North Carolina general assembly, there were fifty members in the senate and 120 members in the house. Unlike the vast majority of other states, legislators in the house and senate serve only two-year terms, so frequent elections increase the potential for rapid political change to occur (see the Web site http://www.ncga.state.nc.us/House/House.html; see also King-Meadows and Schaller 2001). After Reconstruction, Democrats controlled both legislative chambers until the 1994 national Republican landslide, when the GOP won control of the state house. Democrats kept control of the state senate and in 1998 briefly regained control of the state house. The volatile nature of contemporary party politics was reflected in the parties being tied in the number of house seats after the 2002 elections (necessitating a co-speakership arrangement) and Democrats holding only a narrow majority in the senate (Shaffer, Pierce, and Kohnke 2000).

The North Carolina Legislative Black Caucus (NCLBC) did not take on real descriptive meaning until the mid-1980s, when the number of members more than tripled to sixteen. An important event was when the North Carolina legislature switched to single-member districts in 1983, which led to an immediate increase in the number of African American members in both houses (Sullivan 2000). The caucus officially began to operate in 1983, but it was not until 1986 that it was able to gain 501–3 c nonprofit status, which enhanced its ability to raise operating funds. Daniel Blue served as the first chair of the caucus and then rose to the house speaker position from 1990 to 1994. While the NCLBC does not have any racial qualifications for membership, it did reject the application of a white legislator whose districts had a large minority population. Apparently there was some doubt regarding his sincerity. In addition to a chair, the NCLBC also has a vice chair, treasurer, and secretary positions (Sullivan 2000).

As in other Southern states, there has been a dramatic increase in descriptive representation in the North Carolina general assembly. The number of African American lawmakers particularly increased in the 1980s, reflecting the institution of single-member districts. Table 7.5 shows that the number of African Americans elected to serve in the North Carolina house increased from only four in 1980 to fourteen in 1990. The number of senators tripled, from a low base of only one to three. While the redistricting effort following

TABLE 7.5
African Americans in the North Carolina General Assembly

	House		Senate			
	#	% of House	#	% of Senate	Total #	%
1980	4	3.3	1	2.0	5	2.9
1985	13	10.8	3	6.0	16	9.4
1990	14	11.7	3	6.0	17	10.0
1995	17	14.2	7	14.0	24	14.1
2000	17	14.2	7	14.0	24	14.1

Source: Various issues of Black Elected Officials, Joint Center for Political and Economic Studies, http://www.jointcenter.org.

the 1990 census had a large impact on most Southern states, it did not have quite as much overall impact on the North Carolina legislature. However, some effect was evident, as the number of black legislators in the house increased by three members, and African American numbers in the senate more than doubled. These increases allowed African Americans to gain the critical mass that they needed in order to substantively impact legislation. By the turn of the century, African Americans comprised a significant 14% of the state legislature.

African American lawmakers have achieved some notable institutional leadership positions in the North Carolina general assembly. With Democrats controlling both legislative chambers until the 1994 elections, Representative Daniel Blue, elected to the state house in 1981 and serving as the first chair of the NCLBC, assumed the top leadership position of house speaker in 1990. Milton Fitch, a state representative since 1985, served as house majority leader during the 1992–1994 sessions. Both African Americans lost their leadership positions after the Republicans won control of the state house in the 1994 elections (Sullivan 2000). Democrats continued to control the state senate, however, and after the 2002 elections, Democrats maintained a numerical tie with Republicans in the state house delegation. In the 2003–2004 session, each party in the house elected a speaker and a "leader," and all four occupants were white males. Two of the four Democratic whips were African Americans, however: Beverly Earle and Paul Miller. A more significant biracial Democratic leadership team was evident in the senate in the period 2003–2004, where Democrats held a majority of seats. African American Senator Charlie Smith Dannelly served as deputy president pro tempore along with a white male president pro tempore, while black Senator Jeanne Hopkins Lucas served as majority whip along with a white male majority leader (see the Web site http://www.ncga.state.nc.us/NCGAInfo/leadership.html).

When compared to all of the other Southern states, there are more African American committee chairs and vice chairs in the North Carolina house than in any other state. The primary reason for this is the sheer number of committees. In 2000, there were forty-nine house and twenty-three senate committees. In some cases, there were multiple chairs and vice chairs for the same committees. For example, there were eight appropriation committee chairs and eight vice chairs in the house. In addition, there were six house appropriation subcommittees. The total number of committee chairs was seventy-four in the house and twenty-eight in the senate. Such a large number of committees and co-chairs of important committees suggests one strategy whereby other Southern states can increase leadership opportunities for their African American lawmakers, as well as other legislators.

Table 7.6 shows that African Americans in 2000 held the chairmanships of three senate committees and twelve house committees. These assignments included the Ways and Means Committee in the senate, which was ranked fourth among power committees in the senate (Sullivan 2000). In the house, an African American served as one of the chairs of the Appropriations Committee, which was ranked as the most powerful committee in that chamber. In addition, black legislators chaired two appropriations subcommittees in the senate (by 2003, these appropriations subcommittees were officially listed as committees) and chaired three subcommittees in the house. It is also important to point out that in several of the committees and subcommittees in the house and senate, African American chairs played prominent roles in health and welfare, important issue concerns of black constituents. Lastly, African Americans in 2000 served as nine vice chairs of senate committees (plus one subcommittee) and as ten vice chairs of house committees (plus one subcommittee).

Previous studies have pointed out how many of these attributes of descriptive representation can affect the success of Black Caucus public policy goals in North Carolina and other states. In a study of the 1987 North Carolina legislative session, Cheryl Miller (1990) found that the Black Caucus could achieve some legislative successes by having its initiatives referred to committees chaired by African Americans and by forming coalitions with other lawmakers, particularly white Democrats. Miller also suggested that the size of the Black Caucus and its cohesiveness in voting were important factors in legislative success. In a study of roll-call voting in the 1997–1998 North Carolina and Maryland legislatures, King-Meadows and Schaller (2001) found that the NCLBC was very cohesive, particularly in the state senate. Even in the North Carolina house, Black Caucus members were more cohesive than a comparable group of white lawmakers (representing districts with at least a 20% black voting-age population)

TABLE 7.6
Black Committee Chairs and Vice Chairs in the North Carolina General Assembly, 2000

Senate Chairs	House Chairs
Dannelly, Ways & Means	Adams, Highway Safety
Jordan, Appropriations: Justice and	Blue, Small Business
Public Safety (Subcomm.)	Bonner, Preschool Elem., Secondary Ed.
Lucas, Children & Human Resources	(Subcomm.)
Martin, Appropriations, Health, and	Bonner, Election Laws & Campaign
Human Resources (Subcomm.)	Fin. Reform
Shaw, Transportation	Bonner, Univ. Board of Nomina. Comm.
	(Subcomm.)
	Braswell, Judiciary II
	Braswell, Tobacco Settlement
	Earle, Appr. Health and Human
	Services (Subcomm.)
	Earle, Welfare Reform
	Fitch Jr., State Parks and Properties
	Hardaway, Appropriations
	Hunter Jr., Children, Youth, and Families
	McAllister, Public Health
	Michaux, Pension and Retirement
	Wright, Committee on Health

Senate Vice Chairs	House Vice Chairs
Ballance, Public Justice & Safety	Adams, Welfare Reform
Ballance, Judiciary	Bonner, Local Government Reform II
Jordan, State and Local Government	Boyd-McIntyre, Technology
Lee, Appropriations, Higher Education	Boyd-McIntyre, Univ. Board of
(Subcomm.)	Nominating Comm. (Subcomm.)
Lee, Higher Education	Michaux, Judiciary II
Lee, Commerce & Transportation	Oldham, Pensions and Retirement
Martin, Children & Human Resources	Wainwright, Financial Institutions
Martin, Health Care	Wainwright, Insurance
Shaw, Information Technology	Womble, Cultural Resources
Shaw, Pension, Retirement, & Aging	Womble, Econ. Growth and Community Dev.
	Wright, Travel and Tourism

Note: Subcommittee chairs are noted in parentheses.

Source: http://www.ncga.state.nc.us/House/House.html. We also collected data from the staff currently serving the committees' offices.

on about three of four votes. In a study of the perceived "effectiveness" of law-makers, Haynie (2002) found that African American lawmakers were perceived as being more effective by lobbyists, journalists, and other lawmakers when an African American served in the key institutional leadership position of house speaker. Even before Representative Blue became speaker after the 1990 elections, however, Haynie found that the perceived effectiveness of black lawmakers had increased from 1983 to 1989, significantly reducing the gap in effectiveness between black lawmakers and white Democrats, the latter of whom in North Carolina were viewed as more effective lawmakers.

SOUTH CAROLINA

South Carolina is another Deep South state with a history of white opposition to the civil rights of African Americans. Indeed, its Democratic governor in 1948, Strom Thurmond, served as the presidential candidate of the controversial States Rights Party. South Carolina has the third largest African American population in the United States, with a populace about 30% black (Menifield and Jones 2001). The state's constitution has established a general assembly with 124 house members and forty-six senate members. All of the members today are elected from single-member districts. House members serve two-year terms, while senate members serve four-year terms. After Reconstruction, Democrats controlled the state legislature until the 1994 elections, when Republicans gained control of the state house and have maintained control since then. In the 2000 elections, Republicans also gained control of the state senate. South Carolina is therefore a unique Deep South state in its modern flirtation with Republicanism, unlike Alabama, Mississippi, and Louisiana, where the legislature remains under Democratic control (see Kuzenski 2003 for a study of Republican gains in South Carolina).

The South Carolina Legislative Black Caucus (SCLBC) was formally established in 1974. The caucus's number-one goal is "to bring together various segments of the community to inform the public of the need for governmental action to help solve the whole range of racial . . . problems" (Legette 2000, 849). In addition, the organization views itself as the voice of African Americans in the state. The organization works toward this goal with a formal committee system that is based on policy areas. Each committee is responsible for ascertaining the impact of proposed legislation on the black community. Every black lawmaker has been a member of the organization except Mary Miles, a representative from Calhoun County (Legette 2000).

As we have found in other Southern states, descriptive representation in the South Carolina legislature increased over the last two decades of the twentieth century. In 1980, fourteen house members were African Americans, but there were no black senators (see Table 7.7). Over the next twenty years, African American numbers increased in both legislative chambers, but at different times for each chamber. From 1980 to 1990, African American senators went

TABLE 7.7
African Americans in the South Carolina General Assembly

	House		Senate			
	#	% of House	#	% of Senate	Total #	%
1980	14	11.3	0	0	14	8.2
1985	16	12.9	4	8.7	20	11.8
1990	16	12.9	5	10.9	21	12.4
1995	24	19.4	7	15.2	31	18.2
2000	26	21.0	7	15.2	33	19.4

Source: Various issues of Black Elected Officials, Joint Center for Political and Economic Studies, http://www.jointcenter.org.

from zero to five, while house members saw a net increase of only two. The next ten years saw a net increase of only two African American senators, while the number of black house members rose by ten. By the turn of the century, African American lawmakers comprised about 19% of the state legislature, a percentage still significantly below the percentage of blacks in the state population.

In the 1977 house session, when there were only thirteen African American lawmakers, researchers found little difference in the effectiveness of white and black legislators. Hamm, Harmel, and Thompson (1983) found no significant differences between white and black legislators in South Carolina in the number of amendments or bills introduced, or in success in enacting bills. By the 1987–1988 legislative session, Legette's (2000) study suggested that the situation had become more difficult for African American lawmakers. When contrasted with a white comparison group, black lawmakers were found to introduce fewer bills and to enjoy less success in enacting them into law. After the defeat of a Black Caucus member for house speaker pro tempore in the early 1990s, in 1998 the caucus was able to elect one of its own as house Democratic minority leader, Gilda Cobb–Hunter (see Professor Robert E. Botsch's Web site at http://www.usca.edu/aasc/blackcaucus.htm). By 2003, with Republican control of both legislative chambers, all of the key institutional leadership positions were held by white males, including the house minority leadership post.

African American lawmakers have had difficulty acquiring desirable committee chairmanships regardless of the party controlling the legislature. Focusing on the 1970–1988 period, when Democrats controlled both chambers of the legislature, Legette (2000) found that only one African American served as chair of an "exclusive" committee, Representative Juanita M. White, who chaired the

TABLE 7.8
Black Committee Chairs and Vice Chairs in the South Carolina General Assembly,
2000

Senate Chairs	House Chairs
None	Brown, Medical, Military, Public & Municipal Affairs
Senate Vice Chairs	*House Vice Chairs*
None	J. Hines, 2nd Vice, Education and Public Works

Source: http://www.scstatehouse.net/html-pages/house2.html. Also, we interviewed several staff members of the Black Caucus.

Medical, Military, Public, and Municipal Affairs Committee. In the 1987–1988 session that Legette studied, African Americans served as chairs of two house committees: Invitations, and Operations and Management. As the Republicans have risen to control first one and now both chambers of the South Carolina state legislature, African Americans' hopes for committee leadership positions have remained bleak. As Table 7.8 shows, despite fourteen committees in the senate and eleven in the house in 2000, African Americans held none of the committee chairs or vice chairs in the senate and only one of the committee chairs and one vice chair in the house. By 2003, as the Republicans consolidated their control of both legislative chambers, every senate committee and all except two house committees were chaired by Republicans. Since all Black Caucus members were Democrats, this dashed African Americans' hopes for any committee chairmanships in the senate. Interestingly enough, on the house side, however, two African Americans served as committee chairs. Joe E. Brown served as chairman of Medical, Military, Public, and Municipal Affairs, and Mack T. Hines served as chairman of Interstate Cooperation (see the Web site http://www.scstatehouse.net).

TENNESSEE

Tennessee is a Rim South state, which like other Rim South states such as North Carolina and Virginia was not quite as preoccupied historically with opposing the civil rights movement as were the Deep South states. About one-sixth of the state population is African American, a significant proportion but nevertheless smaller than in the Deep South. Consequently, whites did not feel quite as great of a need to unify behind a single party, the old Democratic Party, to maintain white supremacy. Hence, the state enjoyed a more competitive two-party

TABLE 7.9
African Americans in the Tennessee General Assembly

	House		Senate			
	#	% of House	#	% of Senate	Total #	%
1980	9	9.1	3	9.1	12	9.1
1985	10	10.1	3	9.1	13	9.8
1990	10	10.1	3	9.1	13	9.8
1995	13	13.1	3	9.1	16	12.1
2000	13	13.1	3	9.1	16	12.1

Source: Various issues of Black Elected Officials, Joint Center for Political and Economic Studies, http://www.jointcenter.org.

system before the Deep South states did. Yet while the Republican Party has often held over 40% of the state legislative seats, it never was able to hold a majority of seats in either legislative chamber over the last three decades of the twentieth century studied (Shaffer, Pierce, and Kohnke 2000). Tennessee has a bicameral legislature with ninety-nine members in the house and thirty-three members in the senate. House members serve two-year terms, while senators serve four-year terms.

The Tennessee Black Caucus of State Legislators was established in 1975 after a retreat held by eight African American lawmakers the year before (Wright 2000). The primary goal of the organization is to address the needs of African Americans in the state. Since 1975, the caucus has used information from policy experts and eight task forces that focus on different subject areas. This information has been utilized in crafting the legislative agenda of the organization. Membership in the caucus is limited to African Americans serving in the legislature. In addition, former black legislators enjoy emeritus status. The caucus leadership positions include a chairman, vice chairman, treasurer, secretary, and chaplain. Each serves a two-year term (Wright 2000).

African Americans held 9% of state legislative seats in 1980, a respectable proportion given the relatively modest size of the African American population in the state. Given this significant base, the number of African American lawmakers has risen only slightly since 1980 (see Table 7.9). The number of African Americans has remained steady at three in the senate and increased by four members in the house. At the turn of the century, these sixteen African American lawmakers represented 12.1% of the entire legislative body.

Unlike some of the states in our study, African American lawmakers in Tennessee have enjoyed relative success in passing legislation. In a study of the

1987–1988 legislative session, Wright (2000) found that African American legislators were slightly more successful than a comparable sample of white legislators in passing their legislative proposals. African Americans passed 55.8% and 57.2% of their bills in 1987 and 1988, compared to 54.1% and 48.9% of the white lawmakers' legislation in the two years. She found a similar pattern of African American success in passing resolutions. Wright (2000) also found that African American legislators focused more on legislation providing substantive representation to constituents rather than on mere symbolic measures. Hence, their legislation dealt with such important issues as education, health care, economic development, crime, and juvenile problems.

Perhaps one explanation for African American success in legislative affairs in Tennessee has been the success of the Black Caucus in acquiring some key institutional leadership positions. Prior to 1988, African American lawmakers served as house Democratic caucus chairman and as senate Democratic caucus vice chairman (Wright 2000). African American Lois DeBerry from Memphis served as house majority whip and then rose to the number-two house leadership position of speaker pro tempore, which she still held in the 103rd General Assembly during the period 2003–2004. African Americans during this period also held three of the eight Democratic Party leadership posts in the house—majority caucus vice chairman, majority caucus secretary, and majority whip. African Americans in the 103rd general assembly held no chamber leadership positions in the senate, perhaps partly because of the more limited number of such positions. A white female held the speaker pro tem post, and four white males held the Democratic and Republican leader and caucus chairman positions (http://www.legislature.state.tn.us).

There were nine standing and three select committees in the senate and fourteen standing committees in the house in 2000. African Americans chaired two committees in the house and two in the senate. Such a modest number of chairs is nevertheless consistent with the smaller African American share of the population and of the legislative membership in Tennessee, compared to most other Southern states. African Americans gained more committee leadership positions during the 2003–2004 legislative session in the house, as Armstrong and Jones remained chairs of their committees, while African American Representatives John J. DeBerry Jr. and Larry J. Miller served as chairs of the Children and Family Affairs Committee and of the Calendar and Rules Committee, respectively. The senate side of the aisle in the 2003–2004 period saw no change in African American chairmanship of committees, though, with Ford and Harper retaining the committee chairs, as listed in Table 7.10 (see the Web site http://www.legislature.state.tn.us).

TABLE 7.10
Black Committee Chairs and Vice Chairs in the Tennessee General Assembly, 2000

Senate Chairs	*House Chairs*
Ford, General Welfare, Health & Human Resources	Armstrong, Health & Human Resources
	Jones, State and Local Government
Harper, Government Operations	
Senate Vice Chairs	*House Vice Chairs*
None	Bowers, Agriculture
	Turner, Consumer & Employee Affairs
	Miller, Calendar & Rules
	Pruitt, Health and Human Resources
	DeBerry Jr, Children and Family Affairs

Source: http://www.legislature.state.tn.us/. We also collected data from the current committees' offices.

VIRGINIA

By all measures, the state of Virginia is a Rim South state, having an African American population in 2000 of 20% (Menifield and Jones 2001). Unlike the Rim South state of Tennessee, though, by the turn of the century the Republicans held control of a majority of legislative seats in both chambers. Virginia has a bicameral general assembly with 100 seats in the house of delegates and forty in the senate. Members serve two-year terms in the house and four year-terms in the senate, and they are elected in odd-numbered years. The assembly meets for thirty days beginning in January in odd-numbered years and for sixty days in even-numbered years.

With only three African Americans serving in the general assembly until the late 1970s, members interacted only informally. Dr. William Ferguson Reid led this informal grouping of black members, and he also became the first African American to chair a standing committee in the legislature (Clemons and Jones 2000). In the 1980s, an increasing number of blacks were elected to the legislature because of the adoption of single-member districts in 1982 and the inspiration of the Jesse Jackson presidential bid in 1984. Hence, Clemons and Jones report that the Virginia Black Legislative Caucus (VBLC) was officially formed in 1988.

The VBLC is restricted to Democratic legislators. Its main objective is to represent the interests of African Americans in the state population and to protect the interests of those unable to protect themselves, such as the disabled, children, the poor, and the disadvantaged (Clemons and Jones 2000, p. 755). The caucus follows a standard set of officers in its hierarchy, including a chairperson, vice chairperson, and treasurer. Clemons and Jones (2000) indicate that the caucus, given the small number of members and limited budget, did not

TABLE 7.11
African Americans in the Virginia General Assembly

	House		Senate			
	#	% of House	#	% of Senate	Total #	%
1980	4	4.0	1	2.5	5	3.6
1985	5	5.0	2	5.0	7	5.0
1990	7	7.0	3	7.5	10	7.1
1995	8	8.0	5	12.5	13	9.3
2000	10	10.0	5	12.5	15	10.7

Source: Various issues of Black Elected Officials, Joint Center for Political and Economic Studies, http://www.jointcenter.org.

employ an elaborate committee system or task force system to enhance legislative effectiveness.

There has been a slow but steady increase in the number of African American lawmakers in Virginia. Table 7.11 shows how the number of black lawmakers doubled from five in 1980 to ten in 1990, though African Americans still held only 7% of all legislative seats in 1990. By 2000, African Americans gained three more house seats and two more senate seats to comprise close to 11% of the entire legislative membership. This level of descriptive representation is nevertheless barely half of the percentage of African Americans in the state population.

Perhaps the high point of African American influence in institutional leadership was when an African American, Douglas Wilder, served as lieutenant governor of Virginia. In Virginia, as in many states, the lieutenant governor serves as president of the upper legislative chamber. Wilder had served as a state senator from 1970 through 1985, whereupon he was elected lieutenant governor in 1985 and governor in 1989. Despite his service as senate president during the 1987–1988 legislative session, intensively analyzed by Clemons and Jones (2000), these researchers found that blacks chaired none of the committees in the legislature, and that African American lawmakers were less successful than their white counterparts in passing their bills. African Americans' leadership hopes may have become even more bleak in recent years with the capture of both legislative chambers by the Republicans. In 2003, for instance, whites occupied all seven of the key institutional leadership positions of the general assembly. In the house of delegates, the speaker, majority, and minority leaders were all white males. In the senate, white males served as president pro tempore and majority and minority leaders, and a white female served as Democratic caucus chair (see the Web site http://legis.state.va.us).

TABLE 7.12
Black Committee Chairs and Vice Chairs in the
Virginia General Assembly, 2000

Senate Chairs	*House Co-Chairs*
None	Jones, Chesapeake and Its Tributaries
	Christian, Militia and Police
	Robinson Jr., Transportation
Senate Vice Chairs	*House Vice Chairs*
None	Position did not exist in 2000

Source: State of Virginia Senate Legislative Information Office and House Legislative Information Office and Public Relations, http://legl. state.va.us/001/com/COM.HTM.

Virginia had eleven standing committees in the senate and fourteen in the house in 2000. There were no African American committee chairs or vice chairs in the Virginia senate in 2000. However, Yvonne Miller had been chair of the Rehabilitation and Social Services Committee from 1996 to 1999. Committee power was shared in the house in 2000 with a co-chair system existing without vice chairs. African Americans served as co-chairs for three committees in 2000. As Table 7.12 indicates, these included the Chesapeake and Its Tributaries, Militia and Police, and Transportation Committees. The Chesapeake and Its Tributaries Committee was disbanded when the session ended. Republican consolidation of both chambers of the general assembly ended even these limited African American leadership opportunities. After the 2003 elections, all eleven senate committees were chaired by Republicans, as were thirteen of the fourteen committees in the house (one chair was an Independent). Therefore, not one African American served as a committee chair in either legislative chamber (see the Web site http://legis.state.va.us).

CONCLUSION

African Americans have made significant increases in descriptive representation in the state legislatures of the six states examined in this chapter. In the last two decades of the twentieth century, the proportion of state legislators who were African American at least doubled in every state except Tennessee. Tennessee saw more modest gains, only because African Americans were better represented in its state legislature, relative to the black presence in the state population, than in other state legislatures in 1980. Indeed, twenty years before the turn of the century, the highest proportion of black lawmakers in any legislative chamber was only 12% in the Alabama house, and the lowest was zero in the South Carolina

TABLE 7.13
Representation of Black Legislators in the Modern South

	1980			2000		
State/Chamber	Populace (% black)	Members (% black)	Gap (in %)	Populace (% black)	Members (% black)	Gap (in %)
ALAB/House	26	12	−14	26	26	0
ALAB/Senate	26	6	−20	26	23	−3
LA/House	29	10	−19	32	21	−11
LA/Senate	29	5	−24	32	23	−9
N.C./House	22	3	−19	22	14	−8
N.C./Senate	22	2	−20	22	14	−8
S.C./House	30	11	−19	30	21	−9
S.C./Senate	30	0	−30	30	15	−15
TENN/House	16	9	−7	17	13	−4
TENN/Senate	16	9	−7	17	9	−8
VIR/House	19	4	−15	20	10	−10
VIR/Senate	19	3	−16	20	13	−7

Source: Population percentages that are African American are from the text or from the Web site http:// quickfacts.census.gov/qfd/. The percentage of African American legislators is from the text. The gap columns reflect the extent to which the chamber membership that is African American is below the percentage of the population that is black.

senate. Except for Tennessee, African Americans were therefore underrepresented in double digits, ranging from a 14% underrepresentation gap in the Alabama house to a 30% gap in the South Carolina senate. Tremendous change swept over these Southern state legislatures in the last twenty years of the century, as the increased numbers of African Americans serving in the legislatures reduced the underrepresentation gap for blacks in eleven of the twelve legislative chambers (see Table 7.13).

The Deep South state of Alabama made particularly impressive strides in descriptive representation, so by 2000, African Americans were represented in the state house in proportion to the black presence in the population and underrepresented in the senate by only 3%. The South Carolina senate also saw dramatic change, though the underrepresentation gap remained in double digits. Except for the state houses in Louisiana and Virginia, by 2000, the underrepresentation gap between black lawmakers and the African American population in the Southern states studied had fallen into single digits. Though African Americans remained underrepresented relative to the black presence in the state populations in every legislative chamber except the Alabama house, the size of the legislative Black Caucuses in each state had now grown to become a force to be reckoned with.

TABLE 7.14
Representation of Black Legislators in the Modern South in Committee
Chairmanships 2000

State/Chamber	Members (% black)	Comm. Chrs. (% black)	Gap (in %)
ALAB/House	26	25	−1
ALAB/Senate	23	38	+15
LA/House	21	18	−3
LA/Senate	23	12	−11
N.C./House	14	16*	+2
N.C./Senate	14	11*	−3
S.C./House	21	9	−12
S.C./Senate	15	0	−15
TENN/House	13	14	+1
TENN/Senate	9	22	+13
VIR/House	10	11*	+1
VIR/Senate	13	0	−13

Note: The first column indicates the proportion of African Americans legislators. The second column indicates the proportion of African American committee chairs. The gap column reflects the extent to which the percentage of committee chairs that is African American is below the percentage of the chamber's membership that is African American.

* In North Carolina, the denominator in column two reflects the existence of multiple chairs for various committees. In Virginia, the denominator reflects the existence of a co-chair arrangement in 2000.

The situation regarding the extent to which African Americans have achieved descriptive representation regarding legislative leadership positions, such as institutional or party leadership posts or committee chairmanships, is more unclear, and it varies by state and over time (see Table 7.14). An important prerequisite for African Americans to gain leadership positions has been descriptive representation gains in the legislative membership as a whole. In 2000, the proportion of committee chairs held by African Americans was within 5% of the African American share of state legislative seats in both chambers of the North Carolina legislature and the lower chambers of Alabama, Louisiana, Tennessee, and Virginia. African American lawmakers faced double-digit disadvantages (relative to their share of the entire membership) in chairmanships of both legislative chambers of South Carolina and of the senates of Louisiana and Virginia, though they enjoyed double-digit advantages in the senates of Alabama and Tennessee.

As with the case of descriptive representation in numbers of African American lawmakers, there are no consistent differences between Deep and Rim South states in African American leadership posts. African American gains in leadership positions have been most notable in the Deep South state of Alabama and the Rim South state of North Carolina. African Americans currently hold the leadership posts in North Carolina of senate deputy president pro tempore, senate majority whip, two house Democratic whips and in Alabama of house speaker pro tempore. In Alabama, African Americans hold as many house committee chairmanships as their size in the state house warrants, and even more representation than numbers warrant in the senate. Black lawmakers also hold a significant number of committee chairmanships in North Carolina, proportional to the size of the Black Caucus in the legislature.

African Americans' hopes for leadership positions in Louisiana and Tennessee are also relatively positive. Black lawmakers have risen to some key institutional and party leadership posts in both states. In Louisiana, African American lawmakers have historically served as senate president pro tempore and house speaker pro tempore, positions currently held by two black females. In Tennessee, African Americans have been particularly successful in acquiring house leadership posts and currently serve as house speaker pro tempore, majority whip, majority caucus vice chairman, and majority caucus secretary. Though chairing a limited number of legislative committees in both states, those numbers are in line with the size of the Black Caucus in the lower chambers of both states. Descriptive representation of African Americans holding committee chairs varies in the state senates across these two states and over time, however.

African Americans' leadership hopes appear to be most bleak in the Deep South state of South Carolina and the Rim South state of Virginia. Few African Americans have chaired committees in these state legislatures, and with the Republican Party gaining control of these legislative chambers in recent years, descriptive representation of black lawmakers in leadership positions appears increasingly low. Though African Americans at one time served as lieutenant governor and president of the Virginia senate and as house minority leader of South Carolina, today the top institutional and party leadership positions in all four state legislative chambers are occupied by whites. The scarcity of African American leadership opportunities with the advent of Republican Party control of these Southern state legislatures suggests two possible strategies for the African American community. Black political leaders may wish to compromise more with white Democratic lawmakers and defer to their political instincts in an effort to prevent the election of Republican state legislators. The other possibility is to encourage more African Americans who are moderate or conservative in their political philosophy to run for legislative office as Republicans. Hence, African Americans would have the chance of rising to leadership positions not just in the Democratic Party but potentially in the Republican Party as well.

Chapter 8

Politics in the New South:
Looking Ahead

Charles E. Menifield, Stephen D. Shaffer, and Barbara A. Patrick

History has shown that the South not only has a different social culture but a different political culture as well. It has been well documented that the South was the last region in the country to enfranchise African American voters despite federal legislation ensuring these rights decades earlier. This history, and the potential for change, was the main catalyst for not only this research but also for the efforts of many other scholars. Today the states that make up the Deep South continue to have the largest percentage of African Americans in the country. This fact alone has made the region an interesting case study, given the turbulent transition of enfranchising African Americans in the mid-to-late 1960s and the subsequent election of African Americans to public office in large numbers. While our study has primarily centered on five Southern state legislatures, the implications of our analysis can, to a certain extent, be generalized to legislative bodies in non-Southern states.

The main goal of our research was to examine changes in the number of African American legislators and the nature of legislative coalition formations primarily during the last two decades of the twentieth century with respect to African Americans in the South. We chose this time period for two main reasons. First, book-length research analyzing this particular area of African American politics in the South from a broad state legislative level perspective has lagged since the mid-1980s. Thus our objective was to assess change since that period. Second, we concluded that black legislators are a major source of legislation that would prove beneficial to African Americans. Particularly, we posited that African Americans are a major source of redistributive legislation. However, since African American legislators do not constitute the majority of elected officials in any state general assembly, other alternatives to securing the passage of beneficial legislation were considered. These included committee and leadership assignments and legislative coalitions. With those items in mind, our co-authors considered a number of key questions in each chapter.

1. What is the election trend of African Americans?
2. Are African Americans aligned with the Democratic Party?
3. Are African Americans securing leadership positions?
4. Are African Americans chairing committees? If so, what kinds of committees?
5. What has been the impact of the African American presence on different types of key legislation?
6. Are African Americans united within their individual caucuses?
7. Do African American legislators form coalitions with other groups?
8. If so, do these coalitions change when different types of legislation are considered?
9. Are these coalitions permanent?

In addressing each of these questions, we grounded our research primarily in the pioneering work of Hannah Pitkin (1967). Using her representation models, we examined legislative representation from a descriptive and substantive perspective. Descriptive representation is grounded in the belief that a voter should cast her or his vote for someone who possesses demographic characteristics consistent with her or his individual characteristics. This model of representation essentially attempts to maximize the number of minority representatives without much regard for the policy implications (Mansbridge 1999). Unfortunately, this form of symbolic representation has not meant much in terms of redistributive economics in the South or in any other region. While descriptive representation has merit, we as well as other scholars note the limitations of this model (Swain 1993; Whitby 1997; Endersby and Menifield 2000).

Substantive representation espouses the view that it is important for legislators to be responsive to the legislative needs of their constituents and to be able to secure policies that are beneficial to those constituents. Swain (1993) argued that the race of the candidate is not as important as one may perceive when the makeup of the district is considered. She argued that white Democrats in Congress were much more likely to support legislation that was beneficial to African Americans than were Republicans. In addition, she found that white Democrats who had large Africans American constituencies were doing a credible job of representing their constituents.

At minimum, our research has shown that the number of African Americans elected to state assemblies did indeed increase in the last two decades of the twentieth century. In addition, we found that African Americans have made some inroads into the leadership and committee hierarchy and have formed nonpermanent coalitions with other groups in order to shape legislation. Their efforts have primarily hinged on the ability of Democrats to maintain control of the assembly. As previously mentioned, nearly every African American state legislator in each of these case studies is a member of the Democratic Party. This fact, however, has not prevented African Americans from, on occasion, forming coalitions with white Republicans in order to shape legislation.

DESCRIPTIVE REPRESENTATION

African Americans have made progress in terms of descriptive representation in Southern state legislatures, both in membership in legislative bodies and in rising to leadership positions such as committee chairmanships. In the early 1980s, the African American proportion of the legislative chambers included in our study ranged from a low of zero in the Florida, South Carolina, and Texas senates to a high of 13% in the Georgia house (see Tables 8.1 and 7.13). By the

TABLE 8.1
Representation of Black Legislators in the Modern South

State/Chamber	Early 1980s			Late 1990s		
	Populace (% black)	Members (% black)	Gap (in %)	Populace (% black)	Members (% black)	Gap (in %)
AR/House	16	4	−12	16	12	−4
AR/Senate	16	3	−13	16	6	−10
FL/House	14	4	−10	15	13	−2
FL/Senate	14	0	−14	15	13	−2
GA/House	27	13	−14	29	18	−11
GA/Senate	27	4	−23	29	18	−11
MS/House	35	12	−23	36	29	−7
MS/Senate	35	4	−31	36	19	−17
TX/House	12	9	−3	12	9	−3
TX/Senate	12	0	−12	12	6	−6

Source: Population percentage of African Americans is from the U.S. census. The late 1990's population figures are for the 2000 census, available from the Web site: http://quickfacts.census.gov/qfd/. Percentage of state house and senate members who are African American is from the previous state chapters. The gap columns reflect the extent to which the chamber membership that is African American is below the percentage of black population.

close of the century, 13% of the Florida senate, 15% of the South Carolina senate, and 6% of the Texas senate were now African American, while the black membership of the Georgia house had further grown to comprise 18% of that body. However, Louisiana and Alabama had the highest percentages of African Americans in their senates, roughly 23% each.

The magnitude of change was dramatic in other states as well, as the proportion African American doubled in the Arkansas senate, more than doubled in the Mississippi, Virginia, and Louisiana houses, tripled in the Arkansas and Florida houses, and increased even more dramatically in the senates of Alabama, Louisiana, Mississippi, North Carolina, Virginia, and Georgia. With the exception of the Georgia and Mississippi houses, black legislators had started from such a small base of members in the 1980s that any improvement would have been noticeable. Nevertheless, by the turn of the century, the underrepresentation gap of African Americans, calculated by comparing the black proportion of legislative bodies with the black percentage of the state population, had decreased in each state and chamber (except for the Texas house, where the gap had previously been the smallest of the states studied, and the Tennessee senate). Indeed, Florida's African American legislative presence was within two percentages of the population value. Only the Mississippi senate, Georgia house and senate, and Arkansas senate saw a representation gap in double digits, as did the Louisiana and Virginia houses and the South Carolina senate (Menifield and Jones 2001).

These findings were consistent with the growth of African American congressmen during the same period. The most growth among these states came after 1990. More than likely, these increases were the result of legislative redistricting that sought to increase the number of majority-minority black districts (Menifield and Julian 2001). However, the rapid growth rate that occurred in the early 1990s has stabilized at not only the state level but the federal legislative level as well.

African Americans also have made progress in terms of legislative leadership positions. While the early 1980s saw African Americans with no committee chairmanships in six of the ten state legislative chambers examined in our study, by the turn of the century, black lawmakers were shut out of leadership positions in only one state (see Table 8.2). Dramatic change was evident in the Deep South states of Mississippi and Georgia, as the African American proportion of committee chairmanships went from zero to 17% in the Mississippi senate, more than tripled in the Mississippi house, and more than doubled in the Georgia senate. Black legislators went from being completely shut out of committee chairmanships in both Arkansas chambers in the early 1980s to comprise 6% of committee leaders by the late 1990s. The apparent absence of change in Florida, where there were no black chairs at the beginning and end of the period of

TABLE 8.2
Representation of Black Legislators in the Modern South in Committee Chairmanships

State/Chamber	Early 1980s			Late 1990s		
	Members (% black)	Comm. Chrs. (% black)	Gap (in %)	Members (% black)	Comm. Chrs. (% black)	Gap (in %)
AR/House	4	0	−4	12	6	−6
AR/Senate	3	0	−3	6	6	0
FL/House	4	0	−4	13	0	−13
FL/Senate	0	0	0	13	0	−13
GA/House	13	9	−4	18	12	−6
GA/Senate	4	9	+5	18	22	+4
MS/House	12	7	−5	29	23	−6
MS/Senate	4	0	−4	19	17	−2
TX/House	9	10	+1	9	11	+2
TX/Senate	0	0	0	6	7	+1

Source: Percentages are from the previous state chapters. The gap columns reflect the extent to which the percentage of committee chairs that is African American is below the percentage of the chamber's membership that is African American.

study, can be attributed to the Republican takeover of both chambers of the state legislature during the late 1990s. With legislative leadership positions in this competitive two-party state allocated through party-line votes, as is the case in the U.S. Congress, and with no African American lawmakers being Republican, black legislators clearly lost political power with the GOP legislative takeover.

Despite African American gains in committee leadership positions in Southern state legislatures, we should point out that the representation gap between the percentage of the legislative membership that was black and the proportion of chairs that was black was not very great at any point in our study. Even in the early 1980s, the greatest extent of African American underrepresentation in committee chairmanships was only 4–5% in the Mississippi senate and the lower chambers of Arkansas, Florida, Georgia, and Mississippi. Apparently, what has been most critical in promoting African Americans to committee leadership positions in the contemporary Southern state legislature is merely ensuring that a sufficient number of black lawmakers will be elected to office. With seniority and growing legislative experience, African Americans eventually become incorporated into the power structure of state legislatures, as do lawmakers of other races and ethnic groups. Two caveats should be mentioned, however. First, with the exception of a two-year period in Florida, African Americans have never chaired the highly important money committees (finance and appropriations) of any legislative chamber in our study. Second, as a competitive two-party system continues to emerge in Southern state legislative elections, and as Republicans continue to gain control of legislative chambers, African Americans run the risk of being completely shut out of legislative leadership positions, as has occurred in Florida.

SUBSTANTIVE REPRESENTATION—SOME REGIONAL PATTERNS

Substantive representation was studied through an examination of roll-call votes in five key states for black Democrats, white Democrats, and Republicans. A variety of different types of legislation was examined in each state, and to identify patterns that are general to all of the states, we classified each roll-call vote by type of issue area: abortion, crime, economics, education, government reform, health, welfare, and, more directly, race-relevant bills. The authors of this concluding chapter made the final determination of the issue categories in which each bill belonged, drawing on the information provided by the authors of each individual state chapter. The unit of analysis is the individual bill, examined separately for each legislative chamber (except where only one chamber voted on the bill). Roll-call votes where 90% or more of each of the three legislative groups voted in the same direction were excluded from the analysis. The total number of cases analyzed for all five states and for the twenty-year time period is 239, though on six of these bills the Black Caucus vote was split down the middle so that no caucus position could be ascertained.

A key question is whether African American Democrats have been very successful in being in the "winning" coalition of their legislative chamber, and what conditions affect the extent to which the Black Caucuses have been on the winning side. We define each group's (black Democrats, white Democrats, Republicans) position on a bill based on how a majority of that group's members voted on that bill, and the outcome of the bill as whether it passed in the legislative chamber. Victory is defined as a group supporting a bill that passed in the chamber, or opposing a bill that failed to pass in the chamber; defeat is supporting a bill that died, or opposing a bill that passed. On all roll-call votes examined in these five Southern states over the closing decades of the twentieth century, the Black Caucus was successful 71% of the time, a fairly impressive record given the segregationist history of these states. Since some of these measures were consensus measures backed by all three groups, we can gain greater insight into how successful the Black Caucuses really were by comparing their success level with white Democrats and Republicans. White Democrats were the most successful group, winning 95% of the time, but Republicans were less successful than black Democrats, winning only 62% of the time. One explanation for Republicans being the least successful group is that the Democratic party numerically controlled most Southern state legislatures most of the time (90% of the time). Yet the conservative Republican party ideology is probably more in line with the views of average Southerners than is the liberal ideology favored by most African American lawmakers, suggesting that the Black Caucus success level is more impressive than it might appear on the surface.

At first glance, why the success level of the Black Caucus varies across the states is unclear. One might have hypothesized that the Black Caucus would be most successful in Rim South states rather than in the Deep South, given the historic Deep South's greater preoccupation with the race question and its greater resistance to integration. Yet the Black Caucus's highest success rates are in Texas (96%) and Georgia (79%)—Rim and Deep South states—and its lowest success rates are in Arkansas (44%) and Florida (59%)—two Rim South states (see Table 8.3). One possible explanation for the Black Caucus's somewhat greater success level in Georgia than in Mississippi may be that Georgia has modernized and urbanized more rapidly than Mississippi, perhaps reducing the saliency of racial considerations to voters and legislators, thereby enhancing the Black Caucus's political power. Another explanation for inter-state differences is the variation in the mix of issues voted on. Potentially divisive issues such as crime and race comprised 43% of the bills examined in Mississippi, while comprising only 33% of bills considered in all five states. Why the Black Caucus is less successful in Arkansas than in other states is less clear. The debate over education issues appears to have been particularly divisive in Arkansas than in other states, and education bills comprised 32% of the bills examined in Arkansas relative to only 17% of the bills regionwide pertaining to education.

Regionwide, the success of the Black Caucus varies across different types of issues. African American Democrats are most successful on health, welfare, economic, and government reform issues. Measures such as popular health care issues presumably enjoy biracial support, while government reform issues and economic matters may enjoy Democratic Party support regardless of race (see Table 8.3). Illustrating how far the modern South has come from its segregationist history, the Black Caucus's success rate on race-related issues is slightly higher than its overall success rate. Its success is the lowest on potentially divisive issues such as abortion and crime, for reasons that shall soon be illuminated.

The conventional wisdom is that Black Caucus unity enhances its success level, but a contradictory hypothesis is that African American unity may be

TABLE 8.3
Correlates of Black Caucus Victory on Legislation

Predictor	Percentage of Time Black Caucus Is Victorious in Chamber Vote (%)	N Size
On all Bills	71	(233)
State:		
Arkansas	44	(27)
Florida	59	(34)
Georgia	79	(94)
Mississippi	67	(51)
Texas	96	(27)
Issue:		
Abortion	44	(16)
Crime	59	(41)
Economics	81	(36)
Education	62	(39)
Government reform	80	(25)
Health	84	(19)
Race	79	(34)
Welfare	83	(23)
Black Caucus Unity Level:		
Low	46	(48)
Medium	66	(59)
High	83	(126)

Source: Percentages are computed from the roll-call votes reported in the tables from the previous state chapters. A Black Caucus victory is defined as consistency between how a majority of voting African American Democrats voted on a bill and whether that bill passed in the legislative chamber.

counterproductive, as white lawmakers may feel threatened and therefore lash out against the caucus. Unity is defined as how close the African American roll-call vote is to homogeneity—either all members vote for or all against a bill. The unity scale score ranges from 0 for perfect disunity (a 50–50 split among African American Democrats) to 1 for perfect unity (all Black Caucus members voting for or all voting against a bill). When only three-fourths of African American Democrats vote the same way (a low unity score, when the scale is trichotomized), the Black Caucus is successful only 46% of the time. When all African American Democrats vote the same way (a high unity score on the trichotomized scale), the Black Caucus is successful 83% of the time. Hence, maintaining Black Caucus unity is one component of victory. And, indeed, African American Democrats usually vote in a fairly homogenous manner, with about 54% of votes being characterized by high unity scores for the Black Caucus, where all caucus members vote the same way.

As one might expect, the Black Caucus is most united on race-relevant issues (an average scale score of 89 for a scale whose mean is 78 on all issues). The caucus is least united on the divisive issues of crime (63) and abortion (67). While most African American lawmakers generally vote in a liberal direction even on these social issues, fearing that tough-on-crime measures will disproportionately and adversely affect young African American males while pro-life measures may particularly restrict the individual liberties of young black women, some entertain more conservative ideas. Representing majority black districts with growing black-on-black crime, some black lawmakers are as eager to resort to tough crime fighting measures to protect their law-abiding constituents as are white lawmakers. Given the importance of religion in the black community, some pro-life sentiment among African American lawmakers is also understandable. However, since Black Caucus unity tends to be related to caucus success, and caucus unity is lowest on the issues of abortion and crime, these divisions within the Black Caucuses of Southern legislatures may contribute to the caucus being least successful on the issues of abortion and crime.

Linking descriptive with substantive representation, one might expect that Black Caucus success will increase as the size of the Black Caucus increases and decrease as the number of Republicans (a conservative group, unlike the caucus) grows. Surprisingly enough, conventional wisdom was rejected in both cases. Black Caucus success was essentially unrelated to Black Caucus size, as the caucus won 72% of the time when its members comprised 15% or more of the chamber's voting members and won 69% of the time when its members comprised less than 8% of the voting members, a statistically insignificant difference in success level. One possible explanation is that caucus unity may decrease as its size increases, though the Pearson correlation coefficient between the African American percentage of the chamber's voting membership and the extent that the Black Caucus is united is essentially zero (a statistically insignificant −.002). Equally unexpected is the absence of a relationship between Black Caucus success and the size of the *Republican* membership. The Black Caucus is successful 73% of the time when the Republicans comprise over 38% of voting members, compared to a 65% success rate when Republicans comprise 23% of less of the voting members, a statistically insignificant difference in Black Caucus success. One possible explanation for this nonrelationship between the growing GOP membership and Black Caucus success is that a growing Republican Party presents a threat to the Democratic Party, forcing its members to unify regardless of their race. Indeed, the Pearson correlation coefficient for the relationship between the percentage of the voting legislators who are Republican in party membership and the existence of a party vote (a majority of black Democrats joining with a majority of white Democrats to oppose a majority of Republicans) is a statistically significant .158, indicating that a growing GOP caucus is related to a greater tendency for white and black Democrats to vote together in opposition to Republicans.

The emergence of an "unholy alliance" between African American lawmakers and Republicans to shape redistricting so that both groups gain members at the expense of white Democrats has been observed by both scholars and journalists. Such an alliance of ideological opposites occasionally emerges on state legislative roll-call votes, as discussed in each state chapter of our book. Yet one should not overemphasize the frequency or importance of this unique coalition. Regionwide, black Democrats are significantly more likely to vote with white Democrats than with Republicans. A majority of African American Democrats voted in agreement with a majority of white Democrats 75% of the time, while most black Democrats agreed with a majority of Republicans only 36% of the time. Furthermore, some of these bills were popular measures that received widespread support by all three groups of lawmakers.

Turning more explicitly to the coalitions that emerge on roll-call votes in Southern state legislatures, we build on Alexander Lamis's (1990, 1999) studies of electoral politics in the modern two-party states of the South. He points out the importance of Democrats' preserving their biracial coalition in order to defeat a growing Republican Party, and he recounts how some Republican candidates will play the race card in an effort to attract white Democrats away from Democratic Party candidates. We classify a roll-call vote where a majority of white Democrats votes the same way as a majority of black Democrats, with both groups in opposition to a majority of Republican lawmakers as a *party* coalition. Votes where a majority of white Democrats vote the same way as a majority of Republicans, with both groups in opposition to a majority of black Democrats, are referred to as *race* coalitions. As already noted, roll-calls where a majority of each of the three groups votes in the same direction are classified as *consensus* bills. An *unholy alliance* occurs when a majority of black Democrats and a majority of Republicans vote in the same direction, with both groups in opposition to a majority of white Democrats. Finally, any roll-call vote that produces an even split within any of these three groups of lawmakers is regarded as involving an issue that basically elicits an *individualistic* vote on the part of lawmakers. All of our roll-call votes regionwide can be classified into these five categories.

The most frequently emerging coalition in the contemporary Southern state legislatures is the party coalition, which occurs on 39% of the roll-call votes.

The second most common coalition, even after eliminating votes eliciting over 90% support for each of the three legislative groups, is the consensus vote, which emerges 31% of the time (see Table 8.4). Therefore, African American lawmakers today tend to find themselves part of a dominant coalition over two-thirds of the time, quite a change in a Southern society that had fought to prevent black citizens from even exercising the franchise a mere half century ago. Being part of such a dominant coalition was a key factor in producing Black Caucus victories. In the consensus situation, the Black Caucus's position prevailed 100% of the time, as expected, given the definition of this voting pattern, while situations eliciting party coalitions saw the Black Caucus victorious

TABLE 8.4
Coalition Formation in State Legislatures in the Modern South

| Condition | Coalition Type | | | | |
	Party (%)	Race (%)	Consensus (%)	Unholy Alliance (%)	Individualistic Vote (%)
All bills	39	21	31	3	6
State:					
Arkansas	14	39	18	11	18
Florida	38	16	32	3	11
Georgia	47	16	32	2	3
Mississippi	35	33	30	2	0
Texas	45	3	45	0	7
Issue:					
Abortion	25	37	38	0	0
Crime	23	36	32	2	7
Economics	47	17	25	5	6
Education	28	15	40	7	10
Government reform	56	16	20	4	4
Health	43	9	38	0	10
Race	47	21	29	0	3
Welfare	52	13	31	0	4
Frequency of Black Caucus Victories	89	0	100	43	63

Note: The number of votes analyzed is 239. Percentages total 100% across each row. The last row is the percentage of the time that the Black Caucus was victorious, when the coalition listed above emerged. For the last row, the N sizes were small for unholy alliance (7) and individualistic (8).

Source: The roll-call votes are taken from the tables in the previous state chapters. A party coalition is when a majority of black Democrats and a majority of white Democrats ban together to oppose a majority of Republicans. A race coalition is when a majority of white Democrats votes with a majority of white Republicans, in opposition to a majority of black Democrats. Consensus is when a majority of each of these three groups votes in the same direction on a bill. An unholy alliance is when a majority of black Democrats votes with a majority of Republicans, in opposition to a majority of white Democrats. An individualistic vote is when one of these three groups is evenly split on a bill.

89% of the time, as the caucus benefited from membership in a party that controlled the great majority of state legislative bodies.

Race coalitions emerged only 21% of the time, suggesting that when white Democrats were forced to choose between voting with conservative Republicans or liberal African American lawmakers on divisive issues, they were nearly twice as likely to stay with their party colleagues, despite their differences in racial identity, as they were to choose race over party loyalty. However, the consequence of a race coalition emerging was disastrous to the Black Caucus, as the caucus position lost on *every* vote. On the roll calls included in our study that resulted in race coalitions forming, whites of both parties were never so evenly divided that a unified Black Caucus could prevail. The unholy alliance of ideological opposites emerged on only 3% of roll-call votes, a relatively rare occurrence that prompts examination when it does occur but that is thirteen times less likely to occur than is a party vote. Furthermore, when a majority of the Black Caucus joined with most Republicans in opposition to a majority of white Democrats, the Black Caucus position failed to prevail even half of the time, a victory level below the Black Caucus's average on all issues. Individualistic votes that do not fall into these four coalition categories existed on 6% of roll-call votes, and the caucus prevailed on 63% of these bills, a success level that approached its average on all bills.

Intriguing differences emerged across the five states in the frequency of these five coalitions (see Table 8.4). Race coalitions emerged more frequently than the 21% regional average in Arkansas (39%) and Mississippi (33%), helping to explain why the Black Caucus enjoyed the least success on roll-call votes in Arkansas and was slightly below the regional average in Mississippi. Party coalitions were most evident in Texas and Georgia, the two states where the Black Caucus, overall, enjoyed the most legislative success. The frequency of coalition formation in Florida was similar to the region as a whole, producing only 5% more individualistic coalitions and 5% fewer race coalitions than the Southern average.

It is on the potentially divisive issues of abortion and crime that race coalitions are particularly likely to form. Compared to the average bill, where the race coalition emerges only 21% of the time, this coalition emerged 37% of the time on abortion bills and 36% of the time on crime measures (see Table 8.4). The inability of the Black Caucus to retain the support of its white party colleagues is clearly instrumental in accounting for its relatively low success rate, regionwide, on abortion and crime bills. Somewhat intriguing is the fact that on even more potentially divisive issues such as those particularly relevant to race, it is the party coalition that is most likely to emerge, being over twice as frequent as the race coalition. A similar pattern emerges on potentially divisive welfare issues, where party coalitions are clearly dominant, being four times as likely to emerge as are race coalitions. Clearly, Southern Democratic parties have made some impressive strides in preserving unity within their modern biracial party, as many white Democratic lawmakers demonstrate a willingness to stick with their African American party colleagues on issues of special importance to the black community. Other issues on which a particular type of coalition is more likely to emerge relative to the "average" bill are education and health. Given the importance of these issues to constituents of all race, age, and socioeconomic status groups, education and health are more likely than other matters to elicit the formation of a consensus or an individualistic coalition.

The fact that the Black Caucus is most likely to win when it is part of a dominant coalition such as a party vote or a consensus vote, and almost certainly doomed when a racial split emerges among lawmakers, leads one to wonder whether any effort to promote unity within the Black Caucus would make a difference in legislative outcomes. Dichotomizing our Black Caucus unity scale (in order to have enough cases for a multivariate analysis) into high (100% unity) and non-high (under 100% unity) categories, we find that Black Caucus unity does exert some positive effect on the ability of the caucus's position to prevail in the one type of coalition situation that has enough bills to analyze. When a bill produces a party coalition, Black Caucus unanimity does increase the caucus's likelihood of prevailing. The Black Caucus prevailed an impressive 96% of the time on the fifty-six bills where it maintained caucus unanimity, compared to a more average 78% success rate on the thirty-seven bills where caucus unanimity was not achieved (data not shown). The caucus's total lack of success when race coalitions formed was of course unaffected by its main-taining unity among its members, illustrating the importance of the Black Caucus employing strategies and tactics to maintain the biracial Democratic coalition.

SUBSTANTIVE REPRESENTATION—THE UNIQUENESS OF THE STATES

Despite these regionwide patterns, each state has a unique and an interesting political culture that is reflected in distinctive political events, developments, and policy debates. Overall, we have found that several factors affected the extent to which black legislators were elected/selected for leadership positions, and the extent to which they formed coalitions. Some of those factors included redistricting, term limits legislation, the Democratic-Republican ratio, the number of black legislators, and the maturity of the Black Caucus.

Arkansas

While the overall number of African Americans in the general assembly was low, the number steadily increased following the passage of the 1965 Voting Rights Act (VRA). All but one of the black members of the assembly were Democrats. However, Democrats have consistently made up more than 70% of the house and senate. As a result, white Democrats apparently saw no real need to court black legislators when they disagreed with them. Indeed, Arkansas was the only state where the Black Caucus was successful on less than half of the roll-call bills, and the only state where coalitions that divided the races (when white Democrats voted with Republicans instead of black Democrats) were more likely to occur than coalitions that divided the parties.

Overall, African American Democratic lawmakers were more homogeneous and more consistent in their voting behavior than were white Democrats, though there were more recent instances when the group was not completely homogenous. Ultimately, a major barrier to achieving more substantive influence over legislation appears to be the small numbers of black lawmakers. This is further exacerbated by black legislators holding few to no key leadership positions, and a few old "white men" continuing to control the assembly. Even if the number of black legislators matched the percentage of black residents, this number would still be too small to make a significant policy impact given current voting and legislative behavior. On the more positive side, black legislators have been able to bring issues to the table that were not previously considered, and this ability has increased slightly with the implementation of term limits in 1998, as a number of senior "old school" white males left office. Term limits legislation has opened up new opportunities for black legislators, as up until that point only two African Americans (Senator Jewell and Representative Townsend) had held committee chairmanships.

Another possible source of improved power for African American lawmakers is that seniority appears to be the most important determinant in selecting committee chairs in Arkansas, rather than chairs being selected solely based upon race. During the 1990s, several African Americans served as committee vice chairs. They included Representative Irma Hunter Brown (D), who rose to second in command of the House Revenue and Taxation Committee. Senator Jewell (D) was elected president pro tempore of the senate in 1993 for a brief two-year stint. Representative Townsend was elevated to chair the House Aging and Legislative Affairs Committee in the same year and continued in that post through the 1995 session. As the decade came to a close, Senators Roy C. "Bill" Lewellen (D) and Jean Edwards (D) chaired the upper chamber's committees on Aging and Legislative Affairs and City, County, and Local Affairs, respectively, while Representatives Ben McGee (D) and Joe Harris Jr. (D) each served a term heading up the house's Public Transportation Committee.

Though African American legislators in Arkansas have not been able to effectively shape legislation through coalition formation, the Black Caucus has served as a voice to bring issues to the fore that may have been left unattended. This was seen particularly with education reform bills that black lawmakers suspected would have had a disparate impact on African Americans in the state.

Florida

African American lawmakers have faced some real challenges in the Rim South state of Florida as well. Like Arkansas, black legislators in the early 1980s were underrepresented in membership relative to their proportion of the state population, but unlike their fellow Rim South state, African Americans by the turn of the century had achieved near proportional representation in both legislative chambers. And while black lawmakers faced continued challenges in assembling winning coalitions on legislation, their success rate was somewhat higher than Arkansas, though still below the regional average. Yet Florida introduces an intriguing case of the tremendously damaging potential of being in the party that loses control of a legislative body. As Republicans gained control of the legislature in the late 1990s, African Americans were removed from the committee chairmanships they had held. A final special feature of Florida legislative politics was a white Democratic revolt that deposed the newly installed African American minority leader, producing black lawmaker support for the election of a Republican governor, Jeb Bush.

African Americans were selected as committee chairs in the closing decades of the twentieth century, but only one of those committees was viewed as "influential." Joe Kershaw was the first black legislator to chair a committee in the house, when he was selected to lead the Elections Committee from 1974 through 1978. Jamerson (D) made the most of his selection as chair of the House Education Committee during the 1990–1992 and 1992–1994 sessions. He pushed through the house an education reform bill known as "Blueprint 2000". After much negotiation, the bill also passed in the senate. One of the most significant black committee chairs in the house was Willie Logan (D). He was selected chair of the house's Finance Committee and served from 1994 to 1996. He used this position to establish a scholarship fund for minority law students.

Overall, black legislators chaired more committees in the house than in the senate. After serving six years in the senate, Carrie Meek (D-Miami) was selected chair of the Community Affairs Committee. She used this position to bring up issues relevant to African Americans in urban settings. Senator Arnett Girardeau (Jacksonville) was chosen to chair the Ethics Committee the following term. This assignment, however, had no real impact on African Americans specifically. The number of black committee chairs in the senate reached a high during the 1992–1994 session, when five members served as chairs. Most important among these was Senator Hargrett (Tampa), who served as chair of the International Trade, Economic Development, and Tourism Committee.

Similar to other legislative bodies, African Americans lost most of their chair positions when Republicans assumed control of the senate and the house in 1994 and 1996, respectively. However, tradition does allow for some minority party members to serve as chair. As a result, Senator Hargrett (Tampa) was selected to chair the Transportation Committee during the 1996–1998 legislative session.

Despite numerical gains, it is not clear that African American legislators and their minority constituents have benefited significantly. While improvement in descriptive representation is clearly important, there is more of a mixed record with redistributive economic legislation. This, however, does not erase the fact that African Americans have accrued more authority as their seniority rankings have increased. Yet prior to the Republican takeover, conservative white Democrats and Republicans would sometimes constitute the dominant coalition, leaving African Americans and liberal white Democrats in the minority or losing coalition. The Black Caucus found itself in an even worse situation after the Republican takeover, as its legislative success rate plummeted. After winning an impressive 87% of the fifteen votes taken during Democratic legislative control, the Black Caucus won only 29% of the seventeen votes taken under GOP control. (The Black Caucus also won both of the two votes that elicited an equal number of Democratic and Republican votes cast.) On some occasions in the pre– and post–Republican era, the Black Caucus was able to secure enough votes to pass moderate civil rights, taxation, and expenditure bills. Occasionally, particularly after the GOP takeover of the legislature, African Americans voted with white Republicans on some crime and social policy legislation.

Georgia

With the booming metropolitan area of Atlanta, Georgia is a fine example of a modernizing Deep South state that has moved far beyond its agrarian and segregationist heritage. The Black Caucus has become so integral to the life of the state that a concentration on caucus-endorsed legislation produces the same universe of legislation central to the average citizen's quality of life, as does a focus on more generalized bills in other Southern states. With a legislative culture of unanimous consent on many bills, the Black Caucus can sometimes exercise a veto power that is unique to the states studied. Even when unanimity breaks down, African American lawmakers are victorious more frequently than in the average Southern state studied.

The existence of black committee chairs was low, making up only 9% in each legislative chamber in the early 1980s, though even this modest black representation was higher than in any other legislative body studied, except the Texas house. The proportion of black committee chairs nearly doubled by the turn of the century, the result of greater numbers of black candidates being elected to the legislature and African American legislators achieving a degree of seniority and expertise in various substantive policy areas. One important difference between the house and the senate was the selection of Senator Scott to the powerful Rules Committee, a prestige committee leadership position not yet attained by any African American in the house.

In terms of voting behavior and coalition formation, the Georgia legislative chambers quite frequently favored the position of the Black Caucus, so African American legislators have achieved a significant degree of substantive representation. Divisive race coalitions, whereby majorities of white legislators of both parties vote against a majority of African Americans, are somewhat less evident in Georgia than in the typical state studied. With all votes considered, black legislators were moderately independent of the Democratic Party in the house and in the senate. Disagreement between African Americans and their fellow Democrats varied across issue areas, as occurred in other Southern states. For example, on economic development, taxation, and government reform issues, black legislators often voted with other Democrats in the house and the senate.

Mississippi

Unlike the Deep South state of Georgia, Mississippi is dominated by small towns that help preserve a very insular political culture. Sharing with Alabama the dubious distinction of having one of the most troubled racial histories, Mississippi required its African American political leadership to fight relentlessly for civil rights. Dramatic changes have finally come to the Magnolia State, but traces of the state's traditionalistic culture persist. The underrepresentation gap between the proportion of African Americans in the population and in the state legislature remains higher in the Mississippi senate than in any other state studied. Mississippi is also the only state other than Louisiana, South Carolina, and Republican-controlled Florida where the proportion of African American committee chairs fails to accurately reflect the black presence in *both* state legislative chambers. Mississippi is also second only to Arkansas in the emergence of racial coalitions. Indeed, in this Deep South state, racial coalitions are nearly as likely to emerge as party coalitions. In other words, when an African American majority faces off against a white Republican majority, the majority of white Democrats is nearly as likely to vote with the Republicans as it is to vote with its African American party colleagues. Despite these challenges, the Black Caucus has been nearly as successful on legislative roll-call votes as the caucuses in the average Southern state studied.

The growth of African American committee leadership has been dramatic, aided by the growth of the Black Caucus among the legislature's membership and the persistence of an overwhelmingly Democratically controlled house and senate. By the turn of the century, black legislators constituted 29% of the house membership and 19% of the senate and chaired 23% of the standing committees in the house and 17% of the senate committees. Though none of these committees was considered "powerful," an African American did serve as speaker pro tempore of the house, and several others chaired such important committees as Judiciary, Education, and Universities and Colleges. This success is nothing short of remarkable, considering the troubled racial history of the state, reflected in the total absence of any black committee chairs in the senate in 1980 and only two chairmen in the house. Furthermore, African Americans have used their committee chair assignments to help enact a multiyear teacher pay raise and a settlement of the state's higher education desegregation lawsuit. Black committee leaders have also blocked appointments of a few conservatives to key boards and commissions and killed some election measures deemed harmful to the black community. Some successes were also evident in the areas of crime and economic policy.

On the other hand, black lawmakers have expressed concerns over the lack of appointments to committees that control the flow of money. That problem was somewhat alleviated by 2002 when African Americans came to comprise 24% of the slots on the house's Appropriations Committee and 33% of the positions on the house's Ways and Means Committee. In the senate, African Americans now held 23% of the senate's Appropriations Committee positions and 15% of the senate's Finance Committee slots.

African American committee chairs have sometimes benefited politically by having white Democratic mentors and colleagues. This has been particularly true with education reform bills, where they have formed coalitions with white Democratic lawmakers to resist conservative Republican cost-conscious measures. In some instances where white legislators were split, African American legislators have found success as the key element that forged compromises on bills.

Intriguing, given the racially conscious history of the state, African American lawmakers have been successful on several race-related issues. Black lawmakers have benefited from their homogeneous voting orientations and their persistence in convincing white Democrats to stick with them on issues of great importance to the black community. They have also employed intelligent strategies that include creating coalitions with other important interest groups, gaining support from the state media, and changing the focus of the public debate toward a more popular issue. Black Caucus members in other Southern states can learn from the crafty tactics employed by their Mississippi colleagues, who sometimes have been amazingly successful, despite facing enormous obstacles.

Texas

Texas is a Rim South state that has made some dramatic progress in terms of African American representation and power. While the African American presence in the state house remained steady over the last two decades of the twentieth century, black politicians in the senate went from zero to comprise 6% of that chamber in a state with an African American population of only 12%. Similarly, African American committee chairs have also become increasingly evident, though none of the chairs represented a powerful economic redistributive committee. Reflecting African American advances in these committee leadership positions, Texas and Tennessee were the only states examined where black legislators comprised a slightly higher proportion of committee chairs compared to the proportion of each legislative chamber's membership that was black.

On legislative roll calls, the Black Caucus enjoyed the highest success rate in Texas than in any other state studied. Furthermore, consensus coalitions were more likely to form in Texas than in the other states, and race coalitions were the least likely to emerge. The Texas Black Caucus repeatedly expressed solidarity as measured by voting cohesion, being more cohesive than in any of the other four states in our study (exhibiting a mean of 87 on our Black Caucus unity indicator, compared to a regional average of 78). The Black Caucus was the most homogenous when voting on key criminal justice and race-related issues. While still maintaining a high cohesion score, the most disagreement within the caucus occurred on health issues and isolated votes on abortion and economic matters. Quite naturally, bloc voting had a greater impact when white legislators in both political parties were fragmented.

THE FUTURE OF AFRICAN AMERICAN REPRESENTATION IN THE SOUTH

In closing, several general comments are observed. First, as we enter the twenty-first century, it is quite clear that Africans Americans in Southern state legislatures are enjoying some notable electoral and legislative successes. Relative to twenty years ago, African Americans comprise a greater percentage of the membership of Southern state legislatures in twenty of the twenty-two chambers studied, thereby reducing the gap in descriptive representation between the African American state populations and their presence in state legislative bodies. Nevertheless, African Americans have not yet achieved complete descriptive representation in any of the states, though Alabama's and Florida's legislatures are very close to that point.

Regarding descriptive representation in terms of key legislative leadership positions, such as committee chairmanships, gains also have been evident. At the turn of the century, African Americans comprised a higher proportion of committee chairs relative to twenty years ago in four of the five states extensively studied. The absence of black committee chairs in Florida illustrates the devastating effects of black legislators being concentrated in one political party when that party loses control of a legislature. Another problem for the black caucuses has been the dearth of black committee chairs on "power" committees. Appointment to such committees is one of the key elements to shaping redistributive economics in the Southern states.

Turning more toward substantive representation, we find that the Southern black caucuses have experienced many successes, but also some disappointments. African American lawmakers have become a vital part of the governing coalition on most bills that shape the quality of life of their constituents. Even on bills failing to achieve the support of 90% or more of all lawmakers, the Black Caucus position prevails roughly seven out of ten times.

Nearly half of the time the Black Caucus prevails, the issue is backed by a majority of all three legislative groups (black Democrats, white Democrats, and Republicans), but the other half pertains to issues where most white Democrats join with their African American party colleagues rather than with more conservative Republican Party lawmakers who are voting primarily in the opposite direction. Indeed, even when ideological considerations are most evident, as when majorities of black lawmakers and Republicans find themselves on opposite sides of an issue, white Democrats are nearly twice as likely to vote with their African American colleagues than with Republican lawmakers. Nevertheless, black lawmakers also have suffered their share of legislative setbacks, particularly on such divisive issues as crime and abortion.

Further, we note that the formation and aggressiveness of a legislative Black Caucus organization are important to the success of African American legislators. Black lawmakers are extremely homogenous in voting behavior in both chambers and in all of these states. These caucuses are one of the keys to maintaining homogeneity among African Americans. They also serve as a tool to help black lawmakers prepare their legislative agenda and thus espouse the views of their constituents.

Lastly, it is evident that African Americans, despite their generally liberal philosophy in a more conservative region of the nation, have been politically astute in forming coalitions in Southern state legislatures. Normally they form winning coalitions with fellow Democrats who are white, and who today exhibit basically "centrist" viewpoints relative to the white segregationists of decades past. However, on occasion, African Americans have formed coalitions with Republican lawmakers, or even backed a Republican gubernatorial candidate if discontented with their treatment by white Democratic colleagues. Clearly, African American lawmakers in the Southern states have no permanent "friends" or "enemies." Ideally, these coalitions will have greater effects on redistributive economics in the future. As we begin the twenty first century black legislators are an independent force that demands and deserves to be treated as an equal in the legislative process.

References

Albright, Mark. 1993. "Tourism Tax Plan Hits Roadblock." *St. Petersburg Times*, 2 March, p. 1E.

Alexander, Kern, and James Hale. 1978. "Educational Equity, Improving School Finance in Arkansas," Report to the Advisory Committee of the Special School Formula Project of the Joint Interim Committee on Education. Little Rock: Arkansas General Assembly.

Allison, Wes. 2002. "Bush, McBride Didn't Draw Black Voters." *St. Petersburg Times*, 8 November, p. 1A.

Ammerman, Joseph. 1999. "Senate Thwarts Fordice Nominee: Session Goes Nowhere." *The Clarion-Ledger* (Jackson), 4 May, p. 1.

————. 2000a. "Black Lawmakers Express Discontent." *The Clarion-Ledger* (Jackson), 26 January, pp. 1, 7A.

————. 2000b. "Black Caucus Puts Focus on Colleges." *The Clarion-Ledger* (Jackson), 31 January, pp. 1, 3A.

Ammons, James H. 1991. "Reapportionment, Single Member Districts, and Black Representation in the Florida Legislature." In *Reapportionment and Representation in Florida: A Historical Collection*, ed. Susan A. MacManus, 353–365. Tampa, Fla.: Intrabay Innovation Institute.

Arbanas, Michael. 1991a. "Senate Approves 50% Increase in Retirement Pay; Bill Passes 26-8 with No Debate." *Arkansas Gazette*, 15 February. http://web.lexis-nexis.com/universe/printdoc. Accessed electronically 20 May 2002.

————. 1991b. "5 Redistricting Plans Discussed in Committee." *Arkansas Gazette*, 12 March, p. 3G.

Arkansas Legislative Black Caucus. 2002. Official Web site, history. http://www.arklegblackcaucus.org. Accessed electronically 3 June 2002.

Arkansas Legislative Digest. 1981, 1983, 1985, 1987, 1989, 1991, 1993, 1995, 1997, 1999 Arkansas General Assembly.

"Arkansas Ranks 2d in South in Elected Black Officials." 1974. *Arkansas Gazette*, 4 March, p. 5A.

Askari, Emilla. 1983. "Battle Shaping Up on State Multinational Tax." *Miami Herald,* 12 July, p. D1.

Associated Press. 2001. "Blacks Recount Voting Problems to Florida Panel." *St. Louis Post-Dispatch,* 12 January, p. A7.

———. 2003. "New La. Governor Backs Women for Posts." *The Clarion-Ledger,* 1 December, p. 3B.

Bailey, N. Louise, Mary L. Morgan, Carolyn R. Taylor, and Inez Watson. 1986. *Biographical Directory of the South Carolina Senate 1776–1985.* Columbia: University of South Carolina Press.

Barker, Lucius, and Mack H. Jones. 1994. *African Americans and the American Political System.* Englewood Cliffs, N.J.: Prentice Hall.

Barker, Lucius J., Mack H. Jones, and Katherine Tate. 1999. *African Americans and the American Political System.* 4th ed. Englewoods Cliffs, N.J.: Prentice Hall.

Barrett, Edith J. 1995. "The Policy Priorities of African American Women in State Legislatures." *Legislative Studies Quarterly* 20:223–47.

Bass, Jack, and Walter DeVries. 1977. *The Transformation of Southern Politics: Social Change and Political Consequence since 1945.* New York: New American Library.

Bassett, C. Jeanne. 1994. "Comments: House Bill 591: Florida Compensates Rosewood Victims and Their Families for a Seventy-One Year Old Injury." *Florida State University Law Review* 22:503–23.

Becker, Jo. 2000. "Budget Deal Trims Millions in Taxes." *St. Petersburg Times,* 20 April, p. 1A.

Bernd, Joseph L. 1972. "Georgia: Static and Dynamic." In *The Changing Politics of the South,* ed. William C. Havard, 294–365. Baton Rouge: Louisiana State University Press.

Black, Earl, and Merle Black. 1987. *Politics and Society in the South.* Cambridge: Harvard University Press.

———. 1992. *The Vital South.* Cambridge: Harvard University Press.

Blair, Diane D. 1988. *Arkansas Politics and Government: Do the People Rule?* Lincoln: University of Nebraska Press.

Bland, Thyrie. 1998. "Speaker: Conservatives, Blacks Face Collision." *The Clarion-Ledger* (Jackson), 1 February, p. B1.

Blomley, Seth. 2002a. "Candidate Criticizes Lawmakers." *Arkansas Democrat-Gazette,* 5 April, p. B1.

———. 2002b. "Race Emerges as Issue for Democrats Vying in Redrawn LR Senate District." *Arkansas Democrat-Gazette,* 14 May, p. B1.

Boone, William H. 1992. "Georgia Legislative Black Caucus." In *Georgia Legislative Review: 1992,* ed. Bob Holmes and Gretchen E. Maclachlan, Atlanta: Southern Center for Studies in Public Policy.

———. 1993. "Black Caucus." In *Georgia Legislative Review: 1993*, ed. Bob Holmes and Gretchen E. Maclachlan, Atlanta: Southern Center for Studies in Public Policy.

———. 1994. "Black Caucus." In *Georgia Legislative Review: 1994*, ed. Bob Holmes and Gretchen E. Maclachlan, Atlanta: Southern Center for Studies in Public Policy.

———. 1995. "Black Caucus." In *Georgia Legislative Review: 1995*, ed. Bob Holmes and Gretchen E. Maclachlan, Atlanta: Southern Center for Studies in Public Policy.

———. 1998. "Black Caucus." In *Georgia Legislative Review: 1998*, ed. Bob Holmes, Atlanta: Southern Center for Studies in Public Policy.

Bositis, David A. 2002. *Black Elected Officials: A Statistical Summary, 2000.* Washington, D.C.: Joint Center for Political and Economic Studies. http://www.jointcenter. org/whatsnew/beo-2002/index.html. Accessed electronically 10 December 2002.

Botsch, Robert E. 1999. "Legislative Black Caucus." http://www.usca.edu/aasc/ blackcaucus.htm. Accessed electronically 15 November 2003.

Brantley, Max. 1991. "GOP District Plan Has Two Faces." *Arkansas Gazette*, 14 March, p. I1.

Brewer, J. Mason. 1935. *Negro Legislators of Texas and Their Descendants: A History of the Negro in Texas Politics from Reconstruction to Disenfranchisment.* Dallas: Mathis.

Brischetto, Robert, David R. Richards, Chandler Davison, and Bernard Grofman. 1994. "Texas" In *Quiet Revolution in the South: The Impact of the Voting Rights Act, 1965–1990*, ed. Chandler Davison and Bernard Grofman, 233–70. Princeton: Princeton University Press.

Brown, Irma Hunter. 2002. Telephone interview. 5 June.

Browning, Rufus P., Dale Marshall, and David H. Tabb. 1984. *Protest Is Not Enough.* Berkeley: University of California Press.

———. 1997. *Racial Politics in American Cities.* 2nd ed. New York: Longman.

Bullock, Charles S. 1992. "Minorities in State Legislatures." In *Changing Patterns in State Legislative Careers*, ed. Gary F. Moncrief and Joel A. Thompson. 39–58. Ann Arbor: University of Michigan Press.

———. 1995a. "The Impact of Changing the Racial Composition of Congressional Districts on Legislators' Roll Call Behavior." *American Politics Quarterly* 23:141–58.

———. 1995b. *The Georgia Political Almanac: The General Assembly.* Atlanta: Cornerstone.

———. 1999. "The Opening Up of State and Local Election Processes." In *American State and Local Politics: Directions for the 21st Century*, ed. Ronald E. Weber and Paul Brace, 212–40. New York: Chatham House.

Bullock, Charles, and Susan MacManus. 1981. "Policy Responsiveness to the Black Electorate: Programmatic versus Symbolic Representation." *American Politics Quarterly* 9:357–68.

Button, James. 1984. "Blacks." In *Florida Politics & Government, 2nd edition*, ed. Manning J. Dauer, 286–93. Gainesville: University Press of Florida.

Button, James, and David Hedge. 1996. "Legislative Life in the 1990s: A Comparison of Black and White State Legislators." *Legislative Studies Quarterly* 21:199–218.

Caldwell, Elizabeth, and Rachel O'Neal. 1994a. "Bill Cuts Parental Strings on Police Questioning, Would Be OK without Notice." *Arkansas Democrat-Gazette*, 18 August, p. 1A.

———. 1994b. "31 Say Farewells at Legislature." *Arkansas Democrat-Gazette*, 25 August, p. 8A.

Cameron, Charles, David Epstein, and Sharyn O'Halloran. 1996. "Do Majority-Minority Districts Maximize Substantive Black Representation in Congress?" *American Political Science Review* 90:794–812.

Canon, David T. 1999. *Race, Redistricting, and Representation: The Unintended Consequences of Black Majority Districts*. Chicago: University of Chicago Press.

Chachere, Vickie. 1995. "Officials Link Up with Chain Gangs." *Tampa Tribune*, 9 June, p. 1.

Chicago Tribune. 1974. "Blacks Hope LR Sessions Hardworking." *Arkansas Gazette*, 11 March, p. 7A.

The Clarion-Ledger (Jackson, Miss.). Various articles cited as table sources in Mississippi chapter.

Clemons, Michael L., and Charles E. Jones. 2000. "African American Legislative Politics in Virginia." *Journal of Black Studies* 30:744–67.

Clerk of the House. 1968–1970 and 1998–2000. *The Clerks' Manual*. Tallahassee: State of Florida.

Coffey, John Mott. 2002. "Legislature Votes to Reduce IHL Terms." *The Commercial Dispatch* (Columbus), 13 March, pp. 1, 11A.

Colburn, David C., and Richard Scher. 1984. "Florida Politics in the Twentieth Century." In *Florida Politics & Government, 2nd edition*, ed. Manning J. Dauer, 35–53. Gainesville: University Press of Florida.

Cole, Leonard A. 1976. *Blacks in Power: A Comparative Study of Black and White Elected Officials*. Princeton: Princeton University Press.

Coleman, Mary DeLorse. 1993. *Legislators, Law, and Public Policy: Political Change in Mississippi and the South*. Westport, Conn.: Greenwood Press.

"Comments Indicate Job Tough, Not Impossible." 1987. *Arkansas Gazette*, 31 March, p. 9A.

Cox, David, 1998. "Black Caucus Moves Closer to Republicans." *Tampa Tribune*, 4 February, p. 6.

Csar, Trey. 2000. "Education Revamp Advances." *Florida Times Union*, 20 April, p. B1.

Dahl, David. 1987. "A Taxing Problem: Who Will Receive the Exemption?" *St. Petersburg Times*, 15 February, p. 1A.

Davidson, Chandler. 1990. *Race and Class in Texas Politics*. Princeton: Princeton University Press.

Davidson, Chandler, and Bernard Grofman. 1994. *Quiet Revolution in the South: The Impact of the Voting Rights Act, 1965–1990*. Princeton: Princeton University Press.

Davis, Clarice McDonald. 1965. *Legislative Malapportionment and Roll-Call Voting in Texas: 1961–1963*. Austin: Institute of Public Affairs, University of Texas.

Democrat Capitol Bureau. 1991. "Compromise on Clinics Sends Assembly Home." *Arkansas Democrat*, 28 March, p. 1A.

Democratic Party of Arkansas. 2002. Official Web site, history. http://www.arkdems.org. Accessed electronically 7 June 2002.

Desalte, Melinda. 2001. "Louisiana Lawmakers Say Darwin's Ideology Racist." *The Oak Ridger*, 2 May. http://oakridger.com/stories/050201/stt_0502010060.html. Accessed electronically 1 June 2002.

Dillon, Etrenda, and Goro Mitchell. 1995. "Health Care." In *Georgia Legislative Review: 1995*, ed. Bob Holmes and Gretchen E. Maclachlan, Atlanta: Southern Center for Studies in Public Policy.

Duffy, Joan. 1989a. "House Rejects School Settlement." *Arkansas Democrat*, 17 March, p. 1A.

———. 1989b. "68-Day Legislative Session Ends." *Arkansas Democrat*, 18 March, p. 1A.

———. 1993a. "Struggle Looms as Arkansas Houses Pass Separate Civil Rights Bills." *The Commercial Appeal*, 27 February, p. A7.

———. 1993b. "Lack of Action on Civil Rights Bill Leaves Lewellen Measure in Limbo." *The Commercial Appeal*, 10 March, p. A8.

———. 1993c. "Competing Bills, Lawmakers May Doom Law on Civil Rights." *The Commercial Appeal*, 25 March, p. A14.

———. 1993d. "Minority Lawmakers Blast Arkansas Rights Bill; They Say Tucker Let Blacks Down." *The Commercial Appeal*, 28 March, p. B1.

———1993e. "Civil rights law signed to cap Ark. Legislature." *The Commercial Appeal*, 9 April, p. A1.

Dumas, Ernest. 1983. "Enterprise Zones Aid Firms, Not Workers." *Arkansas Gazette*, 9 December, p. 27A.

Dupree v. Alma School District, 279 Ark. 340, 651 S.W.2d 90 (1983).

Dye, Thomas R. 1998. *Politics in Florida*. Upper Saddle River, N.J.: Prentice Hall.

Edmund, Beverly C. 1994. "Human Services." In *Georgia Legislative Review: 1994*, ed. Bob Holmes and Gretchen E. Maclachlan, Atlanta: Southern Center for Studies in Public Policy.

Elazar, Daniel J. 1984. *American Federalism: A View from the States*. 3rd ed. New York: Harper and Row.

Elders, Jocelyn. 2002. Telephone interview. 24 May.

Elliott, Charles P., Kay Hofer, and Robert E. Biles. 1998. *The World of Texas Politics*. New York: St. Martin's Press.

Elliott, Jack, Jr. 1998. "Black Lawmakers Use Vote to Protest Agency." Associated Press article, cited in *The Clarion-Ledger* (Jackson), 2 February, p. 3B.

Endersby, James, and Charles E. Menifield. 2000. "Representation, Ethnicity, and Congress: Black and Hispanic Representatives and Constituencies," In *Black and Multiracial Politics in America*, ed. Yvette Alex-Assensoh and Lawrence Hans, 257–72. New York: New York University Press.

Epstein, Gady A. 1997. "Chiles Vetoes Late Term Abortion Ban." *Tampa Tribune*, 24 May, p. 1.

Feagin, Joe R. 1972. "Civil Rights Voting by Southern Congressmen." *Journal of Politics* 34:484–99.

Ferrell, Lisa. 2002. Telephone interview. 29 May.

Fishman, Robert. 1994. "Governmental Affairs and Ethics." In *Georgia Legislative Review: 1994*, ed. Bob Holmes and Gretchen E. Maclachlan, Atlanta: Southern Center for Studies in Public Policy.

Fleischmann, Arnold, and Carol Pierannunzi. 1997. *Politics in Georgia*. Athens: University of Georgia Press.

Florida Legislature. House of Representatives. 1983–2000. *Journals of the House of Representatives*. Tallahassee: State of Florida.

Florida Legislature. Senate. 1983–2000. *Journals of the Senate*. Tallahassee: State of Florida.

"4 Blacks Lead in Their Races for Legislature." 1972. *Arkansas Gazette*, 8 November, p. 5A.

Francis, Wayne L. 1985. "Leadership, Party Caucuses, and Committees in the U. S. State Legislature." *Legislative Studies Quarterly* 10:243–57.

Georgia House of Representatives. 1999. Text of HR 333. http://www.legis.state.ga.us/legis/1999_00/leg/fulltext/hr333.htm. Accessed electronically 19 November 2002.

Gettleman, Jeffrey. 2000. "Jeb Bush Tries to Hasten Thaw, Gets the Cold Shoulder." *Los Angeles Times*, 15 December, p. A46.

Gibson Jr., L. Tucker, and Clay Robinson. 1999. *Government and Politics in the Lone Star State: Theory and Practice*. Upper Saddle River, N.J.: Prentice Hall.

Grofman, Bernard. 1997. "The 1990s Round of Redistricting: A Schematic Outline of Some Key Features." *The National Political Science Review* 6:17–26.

Grofman, Bernard, and Lisa Handley. 1991. "The Impact of the Voting Rights Act on Black Representation in Southern State Legislatures." *Legislative Studies Quarterly* 16:111–28.

Grofman, Bernard, Lisa Handley, and Richard G. Niemi. 1992. *Minority Representation and the Quest for Voting Equality*. New York: Cambridge University Press.

Guinier, Lani. 1993. "Groups, Representation, and Race Conscious Redistricting: A Case of the Emperor's New Clothes." *Texas Law Review* 71 (June): 1589–1642. Accessed through Lexis-Nexis Academic Universe, 2 May 2001.

Hamm, Keith E., and Robert Harmel. 1993. "Legislative Party Development and the Speaker System: The Case of the Texas House." *Journal of Public Policy* 13:1:1140.

Hamm, Keith E., Robert Harmel, and Robert Thompson. 1983. "Ethnic and Partisan Minorities in Two Southern State Legislatures." *Legislative Studies Quarterly* 8:177–89.

Handley, Lisa, and Bernard Grofman. 1994. "The Impact of the Voting Rights Act on Minority Representation: Black Officeholding in Southern State Legislatures and Congressional Delegations." In *Quiet Revolution in the South: The Impact of the Voting Rights Act of 1965–1990*, ed. Chandler Davidson and Bernard Grofman, 335–50. Princeton: Princeton University Press.

Harmel, Robert, Keith Hamm, and Robert Thompson. 1983. "Black Voting Cohesion and Distinctiveness in Three Southern Legislatures." *Social Science Quarterly* 64:183–91.

Harris, Robert. 1970. "Black Legislators and Their White Colleagues." *The Black Politician* 2:15–16.

Havard, William C., and Loren P. Beth. 1991. "Representative Government and Reapportionment: A Case Study of Florida." In *Reapportionment and Representation in Florida: A Historical Collection*, ed. Susan A. MacManus, 21–76. Tampa: Intrabay Innovation Institute.

Haynie, Kerry L. 2001. *African American Legislators in the American States*. New York: Columbia University Press.

———. 2002. "The Color of Their Skin or the Content of Their Behavior? Race and Perceptions of African American Legislators." *Legislative Studies Quarterly* 27:295–314.

Hedge, David, James Button, and Mary Spear. 1996. "Accounting for the Quality of Black Legislative Life: The View from the States." *American Journal of Political Science* 40:82–98.

Herring, Mary. 1990. "Legislative Responsiveness to Black Constituents in Three Deep South States." *Journal of Politics* 52:740–58.

Hill, Kevin. 1995. "Does the Creation of Majority Black Districts Aid Republicans?" *The Journal of Politics* 57:384–401.

Hollis, Mark, 1997. "Black Caucus Faces Test of Political Clout." *Sarasota Herald-Tribune*, 7 April, p. 1B.

Holmes, Robert A. 1992. "Reapportionment and Redistricting." In *Georgia Legislative Review: 1992*, ed. Bob Holmes and Gretchen E. Maclachlan, Atlanta: Southern Center for Studies in Public Policy.

————. 1994. "The Georgia Legislative Black Caucus and the Office of the Governor: 1975–1994." In *Black Politics and Black Political Behavior*, ed. Hanes Walton Jr., 137–53. Westport, Conn.: Praeger.

————. 1997. "Georgia's Reapportionment and Redistricting Process in 1995: Reflections of a Participant Observer." *The National Political Science Review* 6:72–93.

————. 2000. "The Georgia Legislative Black Caucus: An Analysis of a Racial Subgroup." *Journal of Black Studies* 30:768–90.

Houston Chronicle News Services. 1994. "Election '94: Nation." *Houston Chronicle*. 9 November, p. A42.

James, Meg. 1995. "Conservative Christians Gaining Legislative Clout." *Palm Beach Post*, 15 May, p. 1A.

————. 1996. "Senate Approves Open Enrollment." *Palm Beach Post*, 1 May, p. 1A.

Jeffers v. Clinton (E.D.Ark. 1989) 730 F. Supp. 196.

Jeffrey, Laura S. 1997. *Barbara Jordan: Congresswoman, Lawyer, Educator*. Berkeley Heights, N.J.: Enslow.

"Jewell Defeats Sparks to Win Senate Race." 1972. *Arkansas Gazette*, 8 November, p. 10A.

Jewell, Malcolm, E. 1982. *Representation in State Legislatures*. Lexington: University of Kentucky Press.

John, Butch. 1996. "Even Hand Cited in Turner's Rise." *The Clarion-Ledger* (Jackson), 28 January, pp. 1, 15A.

John, Butch, and Emily Wagster. 1998. "Black Caucus Takes Issues to Public with Hearings." *The Clarion-Ledger* (Jackson), 15 February, p. 2H.

Johnston, Robert, and Mary Storey. 1983. "The Arkansas Senate: An Overview." *Arkansas Political Science Review* 4:69–81.

Joint Center for Political and Economic Studies. *Black Elected Officials: A National Roster*. http://www.jointcenter.org.

Jones, Charles. 2000. "African American State Legislative Politics: An Introduction." *Journal of Black Studies* 30:741–43.

Kanengiser, Andy. 2002. "Ayers Deal Sets Stage for Major Growth, Colleges Say: JSU Counting on School of Engineering." *The Clarion-Ledger* (Jackson), 10 March, p. 1.

Kassab, Beth. 1999. "3-Strikes Bill Passes House with Less Bite." *Florida Times-Union*, 27 April, p. A6.

Kern, David F. 1991. "Brownlee Opposes Condom Ban." *Arkansas Democrat*, 27 March, p. E1.

Kern, David, and Noel Oman. 1991. "With Day Left, Chambers Split on Condom Ban." *Arkansas Democrat*, 27 March, p. 13A.

Key, V. O., Jr. 1949. *Southern Politics in State and Nation*. New York: Vintage, a division of Random House.

King-Meadows, Tyson, and Thomas F. Schaller. 2001. "Black State Legislators: A Case Study of North Carolina and Maryland." In *Representation of Minority Groups in the U.S.: Implications for the Twenty-First Century*, ed. Charles E. Menifield, 163–88. Lanham, Md.: Austin and Winfield.

Kirkpatrick, Jeanne. 1975. "Representation in the American National Conventions: The Case of 1972." *British Journal of Political Science* 5:265–322.

Klas, Mary Ellen, 2001. "Election Reform Package Marred by Partisanship, Weakens Finance Rules." *Palm Beach Post*, 25 April, p. 3A.

Knight News Service. 1989. "School Case Cost May Hit $59 Million." *Arkansas Gazette*, 9 February, p. 1A.

Kraemer, Richard H., Charldean Newell Charldean, and David F. Prindle. 1998. *Essentials of Texas Politics*. 7th ed. Belmont, Calif.: Wadsworth.

Krane, Dale, and Stephen D. Shaffer. 1992. *Mississippi Government and Politics: Modernizers versus Traditionalists*. Lincoln: University of Nebraska Press.

Kuzenski, John C. 2003. "South Carolina: The Heart of GOP Realignment in the South." In *The New Politics of the Old South: An Introduction to Southern Politics*, 2nd ed. Charles S. Bullock III and Mark J. Rozell, 23–51. Lanham, Md.: Rowman and Littlefield.

Lamare, James W. 1998. *Texas Politics: Economics, Power, and Policy*. 6th ed. Belmont, Calif.: Wadsworth.

LaMarr, Ecitrym S. 2002. *The Florida Conference of Black State Legislators*. Tallahassee: The Florida Conference of Black State Legislators.

Lamis, Alexander P. 1990. *The Two-Party South*. 2nd expanded ed. New York: Oxford University Press.

———. 1999. *Southern Politics in the 1990s*. Baton Rouge: Louisiana State University Press.

Landry, Sue. 1989. "Kids' Access to Weapons Comes Before Legislature." *St. Petersburg Times*, 19 June, p. 1A.

Legette, Willie E. 2000. "The South Carolina Legislative Black Caucus, 1970–1988." *Journal of Black Studies* 30:839–58.

Liston, Brad. 2000. "Thousands March on FLA Capitol." *Boston Globe*, 8 March, p. A3.

Lublin, David. 1997. *The Paradox of Representation: Racial Gerrymandering and Minority Interests in Congress*. Princeton: Princeton University Press.

Maclachlan, Gretchen E. 1998. "Employment and Labor." In *Georgia Legislative Review: 1998*, ed. Bob Holmes, Atlanta: Southern Center for Studies in Public Policy.

MacManus, Susan. 2002a. "1992 Congressional Redistricting: A Decade Long Battle." In *Mapping Florida's Political Landscape: The Changing Art of Politics of Reapportionment and Redistricting*, ed. Susan A. MacManus, 117–75. Tallahassee: Florida Institute of Government.

————. 2002b. "State Legislative Redistricting in 1992: Precedent-Setting Decisions in a Diverse Florida." In *Mapping Florida's Political Landscape: The Changing Art of Politics of Reapportionment and Redistricting*, ed. Susan A. MacManus, 176–235. Tallahassee: Florida Institute of Government.

Mansbridge, Jane. 1999. "Should Blacks Represent Blacks and Women Represent Women? A Contingent 'Yes'." *Journal of Politics* 61:628–57.

Marable, Manning. 1991. *Race, Reform and Rebellion: The Second Reconstruction in Black America, 1945–1990*. Rev. 2nd ed. Jackson.: University Press of Mississippi.

Maxwell, William Earl, and Ernest Crain. 1995. *Texas Politics Today*. 7th ed. St. Paul, Minn.: West.

May, A. L. 1977. "Senate Has Long, Full Day of Work." *Arkansas Democrat*, 18 March, p. 12B.

McClain, Paula D. 1990. "Symposium: Agenda Setting, Public Policy and Minority Group Influence: An Introduction." *Policy Studies Review* 9:263–72.

McDonald, Laughlin, Michael B. Binford, and Ken Johnson. 1994. "Georgia" In *Quiet Revolution in the South: The Impact of the Voting Rights Act of 1965–1990*, ed. Chandler Davidson and Bernard Grofman, 67–102. Princeton: Princeton University Press.

McElroy, Lori. 1991. "Education Bills Fly by Panel in Senate." *Arkansas Gazette*, 31 January. http://web.lexis-nexis.com/universe/printdoc. Accessed electronically 20 May 2002.

McGee, Ben. 2002. Telephone interview. 25 May.

McKinnon, John. 1991. "Governor Vetoes Anti-Bias Bill." *St. Petersburg Times*, 25 May, p. 1A.

Menifield, Charles E. 2000. "Black Political Life in the Missouri General Assembly." *Journal of Black Studies* 31:20–38.

————. 2001. "Minority Representation in the Twenty-First Century." In *Representation of Minority Groups in the U.S.: Implications for the Twenty-first Century*, ed. Charles E. Menifield, 1–11. Lanham, Md.: Austin and Winfield.

Menifield, Charles E., and Charles E. Jones. 2001. "African American Representation in Congress, Then and Now." In *Representation of Minority Groups in the U.S.: Implications for the Twenty-first Century*, ed. Charles E. Menifield, 13–36. Lanham, Md.: Austin and Winfield.

Menifield, Charles E., and Frank Julian. 1998. "Changing the Face of Congress: African Americans in the Twenty-first Century." *Western Journal of Black Studies* 22:18–30.

————. 2001. "The Effects of Redistricting on the Underrepresented." In *Representation of Minority Groups in the U.S.: Implications for the Twenty-first Century*, ed. Charles E. Menifield, 149–62. Lanham, Md.: Austin and Winfield.

Menifield, Charles E., and Kwame Badu Antwi-Boasiako. 2002. "African Americans in the Mississippi Legislature: Representation from Two perspectives." In *Mississippi Votes*, 2000: A Comprehensive Examination of Politics and Elections., ed. Charles E. Menifield, 54–59. Stennis Institute of Government: Mississippi State.

Menifield, Charles E., Stephen Shaffer, and Charles E. Jones. 2000. "Voting Behavior among African Americans in Southern State Legislatures." Paper presented at the 2000 Annual Meeting of the American Political Science Association, August 31–September 3.

Metz, Kevin. 1995. "Welfare Benefits Targeted in Bill Headed to Chiles." *Tampa Tribune*, 6 May, p. 4.

Middlemass, Keesha. 2000. "Redistricting: Georgia's Experience." Paper presented at the Southern Political Science Association Meeting, November.

Miller, Cheryl. 1990. "Agenda-Setting by State Legislative Black Caucuses: Policy Priorities and Factors of Success." *Policy Studies Review* 9:339–54.

———. 1993. "Issue Selection by State Legislative Black Caucuses in the South." In *Minority Group Influence: Agenda Setting, Formulation, and Public Policy*, ed. Paula D. McClain, 111–25. Westport, Conn.: Greenwood Press.

———. 1994. "State Legislative Black Caucuses Influence on Legislative Policy Agendas: Continuities and Variations in North Carolina." In *Black Politics and Black Political Behavior: A Linkage Analysis*, ed. Hanes Walton Jr., 155–68. Westport, Conn.: Praeger.

Miller, Sabrina. 1995. "Bill Makes Way for a Revival of Chain Gangs by December." *St. Petersburg Times*, 7 May, p. 5B.

Mississippi Official and Statistical Register, 1980–1984, 1984–1988, 1988–1992, 1992–1996, 1996–2000. Jackson Mississippi Secretary of State's Office.

Mitchell, Goro. 1999. "Rating the Legislators." In *Georgia Legislative Review 1999*, ed. Bob Holmes, Atlanta: Southern Center for Studies in Public Policy.

Mitchell, Goro, and Etrenda Dillon. 1996. "Rating the Legislators." In *Georgia Legislative Review 1996*, ed. Bob Holmes and Gretchen E. Maclachlan, Atlanta: Southern Center for Studies in Public Policy.

Mitchell, Goro, and Shelly Broomes. 1997. "Rating the Legislators." In *Georgia Legislative Review 1997*, ed. Bob Holmes and Gretchen E. Maclachlan, Atlanta: Southern Center for Studies in Public Policy.

Moncrief, Gary, Joel A. Thompson, and William Cassie. 1996. "Revisiting the State of U.S. State Legislative Research." *Legislative Studies Quarterly* 21:301–35.

Moncrief, Gary, Joel Thompson, and Robert Schuhmann. 1991. "Gender, Race, and the State Legislature: A Research Note on the Double Disadvantage Hypothesis." *The Social Science Journal* 28:481–87.

Moreland, Lawrence W., Robert P. Steed, and Tod A. Baker. 1987. "Black Party Activists: A Profile." In *Blacks in Southern Politics*, ed. Moreland, Lawrence, Robert P. Steed, and Tod A. Baker, 112–32. New York: Praeger.

Morgan, Lucy. 1998. "After 22 Years, Bill Passes on Claim of Ex-Death Row Inmates." *St. Petersburg Times*, 1 May, p. 1B.

———. 2000. "Partisan Is This Year's Buzzword for Session." *St. Petersburg Times*, 4 March, p. 1B.

Morris, Scott. 1991a. "House Decides to OK 2 Redistricting Plans." *Arkansas Gazette*, 22 March, p. I2.

———. 1991b. "Session Comes to an End." *Arkansas Gazette*, 28 March, p. 1A.

———. 1991c. "12 Blacks Ask to Intervene in Redistricting Suit." *Arkansas Gazette*, 19 June, p. B6.

Moser, Tony. 1995. "Arkansas Case Lies at Heart of Fight over Redistricting." *Arkansas Democrat-Gazette*, 20 February, p. 1A.

Moss, Bill. 1993. "Jamerson Once Again Fights for His Dream." *St. Petersburg Times*, December 20, p. 1B.

Murphy, C. S. 2002. "Steele's Style Found Favor with Voters, Pundits Say." *Arkansas Democrat-Gazette*, 23 May. http://web.lexis-nexis.com/universe/printdoc. Accessed electronically May 24 2002.

Nelson, Albert J. 1991. *Emerging Influentials in State Legislatures: Women, Blacks, and Hispanics.* New York: Praeger.

Nieman, Donald G. 1990. "Black Political Power and Criminal Justice: Washington County, Texas, 1868–1884". *The Journal of Southern History* 55:3:391–420.

Nye, Mary Alice, and Charles S. Bullock III. 1992. "Civil Rights Support: A Comparison of Southern and Border State Representatives." *Legislative Studies Quarterly* 17:81–94.

Oman, Noel. 1994. "Voter Outrage at Jewell Helped Push Walker over Top." *Arkansas Democrat-Gazette*, 29 May. http://web.lexis-nexis.com/universe/printdoc. Accessed electronically December 22 2002.

O'Neal, Rachel. 1995. "Seven Freshman Senators Take Oath". *Arkansas Democrat-Gazette*, 10 January, p. 5B.

Orey, Byron D'Andra. 2000. "Black Legislative Politics in Mississippi." *Journal of Black Studies* 30:791–814.

Osborne, David. 1990. *Laboratories of Democracy: A New Breed of Governor Creates Models for National Growth.* Boston: Harvard Business School Press.

Oswald, Mark. 1980. "Blacks Must Stand Up for Rights to Achieve Success, Lawyer Says." *Arkansas Gazette*, 22 September, p. 4A.

———. 1991a. "New District Plan Issued." *Arkansas Gazette*, 2 March, pp. B1–B2.

———. 1991b. "Black House Members, GOP Join Forces." *Arkansas Gazette*, 13 March, p. 31.

Oswald, Mark, and Scott Morris. 1991. "House Accepts Plan for Districts." *Arkansas Gazette*, 27 March, p. H3.

Pacenti, John. 1998. "Bush Pulls Key Voters Away from McKay." *Associated Press.* November 3.

Parent, Wayne, and Huey Perry. 2003. "Louisiana: African Americans, Republicans, and Party Competition." In *The New Politics of the Old South: An Introduction to Southern Politics,* 2nd ed, ed. Charles S. Bullock III and Mark J. Rozell Lanham, Md.: Rowman and Littlefield. 113–31.

Parker, Frank R. 1990. *Black Votes Count: Political Empowerment in Mississippi after 1965.* Chapel Hill: University of North Carolina Press.

Pennington, John V. 2002. "Legislative Black Caucus Meeting Draws Competitors in Senate Race." *Sentinel-Record,* 3 August, p. B1.

Perez, Arturo. 1996. "State of the States." *State Legislatures* (March): 14–15.

Perry, Robert T. 1976. *Black Legislators.* San Francisco: R and E Research Associates.

Persons, Georgia A., ed. 1997. *Race and Representation.* New Brunswick, N.J.: Transaction.

Pinney, Neil, and George Serra. 1999. "The Congressional Black Caucus and Vote Cohesion: Placing the Caucus within House Voting Patterns." *Political Research Quarterly* 52:583–608.

Pitkin, Hanna. 1967. *The Concept of Representation.* Berkeley: University of California Press.

Pohlman, Marcus D. 1990. *Black Politics in Conservative America.* New York: Longman.

Radelat, Ana. 2002. "Senate Panel KOs Pickering." *The Clarion-Ledger* (Jackson), 15 March, pp. 1, 7A.

Rado, Diane. 1994. "Bush Alienates Black Lawmakers." *St. Petersburg Times,* 28 October, p. 2B.

———. 1995. "Law Stipends for Minorities Flow to Non-Florida Students." *St. Petersburg Times,* 23 March, p. 1B.

Ranchino, Jim. 1977. "The Arkansan of the '70s: The Good Ole Boy Ain't Whut He Used To Be." *Arkansas Times* (September), vol. 4, no. 1, pp. 40–43.

Reed, John. 1989. "School Choice Passes Senate after Tie Vote." *Arkansas Gazette,* 10 March, p. A11.

"Resolution Supports Call for Session." 1980. *Arkansas Gazette,* 15 March, p. 6A.

Rogers, Mary Beth. 1998. *Barbara Jordan: American Hero.* New York: Bantam Doubleday Dell, a division of Random House.

Rossilli, Mario. 1998. "Disappointment, Frustration Voiced over Welfare Reform." *The Clarion-Ledger* (Jackson), 7 February, p. 1.

"Senate Passes Diluted Building Code, Fair Housing Code." 1983. *St. Petersburg Times,* 1 June, p. 5B.

Salter, Sid. 1999. "Sen. Horhn Has 'Special' Legislative Power?" *The Clarion-Ledger* (Jackson), 2 May, p. 3H.

Satter, Linda. 2002. "Lawsuit Says Bias Corrupted Primaries." *Arkansas Democrat-Gazette*, 24 May, p. 15A.

Sawyer, Patrice. 2001. "Panel Rejects All 3 Redistricting Proposals." *The Clarion-Ledger* (Jackson), 6 October, p. 1.

Shaffer, Stephen D., Stacie Berry Pierce, and Steven A. Kohnke. 2000. "Party Realignment in the South: A Multi-Level Analysis." *The American Review of Politics* 21:129–54.

Shaw, Robert D., Jr. 1978. "House Passes Election Reform." *Miami Herald*, 8 April, p. 25A.

Silva, Helga. 1982. "A First for Florida Legislature." *Miami Herald*, 21 November, p. 2B.

Singh, Robert. 1998. *The Congressional Black Caucus: Racial Politics in the U.S. Congress.* Thousand Oaks, Calif.: Sage.

"Some Praise, Others Bemoan Session's Work." 1991. *Arkansas Democrat-Gazette*, 31 March. http://web.lexis-nexis.com/universe/printdoc. Accessed electronically 20 May 2002.

Southern Poverty Law Center. 2002. "Julian Bond" (biography). http://www.splcenter.org/cgi-bin/goframe.pl?refname=/centerinfo/julian.html. Accessed 12 September 2002.

Stanley, Harold W. 2003. "Alabama: Republicans Winning the Heart of Dixie." In *The New Politics of the Old South: An Introduction to Southern Politics.* 2nd ed, ed. Charles S. Bullock III and Mark J. Rozell, 75–94. Lanham, Md.: Rowman and Littlefield.

"Senators Reject Fordice Nominations." 1996. *Starkville Daily News*, 12 July, p. 1.

"State Second in Electing Black Officials." 1973. *Arkansas Gazette*, 4 February, p. 18A.

Statistical Abstract of the United States. 1995. Washington, D.C.: United States Bureau of the Census.

———. 2002. Washington, D.C.: United States Bureau of the Census.

Steele, Tracy. 2002. Telephone interview. 3 June.

Stone, Clarence. 1989. *Regime Politics.* Lawrenceville: University of Kansas Press.

Strickland, Pam. 1987. "Panel's Approval Moves Sales Tax Closer to Final Test in Full House." *Democrat*, 3 April, p. 1A.

Stringfellow, Eric. 1999. "Killed Nominations Reflect Problems in Committee System." *The Clarion-Ledger* (Jackson), 13 May, p. 11A.

Strong, Donald S. 1944. "American Government and Politics: The Poll Tax: The Case of Texas." *The American Political Science Review*. 38:4:693–709.

Stumpe, Joe. 1991. "House Passes Senate Redistricting Plan." *Arkansas Democrat*, 27 March, p. 1A.

Sullivan, Brenda. 2000. "Even at the Turning of the Tide: An Analysis of the North Carolina Legislative Black Caucus." *Journal of Black Studies* 30:815–38.

Swain, Carol M. 1993. *Black Faces, Black Interests: The Representation of African Americans in Congress.* Cambridge: Harvard University Press.

———. 1998. "The Rise and Decline of the Congressional Black Caucus." In *Politicians and Party Politics,* ed. John G. Geer, 294–308. Baltimore: Johns Hopkins University Press.

Talev, Margaret. 1998. "Logan Abandons McKay for Bush." *Tampa Tribune,* 2 October, p. B2.

Tennille, Grant. 1995. "Necessary Taxes or Highway Robbery? Better Roadways Carry Divisive Price." *Arkansas Democrat-Gazette,* 20 March, p. 1A.

Texas Legislative Council. 1999. http://www.tlc.state.tx.us/. Accessed electronically 8 March, 1999.

Texas Legislative Reference Library Online: http://www.lrl.state.tx.us/lrlhome.cfm. Accessed electronically 8 March, 1999.

Tharpe, Jim. 2003a. "House Chairmanships Go to Democrats Only." *Atlanta Journal-Constitution,* 18 January. http://www. accessatlanta.com/ajc/metro/politics/0118bipartisan.html. Accessed electronically 4 February, 2003.

———. 2003b. "Coleman Names Committee Chairs—All Democrats." *Atlanta Journal-Constitution,* 16 January. http://www.accessatlanta.com/ajc/metro/politics/0117legis.html. Accessed electronically 4 February, 2003.

Thielemann, Gregory S. 1992. "Minority Legislators and Institutional Influence." *The Social Science Journal.* 29:4:411–21.

Thompson, Doug. 2001. "Tax Cuts Not High on List for Legislators This Year". *Arkansas Democrat-Gazette,* 9 January, p. A1.

Tucker, Harvey J. 1989. "Legislative Calendars and Workload Management in Texas." *Journal of Politics* 51:3:631–45.

Tucker, Ronnie Bernard. 2000. *Affirmative Action, the Supreme Court, and Political Power in the Old Confederacy.* Lanham, Md.: University Press of America.

"Two Blacks, Johnston Win in District 3." 1972. *Arkansas Gazette,* 8 November, p. 11A.

U.S. Bureau of the Census. 2000. Summary File 1, Matrices P3, P4, PCT4, PCT5, PCT8, and PCT11. Washington, D.C.

Wagster, Emily. 1998a. "Black Caucus, Constituents in Town This Weekend for Annual Forum." *The Clarion-Ledger* (Jackson), 31 January, p. 1.

———. 1998b. "Black Mississippi Lawmakers Elected to National Posts." *The Clarion-Ledger* (Jackson), 12 December, p. B1.

———. 1999. "Election Chairmen's Relationship Reflection of Mississippi." *The Clarion-Ledger* (Jackson), 24 January, p. 1, 7A.

Wagster, Emily, and Bruce Reid. 1998. "Black Caucus Calls for Wildlife Resignations." *The Clarion-Ledger* (Jackson), 13 March, p. B1.

Wall, Dennis J. 1977. "Multi-Member Legislative Districts: Requiem for a Constitutional Burial." *University of Florida Law Review* 29:703–29.

Wallsten, Peter, 1998. "4 Senators Split from Black Caucus." *St. Petersburg Times*, 6 February, p. 1B.

Wallsten, Peter, and Adam C. Smith. 1998. "Black Caucus, GOP Ally on Budget." *St. Petersburg Times*, 21 March, p. 1B.

Walton, Hanes, Jr. 1985. *Invisible Politics: Black Political Behavior*. Albany: State University of New York Press.

Wells, Bob. 1983. "Black Caucus Listens to Clinton; Pay Plan, Tax, Tests Opposed." *Arkansas Gazette*, 2 October, p. 4A.

Whitby, Kenneth J. 1997. *The Color of Representation: Congressional Behavior and Black Interests*. Ann Arbor: University of Michigan Press.

Wielhouwer, Peter W., and Keesha M. Middlemass. 2002. "Party Voting and Race in the Georgia General Assembly." Paper presented at the Citadel Symposium on Southern Politics. March 2002.

Wiggins, Charles W., Keith E. Hamm, and Charles G. Bell. 1992. "Interest Group and Party Influence Agents in the Legislative Process: A Comparative State Analysis." *The Journal of Politics* 54:82–100.

Wink, Kenneth A., and Allison L. Hayes. 2001. "Racial Redistricting and Ideological Polarization in Southern U.S. House Delegations." *Politics and Policy* 29:361–84.

Wright, Sharon D. 2000. "The Tennessee Black Caucus of State Legislators." *Journal of Black Studies* 31:1–19.

About the Contributors

Brandi J. Brassell completed a B.A. in psychology from the University of Memphis in 1998. She then went on to work for the state of Tennessee as a probation officer for four years. Currently, she is pursuing a master's degree in public administration at the University of Memphis. She is expected to finish the degree in the spring of 2005.

Michelle G. Briscoe is an assistant professor of political science at Miami University of Ohio. Prior to going to Miami University, she taught at Benedict College. Her main teaching interests lie in the study of American politics, comparative politics, African American/minority politics, urban politics, and policy/social stratification and social inequality. Her research has appeared in the *Journal of Colonialism and Colonial History* and *International Politics*. She has presented numerous papers examining issues from the federal courts to the Texas Legislative Black Caucus. Briswe received her Ph.D. from Northern Arizona University in 1997 and her M.A. in educational psychology in 1991.

Charles E. Menifield is an associate professor at the University of Memphis, where he teaches research methods, political statistics, budgeting and finance, and public management information systems. He spent the 2002–2003 academic year as a visiting scholar at the Congressional Budget Office in Washington, D.C., where he conducted budget analysis on SCHIP programs and served as an adjunct professor at Howard University. Previously he was an associate professor of political science and public administration at Mississippi State University and an assistant professor at Murray State University. His research interests lie primarily in the area of minority group behavior and budgeting and financial management. His research has appeared in *Public Administration Times, Public Choice, Western Journal of Black Studies, Latino Studies Journal, Journal of Black Studies, Congress and the Presidency, Deviant Behavior*, and the *Policy Studies Journal*. In addition, he has edited two books: *Representation*

217

of Minority Groups in the U.S.: Implications for the Twenty-first Century and *MS Votes*. He is currently working on *A Beginner's Guide to Practical Budgeting in State and Local Government*. Menifield received his Ph.D. from the University of Missouri-Columbia in 1996.

Keesha M. Middlemass is an assistant professor of political science at the University of Kansas in Lawrence. Beginning in the fall of 2004, she will be on leave from KU and doing research on disenfranchisement laws and voting rights of black men at the Vera Institute of Justice in New York City. Previously she was an American Political Science Association Fellow in Washington, D.C. She has presented research on legislative redistricting, the Voting Rights Act, presidential elections, and representation at the national and state levels at the Midwest Political Science Association Conference, American Political Science Association Conference, Western Political Science Association Conference, Citadel Symposium on Southern Politics, and Southern Political Science Association Conference. She has a book chapter examining redistricting in Georgia published in *Selected Bibliography of the State Legislature as an Institution* and has several other pieces of research under review. Middlemass completed her Ph.D. from the University of Georgia in 2004.

William Miller is a professor of political science at the University of Arkansas. Prior to that he worked as a policy analyst for St. Louis University as well as with numerous community-based advocacy and service groups. He has published generally on public policy in such areas as desegregation policy, church and state issues, citizen participation in economic development, financial ratios, equal employment, and the use of race in research. His work has appeared in *Public Administration Review, American Review of Public Administration, Women and Politics, State and Local Government Review, American Journal of Political Science*, and elsewhere. Miller is the director of the public policy Ph.D. program at the University of Arkansas. He received his Ph.D. from St. Louis University.

Janine A. Parry is an assistant professor of political science and director of the Arkansas Poll. Before her post at the University of Arkansas in 1998, she worked in a number of government settings, including the U.S. House of Representatives for Speaker Tom Foley in 1993 and the Washington state senate in 1992. Her fields of teaching and research include gender, politics, and policy, state, and local government (including Arkansas politics), parties and interest groups, and American national government. Her work has appeared in the *Policy Studies Journal, Social Science Quarterly, Arkansas Historical Quarterly, Midsouth Political Science Review, National Women's Studies Association Journal,* and elsewhere. She was awarded the Fulbright College's Master Teacher Award for 2002. Parry received her Ph.D. from Washington State University in 1998.

Barbara A. Patrick is a Ph.D. student in the public policy and administration doctoral program in the Political Science Department at Mississippi State University. She holds a doctoral fellowship awarded by the Atlanta-based Southern Regional Education Board. She also has a master's degree in public administration from Mississippi State and a bachelor's degree from Rust College in Holly Springs, Mississippi.

Stephen D. Shaffer is a professor of political science at Mississippi State University, where his research focuses on American politics, particularly, Mississippi politics and public opinion polling. He received his Ph.D. from Ohio State University and has been at MSU since 1979. Shaffer teaches specialized courses in campaign politics, public opinion, political behavior, political parties, and Southern politics, as well as more introductory classes in American government, political analysis, and graduate research methods. He has published extensively on Mississippi party organizations and political campaigns, as well as national public opinion and federal elections. He maintains a national reputation in research, having co-authored the book *Mississippi Government and Politics*, and has been published in such recognized journals as *American Journal of Political Science*, *Public Choice*, *American Review of Politics*, *Southeastern Political Review*, *American Politics Quarterly*, *Western Political Quarterly*, and *Social Science Quarterly*. Shaffer has been recognized as an outstanding teacher on three different occasions.

Steven Tauber is an associate professor of political science at the University of South Florida in Tampa, Florida. His research focuses on judicial behavior, the politics of race, and Florida government. He has published the results of this research in scholarly journal articles and chapters in edited volumes. His published articles have appeared (or will appear) in *Political Research Quarterly*, *Social Science Quarterly*, *American Politics Quarterly*, and *Politics and Policy*. Tauber also serves as the methodologist on a large-scale project investigating nations' ability to adapt to the HIVAIDS crisis.

Peter W. Wielhouwer is on the faculty of Western Michigan University's Department of Political Science. Previously, he taught at the Regent University School of Government, where he directed the graduate program in Political Management, and at Spelman College. Most recently he was the chief writer and speechwriter for Major General John R. Wood, Director of Joint Experimentation at United States Joint Forces Command. Wielhouwer's areas of expertise include campaigns, political behavior, electoral mobilization, and racial politics. His research has appeared in the *American Journal of Political Science*, the *Journal of Politics*, *American Politics Quarterly*, and *Social Science Quarterly*, among others. He has also been a political consultant for several state and local political campaigns. He received his Ph.D. from the University of Georgia.

Index

1990 Census, 165
2000 Presidential Election, 52, 54,
385 U.S. 440, 45,
501-3c nonprofit, 164

abortion, 18, 24, 28, 62, 63, 119, 120,
    128, 184, 185, 187, 190, 198, 199
Abrams, Mike, 56
Adequate Education Bill, 118, 123, 128
ADA Scores, 8
affirmative action, 52, 67, 121
African American Legislators in the
    American States, 13
Agent Orange Bill, 147
Aid for Students with Children Bill, 145,
    146
Aid to Families with Dependent
    Children, 86, 93
Allain, Bill, 123
Americans for Democratic Action, 6, 8, 15
amusement ride regulation, 152
Anderson, Doug, 108, 112
anti-discrimination statute, 31,
appellate court, 39
Arkansas Civil Rights Act, 38
Atlanta City Council, 79
Ayers Case, 118

Bagneris, Dennis, 162
Bajoie, Diana, 162
Banks, Fred, 108, 110, 111
Beard, Malcolm, 68
bicameral legislature, 171, 173

Biennial Symposium on Southern
    Politics, 1
Birmingham Urban League, 159
Birmingham, Alabama, 159
black belt, 75, 137
black-majority districts, 34, 36, 38, 111,
    133
black-on-black crime, 187
Blanco, Kathleen, 163
bloc voting, 198
Blue, Daniel, 164, 165, 167
Blueprint 2000, 56, 193
Bond, Julian, 78
Bradley, Rudy, 54, 59, 60
Briggs, Eddie, 113
Brogan, Frank, 56
Broome, Sharon W., 162
Brown, Corrine, 48
Brown, Irma, 22, 26, 30, 32, 33, 39, 192
Brown, Joe E., 170
Brownlee, Christine, 18, 28
Bryan, Hob, 114
Buckley, Horace, 108
Bullard, Larcenia, 49
Bullock, Charles, 5, 9, 15
Burke, James, 48
Bush, George W., 55, 127
Bush, James, 49
Bush, Jeb, 52, 53, 54, 55, 60, 63, 64, 66,
    193

Carter, Jimmy, 77
Cassie, William, 8

Castor, Betty, 56
Catholic, 160
Caucus
  Alabama Legislative Black, 158
  Arkansas Legislative Black, 23, 25, 37
  Black, 10, 12, 25, 30, 36, 38, 39, 44,
    50, 68, 70, 91, 94, 96, 107, 115, 118,
    120, 114, 124–128, 157–161, 166,
    169–172, 176, 184–190, 192, 196–
    199
  Congressional Black, 7, 8, 34, 50–53,
    104
  Florida Legislative Black, 50–53, 72
  Georgia Legislative Black, 74, 80, 83,
    85, 86, 88, 91, 93, 94, 96, 103, 104
  Hispanic State Legislative, 138
  House Democratic, 7
  Louisiana Legislative Black, 161, 162
  Mexican American, 134
  Mississippi Legislative Black, 108, 110
  North Carolina Legislative Black, 164,
    165, 166
  South Carolina Legislative Black, 168
  Texas Legislative Black, 134, 138, 141,
    144, 153, 154, 197
  Virginia Black Legislative, 173
  Women's, 39
Central High School, 17
chain gangs, 63, 96
Charles, Dale, 36
charter schools, 67
Chestnut, Cynthia, 48, 49
Child Health Insurance Plan, 126
Chiles, Lawton, 53, 54, 63, 67, 70
Circuit Court of Appeals, 162
Citadel, 1
Civil Rights Act (1993), 31, 38
civil rights movement, 10, 18, 32, 53, 61,
    62, 69, 70, 72, 78, 80, 170
Civil War, 43, 134, 144, 146
Clark, Bill, 48
Clark, Robert, 107, 110, 111
Clark-Atlanta University, 85
class action suit, 152
Clinton, Bill, 18, 25, 32, 34, 45

Clinton, Hillary, 25
coalition [s]
  biracial, 1, 10–12, 44, 78, 79, 100, 101,
    119, 125, 128
  biracial Democratic, 116, 118
  formation of, 62, 179, 184
  liberal, 65
  nonpermanent, 181
  Progressive, 61, 69, 71, 181
  race, 188, 189, 190, 191, 195, 196, 197
Cobb-Hunter, Gilda, 169
Coleman, Mary H., 127
Coleman, Terry, 102
College Board, 115, 126
Commission
  Civil Rights, 30
  Human Resources, 30
  Little Rock Civil Service, 19
  Martin Luther King Jr., 36, 39
  Workers Compensation, 114
committee
  Aging ad Legislative Affairs, 193
  Agriculture and Economic Develop-
    ment, 22
  Appropriations, 15, 55, 56, 160, 166,
    196, 197
  budget, 55, 59
  Calendar Affairs Committee, 172
  Children and Family Affairs, 59, 172
  Children and Youth Committee, 84
  City, 22
  City, County, and Local Affairs, 193
  Conference, 139
  Community Affairs, 55, 58, 194
  Conference, 139
  County, 22,
  Cultural Affairs, 163
  Democratic Party Executive, 56
  Development, 59
  Economic Development, 58, 113, 114,
    194
  Education, 20, 40, 55, 108, 111, 114,
    127, 160, 193, 19
  Education Standards, 25
  Elections, 56, 113, 114, 125, 193

Ethics, 58, 111, 194
Federal, 137
Finance, 56, 114, 115, 193, 197
Government Finance, 160
Governmental Affairs, 84
Health and Human Services, 85
Municipal Affairs, 170
Municipal and Parochial, 163
Municipalities, 112, 113
House Aging and Legislative Affairs, 22
House Revenue and Taxation, 22
Housing, 55
Labor and Industrial Relations, 163
Labor, 40,
Institutions and Property, 84
International Relations, 139
International Trade, 58, 59, 194
Interstate Cooperation, 85, 170
Joint Legislative Budget, 115, 125
Legislative Affairs, 20,
Legislative Budget, 115
Local and Municipal Affairs, 163
Judiciary, 20, 32, 111–115, 127, 39, 196
Management, 40, 111
Medical, 170
Military, 170
Natural Resources, 163
Operations, 170
Public Affairs, 55
Public Health, 32, 40
Public Property, 113
Public Transportation, 22, 193
Retirement, 163
Revenue and Taxation, 192
Rules, 85
Rules and Resolutions, 55, 56, 83, 139, 195
Senate and Government Affairs, 163
State, 139
State and Local Government Operations, 85
Tourism Committee, 58, 194
Transportation, 55, 59, 163, 194

Universities and Colleges, 112, 127, 196
Veterans and Consumer Affairs, 85
Ways and Means, 115, 166, 197
Welfare, 40,
committee chairs
    Alabama legislature, 159, 160
    Arkansas legislature, 21–23, 44
    Florida legislature, 50, 55, 59
    Georgia legislature, 77, 82, 102
    Louisiana legislature, 163
    Mississippi legislature, 11–116
    North Carolina legislature, 166–168
    positions, 13, 177, 180–182, 192–195, 198
    prestige, 13, 107
    South Carolina legislature, 169,170
    standing, 77, 82, 127, 159, 172, 196
    Texas legislature, 131, 134, 139
    Virginia legislature, 175
Confederate Flag, 126
Confederate state, 43
consensus bill, 188
consensus coalition, 197
Constitutional Convention, 19, 78, 113, 123, 160
Copelin, Sherman M., 162
county unit system, 75, 79
Court of Appeals, 127
Crenshaw, Andrew, 45
crime, 18, 24, 28, 61, 63, 103, 119, 120, 128, 146, 172, 184, 185, 187, 190, 194, 196, 199
criminal justice, 49, 96, 100, 133, 146, 152, 198
Cuban Americans, 49
Cuban refugees, 44

Dannelly, Charlie S., 165
Dawson, Muriel, 49
DeBerry, John J., 172
DeBerry, Lois, 172
Delpit, Joseph A., 162
Democratic Black Caucus, 24,
Democratic Party Caucus, 80

Democratic Party of Arkansas, 24,
Dennis, Willye, 49,
Department of Justice, 88
desegregation, 26, 67, 116, 118, 127, 196
designer drugs, 63
diesel gasoline tax, 34,
discrimination, 26, 44, 53, 70, 114, 122,
    129, 133
discriminatory laws, 74
disenfranchised voters, 1, 43, 52, 55, 78,
    84, 107, 132
district boundaries, 45
Dixiecrats, 2
Dumas, Ernie, 32, 33
Dupree v. Alma School District (1983), 25

Earle, Beverly, 165
Ebonics, 94
Economic Development Conference,
    161
economic development programs, 55
economic development, 1, 18, 24, 32, 34,
    80, 100, 121, 123, 128, 133, 151,
    161, 172, 195
education, 7, 11, 18, 24, 25, 61, 65, 66,
    86, 93, 102, 116, 117, 133, 144, 172,
    184, 185, 191
education commissioners, 56
education reform, 18, 116, 124, 193, 197
Edwards, Jean, 22, 193
Eggelletion, Josephus, 49,
Eisenhower, Dwight D., 44
Elazar, Daniel, 132
Elders, Jocelyn, 28, 38
election legislation, 84
election procedure, 44, 149
election Process bill, 150
election reform, 55, 86, 101
election regulations, 56,
Electoral College, 56
Emancipation (1863), 131, 132
Emeritus status, 171
End-Stage motions, 141
enfranchise, 179
enterprise zones, 32, 34

environmental policy, 61, 133
equal funding, 146

fair housing, 69
Fairchild, Bob, 31, 32
Farm Bureau, 123, 128
federal appeals court, 126
Federal Court, 31, 49
federal government, 44,
federal mandate, 144
federal minimum wage, 94
federal supervision, 44,
federalism, 134
Ferrell, Lisa, 29, 30, 39
Fifteenth Amendment, 132
Figure, Vivian, 159
Figures, Michael A., 158
finance reform, 125
Florida Constitution, 63
Florida Supreme Court, 49, 63
Ford, Johnny, 160
Ford, Tim, 111
Fordice, Kirk, 114–116, 117, 118, 122,
    123, 125, 127
foreign policy, 8
Frazier, Hillman, 113, 127
Fredricks, Francis, 127
Free Federal Breakfast Participation Bill,
    144
frontier state, 43
fund raising, 54

gas tax, 123
gay marriage, 68
gay rights, 68
George, Lloyd, 38, 39
Georgia Legislative Review, 85, 96
gerrymander, 1, 49
Girardeau, Arnett, 46, 48, 50, 51, 58, 194
Gordon, Elaine, 49, 50
government reform, 18, 24, 34, 68, 125,
    184, 185
Graham, Bob, 65
Gray v. Sanders, 79
great depression, 43

Great Emancipator, 43
Great Negro state, 17
Greene, Addie, 49
Grofman, Bernard, 9, 16
group politics, 73

Hamm, Keith, 9, 10, 16
Handley, Lisa, 9, 16
Harden, Alice V., 114, 127
Hargrett, James, 48, 50, 54, 58, 194
Harmel, Robert, 9, 10, 16
Harris, Joe F., 85
Harris, Joe Jr., 193
Harris, Joe, 22,
Harris, Katherine, 55
Harris, Robert, 8
hate crimes, 31, 123
Haynie, Kerry L., 13, 14, 15, 24, 59, 61,
     167
Haynie's political incorporation index, 59
Health Plan Act (1995), 91
Healthcare, 11, 18, 24, 28, 80–91, 125,
     134, 149, 166, 172, 184, 185, 91,
     198
Healthy Kids Bill, 149
Herring, Mary, 157
higher education, 14, 96, 116
highway bill, 128
Hill, Anthony, 49
Hines, Mack T., 170
Hispanic Caucus, 154
Historic disenfranchisement, 34
historically black university, 86, 110, 115,
     119, 126, 145, 153
historically underutilized business, 151
historically white universities, 126
Holzendorf, Betty, 50, 58
Hooks, Benjamin, 32
Horhn, John, 114, 127
Howard, Pierre, 77
Huckabee, Mike, 36,

income tax, 66, 123, 128
individual liberty, 70
individualistic vote, 188, 191

infant mortality, 129
institutional racism, 25,
intangibles tax, 66
interest rates, 151

Jackson State University, 110
Jackson, Jesse, 173
Jackson, Maynard, 79
Jamerson, Doug, 48, 49, 56, 193
Jefers v. Clinton, 19,
Jennings, Harry, 63
Jennings, Toni, 59
Jewell, Jerry, 19, 21, 22, 26, 30, 32, 34,
     36, 192
Jim Crow laws, 17
job-training, 70, 93
Johnson, Leroy, 78
Jones, Daryl, 48–50, 172
Jordan, Barbara, 135
Journal of the House of Representatives,
     61, 85
Journal of the Senate, 61, 85
Justice Department, 78, 80, 101, 107
juvenile court judge, 161

Kershaw, Joe, 46, 56, 193
Key, V.O., 1, 16, 17, 75, 76

Lamis, Alexander, P., 16, 188
land speculation, 43
Lawson, Alfred, 48, 49, 53, 55
Leadership Conference on Civil Rights, 7
Leadership Experience program, 159
leadership position, 13, 70, 131, 162,
     165, 167, 169, 171, 172, 174, 177,
     178, 180, 181, 182, 183, 184, 191,
     192, 195, 197, 198
Lee, Wilbur, 70
Legislation of Laetrile, 147
lesbians, 31
Lewellen, Bill, 40,
Lewellen, Roy, 22, 31, 32, 36, 193
Lincoln, Abraham, 160
literacy tests, 44, 78, 114
living wage, 94

lobbyist, 167
Logan, Willie, 48, 52, 54, 56, 57
Long, Huey P., 160
longitudinal examination, 152
Lott, Trent, 127
lottery, 124
Louisiana, 10, 78, 176, 177, 178, 182
Lucas, Hopkins, 165
lynching, 17,
Lyra, Logan, 57

Mabus, Ray, 120, 124
Mackenzie, Anne, 52, 54
MacManus, Susan, 9
Magnolia State, 196
majority-black district, 48, 49, 52, 71, 88,
    161, 187
majority-Latino districts, 49,
majority-minority districts, 49, 80, 101,
    111, 131, 182
Mankin, Helen, 78
Martin Luther King Holiday, 51, 85
Martinez, Robert, 63, 66
Mays, Richard, 19
McBride, Bill, 55
McGee, Ben, 22, 26, 30, 34, 35, 36, 38,
    193
McKay, Buddy, 53, 54,
Meadows, Mathew, 50
Medicaid, 149
Meek, Carrie, 48, 50, 51, 58, 69, 194
Meek, Kendrick, 50, 54, 70
Menifield, Charles, 7, 8, 14
Mexico, 147
Michel A. Figures Legacy Education
    Fund, 159
Miles, Mary, 168
military personnel, 150
Miller v. Johnson, 80
Miller, Cheryl, 10, 166
Miller, John, 28, 39,
Miller, Larry J., 172
Miller, les, 49, 54, 60
Miller, Paul, 165
minimum prison sentence, 28

minimum wage, 94
Minor privacy rights, 149
Mississippi Black Caucus, 107, 127
Mississippi Delta, 116
Mississippi, 9, 11, 12, 16, 78, 158, 162,
    182, 183, 185, 190
Missouri, 11, 12, 137
Moncrief, Gary, 8
Morial, Ernest, 161
Morrill Land Grant College Act, 145
motor vehicle liability, 152
Motor Voter Act, 125
Motor Voter legislation, 88
multicultural education, 56
multi-member district, 46, 108, 133
multivariate analysis, 191
Musgrove, Ronnie, 113, 114, 118, 126

National Association for the Advance-
    ment of Color People (NAACP),
    19, 32, 36
National Black Caucus of State Legisla-
    tors, 127
National Conference of State Legisla-
    tures, 20,
National Rifle Association, 63
National Voter Registration Act, 88
Negro vote, 78
Nelson, Alert J., 13
Nelson, Bill 54
Newman, Buddie, 116
Newton, Demetrius C., 159
Nixon, Richard M., 44,
North Carolina, 10, 11, 13, 60, 178
Nye, Mary A., 5, 15

Office of Public Information, 161
Old South Democrats, 44,
One Florida executive order, 54,
one-party state, 43,

parental consent, 119
parental control, 149
Parental Notification of Abortion on
    Minors, 148

parole, 84, 120, 129
party coalition, 11, 188, 196
party control, 61
party loyalty, 190
Permanent University Fund, 146
Pickering, Charles, 127
Pickering, Chip, 127
Pitkin, Hanna, 2, 107, 180
Pitts, Freddie, 70
Pitts-lee Compensation Law, 72
Plummer, John, 46,
political activism, 78
political culture, 43,
political discrimination, 44
Political Education and Economic
    Development Foundation, 110, 125
political incorporation index, 59–61
political marginalization, 105
poll tax, 78, 132
populist, 160
pork barrel projects, 55, 56
Prairie View A & M, 145
prayer in school, 52, 67
presidential election, 161
Priest, Sharon, 36,
primary candidates, 56,
prison, 64, 128, 129, 146
privatization, 146
probation, 84
property tax, 116, 146
Pryor, David, 30
Pryor, Mark, 36
public defender program, 115
public education, 25, 116, 118, 144
public services, 17, 25, 56, 76, 123, 149, 159
Pulaski County Schools, 31
punitive damages, 53, 70, 125

race, 18, 24, 30, 44, 79, 184, 185, 187,
    191, 197, 198
racial
    equity, 17
    politics, 79
    preferences, 54
    toleration, 17

Ranchino, Jim, 19
Re T.W., A Minor, 63
Reagan, Ronald, 13, 44
reapportionment, 71, 79, 88, 111,161
Reaves, Jefferson, 48
recession, 116, 118
reconstruction, 18, 30, 43, 45, 46, 48, 78,
    116, 118, 132, 134, 158, 161, 164
Reddick, Alzo, 48, 58, 67
redistributive economics, 170, 180, 194,
    198, 199
redistricting, 19, 34, 36, 38, 44–46, 48,
    49, 50, 51, 61, 68, 72, 80, 88, 100–
    102, 111, 126, 136, 164, 182, 188
Reid, William F., 173
religious fundamentalism, 44
representation, 152, 180
    descriptive, 2–6, 10, 12, 13, 16, 37, 44,
        50, 51, 61, 72–74, 85, 101, 102, 104,
        107, 108, 112, 162, 166, 168, 174,
        175, 177, 180, 187, 194
    substantive, 4–7, 12, 13, 16, 37, 44, 50,
        51, 55, 57, 61, 72–74, 85, 86, 89, 96,
        102–105, 107, 108, 180, 187, 195,
        198,
    symbolic, 2–5
    virtual, 2, 3
right to citizenship, 78
right to hold office, 78
right to vote, 78
riot, 52,
Ritchie, Buzz, 59
riverboat gambling, 124, 128
road improvements, 34, 66
Roberts-Burke, Beryl, 49, 52, 59, 60, 64
roll call votes, 6, 62, 85, 86, 92, 94, 96,
    102, 108, 134, 139, 140, 149, 152,
    166, 184, 186, 188
Rosewood massacre (1923), 53, 70

sales tax holiday, 66
sales tax, 25, 34, 66, 117
same sex marriage, 52
scholarship fund, 57, 194
scholarship program, 159

school based health clinics, 28
School
    Choice, 26, 39
    Choice Act, 26
    desegregation, 30
    district, 31, 56
    Equity Funding Act (1989), 116
    finance, 25, 146
    Safety Act (2001), 120
    vouchers, 52, 66
Scott, David, 83, 195
segregation, 17, 26, 31, 129, 160, 184,
    195, 199
seniority, 59
sentencing, 84, 128
separation of church and state, 66
sex education, 28, 88
Shows, Ronnie, 126
Singh, Robert, 7, 15
single-member district, 9, 44, 46, 108,
    164, 168, 173
Sinkfield, Georgianna, 93
Smith v. Allwright, 76
Smith, Christopher, 64
social issues, 44
social welfare legislation, 91, 100, 102
solidarity, 8
South Africa, 86
Southern Center for Studies in Public
    Policy, 85
Sparks, Sam, 19
stagflation, 1, 13
State
    contract awarding, 54,
    correctional institutions, 84
    Funding for Full Day Kindergarten
        Bill, 149
    of the State, 125
    University Board of Regents, 66
State's Rights Party, 168
Steele, Tracy, 24, 36, 39
Stone, Clarence, 4
Street-Gang Act (1996), 120
structural unemployment, 32
subjugation, 76
succession, 134

Supreme Court, 111
Swain, Carol, 6, 14, 15
Swann v. Adams, 45,

Talmadge, Eugene, 75, 76
taxation, 25, 32, 55, 56, 57, 61, 66, 75,
    123
Taylor, Dorothy M., 161
Teacher Testing Bill (1983), 25
teachers unions, 56
Telecommunications Bill, 121, 128
Temporary Absentee Polling Places bill,
    149
Tennessee Black Caucus of State
    Legislators, 171
term limits, 20, 164, 192
Texas, 10, 138, 160, 181, 182, 185, 190
Thomas, John, 46, 48, 51
Thomas, Pat, 45,
Thompson, Bennie, 119
Thompson, Joel A., 8
Thompson, Robert, 9
Thompson, Senfronia, 147
Thornburg v. Gingles, 48, 80
Thrasher, John, 59
Three Strikes Bill, 64
Thurmond, Strom, 168
tobacco settlement, 24, 39,
Tollison, Gray, 115
Toombs v. Fortson, 79
Tort Reform Bill (125), 125
tourism, 43, 58
Townsend, William, 19, 21, 22, 192, 193
traditionalistic culture, 196
Tuck, Amy, 113, 114, 116, 118
Tucker, Guy, 28, 30, 32, 34,
Turner, Bennie, 114
Turner, Bill, 50,
Two Party South, 16
Two Strikes Legislation, 28, 30, 96

U.S. Supreme Court, 36, 48, 49, 55, 76,
    79, 80, 94, 102, 108
Under-representation gap, 182, 183, 193
unemployed parents, 70
unholy alliance, 188, 190

Uniform Admission and Reporting Bill, 146
unit votes, 75
United States Constitution, 94
unity indicator, 198
unity scale, 186
unity score, 187
University of Arkansas at Pine Bluff, 19
University of Mississippi, 115
University of Nebraska, 16

Vietnam War, 79, 147, 148
violent crime, 28, 120, 146
Virginia, 11, 78, 176, 182
Virtual South, 1
Voter
  behavior, 18, 44
  bloc, 45
  cohesion, 198
  discrimination, 49
  identification, 128
  registration, 126
voting
  rights, 37, 53, 76, 132, 153
  solidarity, 134

Voting Rights Act (1965), 2, 9, 16, 19,
  44, 48, 77, 78, 92, 107, 108, 131,
  133, 137

Walker, Bill, 20, 30, 31, 32, 34, 38
Walker, John, 36
Walker, Wilma, 36,
Walton, Hanes, 12, 14
Webster, Daniel, 59
welfare to work programs, 85, 96
Whitby, Kenneth, 7, 14, 15
white
  accommodation, 157
  flight, 26, 76
  opposition, 168
  primary, 17, 132
  supremacy, 1, 17, 75, 170
White, Juanita, M., 169
Wilkins, Henry III, 19, 30, 36
Wilson, Jimmie, 32
Wingfield, Gus, 28
Wink, Kenneth, 6, 15
Winter, William, 116
World War II, 43